THE NEGRO NOVELIST

The Negro Novelist

A Discussion of the Writings of American
Negro Novelists
1940—1950

by
CARL MILTON HUGHES

With a new Introduction by Arthur Ashe

A CITADEL PRESS BOOK
Published by Carol Publishing Group

First Carol Publishing Group Edition 1990

A Citadel Press Book
Published by Carol Publishing Group

Editorial Offices
600 Madison Avenue
New York, NY 10022

Sales & Distribution Offices
120 Enterprise Avenue
Secaucus, NJ 07094

In Canada: Musson Book Company
A division of General Publishing Co. Limited
Don Mills, Ontario

Manufactured in the United States of America
ISBN 0-8065-0006-9

10 9 8 7 6 5 4 3 2 1

Carol Publishing Group books are available at special discounts
for bulk purchases, for sales promotions, fund raising, or
educational purposes. Special editions can also be created to
specifications. For details contact: Special Sales Department,
Carol Publishing Group, 120 Enterprise Ave., Secaucus, NJ 07094

To the spirit of motherhood exemplified in

EMMA G. TROY

and

MATTYE C. WATSON

INTRODUCTION BY ARTHUR ASHE

In his critique and review of prominent African-American novelists and essayists, Carl Milton Hughes centers on a unique decade. Before 1940 the pens of many black writers were focused on several common themes: the difficulties inherent in the great migration from the segregationist South to the more promising northern cities; the literary legacy left by the ideas of the Harlem Renaissance covey of authors; and the particularized effects of the Great Depression on black America and race relations.

After 1950 these same writers and their newer colleagues turned angrier as World War II raised expectations, hopes, and horizons. Unquestionably the black writers of the decade 1940–1950 helped frame the emotional and spiritual mindset for the legal gains of the 1950s. In retrospect, it seems almost inevitable that Chief Justice Earl Warren's Supreme Court would hand down the *Brown v. Board of Education* decision in 1954 partially because of the fictionalized moral arguments proffered by the novelists in this book.

It was never easy or comfortable for black critics of American foreign or domestic policies and customs to be objective *and* secure. The Negro literati and intelligentsia had flirted with Communism in the 1930s. Some like Paul Robeson actually moved to the Soviet Union for a time, not so much because of a primal love for Communism or the Soviets but rather because racism seemed so intractable stateside. Entire subject areas, geographical regions, colleges and universities, public accommodations et al. were simply off-limits to blacks, and there seemed little hope that change for the better was imminent.

One subject area that experienced constant change and examination was the very nomenclature of ethnic self-definition. In the white press of the 1940s and earlier, the word "negro" was spelled with the *n* in lower case. Southern papers, of course, did so intentionally as a sign of white racial superiority. Others did so because negro was not considered a proper noun. In textbooks or anthropological works the appellation "Negroid"—referring to a particular or distinct race of people—was spelled with the upper case *n*.

This exercise was not done for semantics' sake alone. The arguments had to do with the etymology of how whites—or Caucasians—labelled their darker brethren. Concurrent with the new sense of liberation felt just after World War II, Negroes wanted to—even insisted on—being able to define themselves instead of accepting whatever name—or label—was given to them by whites. There could be little meaningful political liberation without true cultural liberation. This cultural metamorphosis began with self-definition. At the beginning of the Depression in 1931, George Schuyler had written *Black No More* in which he railed against equivocating Negro leadership, and satirized America's fear of yellow, black, and brown peoples. The *Black* in his title was intentional and more biting than *Negro* would have been.

Negro novelists also had to contend with the burgeoning political liberation on the other side of the Atlantic Ocean. In West and East Africa, the immediate post-World War II era was the backdrop of the beginning of the end of European colonialism. When Great Britain's Prime Minister Harold McMillan spoke in the early 1960s of "the winds of change" sweeping across the African continent, rustlings had been felt as early as the late 1940s. In anglophone Africa in particular, there was no hint of uncertainty over nomenclature or self-definition. Africans were "black," proud of it, and centuries-old tribal loyalties actually favored ethnic purity. While Negro writers in America wrestled with the dilemma of light-skinned versus darker-skinned blacks, African novelists exposed the effects of colonialism in the Portuguese, French, English, and Afrikaans languages.

The 1940s in America had an even further distinction. It was the last full expanse of time before the advent of television and the portable radio. Radio was still king but one listened to it at home. *Amos 'n' Andy* and *Beulah* were popular caricatured Negro characters but without any lasting or redeeming import. They seemed to be faceless audio versions of the old *Coontown* series of cartoons in *Harper's Magazine* in the 1880s. Against this feckless exploitation of black people, the Negro novelist strained to be read, heard, and understood. Negro history in segregated or nominally integrated public schools was limited to acceptable figures like Booker T. Washington, George Washington Carver, and Mary McCloud Bethune. Richard Wright's *Native Son* was seen as threatening.

Richard Wright himself was easily the most famous Negro novelist of the decade, if not the most prolific. Bigger Thomas, the central character in *Native Son*, is posited as the embodiment of the contradiction inherent in male Negro America. There is on the one hand a striving for acceptance as an American with all that it includes. But juxtaposed alongside this yearning is the stark and graphic realization that being a true or real American is for white folks only. While some said that Wright reached stardom because white critics annointed him, there is no doubt that *Native Son* struck discordant notes of anguish, despair, and pathos.

Wright and other male writers also described the ambig-
uous, exploited, and tenuous position of black women. But
none could match the incisiveness, clarity, and attention to
detail that was etched by Zora Neale Hurston. It had been
historically difficult for black men to accurately portray black
women both because of the normal American relegation of all
women to second class status, and because black men have
nearly always felt a visceral competitiveness with their mates.
America had never let black men be "real men" without
paying a dear price that included neuroses, sociopathological
behavior, and psychological dysfunction. Indeed, there was no
archetypal black woman analagous to the fictionalized and
romanticised Southern white virginal belle.

There were precious few black women of education, wealth,
and social status who could serve as paradigms for all other
black womenhood. These roles were served variously by
ministers' (ordained or not) wives and daughters, black
college presidents' wives and daughters, and perhaps the wife
and/or daughter of the handful of black doctors. The tenacity
with which this ambiguity remained is somewhat evident by
the lukewarm reception accorded the feminist movement of
the 1970s by black women. No novel of the 1940s even hinted
at a nascent but coordinated black feminist movement with
the same goals as their white sisters. Perhaps it was precisely
this void that inspired the prose and poetry of black women
writers that began in earnest during the black social revolution of the 1960s.

For black men and women novelists of the 1940s there was
seldom enough economic and psychic breathing space to
write full-time. As is pointed out, no one wrote more than two
novels in this ten-year period. Though thought of as a
profession by the authors themselves, writing did not pay well
"up front," and there was a clear past history of competition
among blacks for patrons. Arnold Rampersad's *The Life of
Langston Hughes: 1902–1941* makes note often of a "godmother"

shared by Hughes and Alain Locke. Most black novelists had no such assistance, and frequently wrote with only a remote possibility of begin published. According to Charles Harris, the black publisher of Amistad Press's *Daemonic Genius* by Margaret Walker, "the vast majority of black authors up through today feel that for them there may be no second chance; that one flop may mean no more published works." In other words, the godmother for Hughes and Locke in the pre-World War II era has been replaced by giant bottom-line-oriented publishing firms in the 1980s. Consequently, even writers like Frank Yerby, who was considered very prolific in the 1940s, could hardly subsist completely on commissions alone.

The themes expressed in this decade can now be viewed somewhat objectively and part of a continuum right up to the 1990s. Barbara Chase-Riboud has certainly learned and followed the rich detail of Zora Neale Hurston. In both *Sally Hemmings* and *The Echo Of Lions*, Chase-Riboud borrows from historical omissions of seminal figures in African-American history who have been studiously demoted to footnote status. David Bradley and John Edgar Wideman in the 1980s showed more than a trace of Richard Wright, though Bradley and Wideman tend more to non-fiction. Wideman has written of his imprisoned brother (in real life) in vivid detail, and one can think of him as a Bigger Thomas (in *Native Son*) from a middle-class family. With the same fortunate opportunities open to his sibling, Wideman makes a good case that racism remains so pervasive that black sociopaths will still emerge even in culturally advantaged families.

Finally, the novelists herein write of what Dr. Maulana Karenga of the Institute of Pan African Studies calls "the black masses." The subject matter is real people with real problems with unreal expectations. America has teased and formally indoctrinated blacks with the exalted notions of equality and freedom, yet these highly desirable states always seem just barely out of reach: theoretically possible but practically wanting.

I am, in 1990, struck by the way most of the works of this decade were ended. Was the "happy ending" typical? As a matter of fact, no. Nearly all left the reader with a graphic account of the anguish and pain and suffering, but few solutions that did not seem incongruent or born of wistful fantasies. Those resolutions had to wait another fifteen to twenty-five years when the anger of the 1960s had been synthesized. Without that sea change in awareness brought about by television, the writers in this book conjured up detailed but true portraits of life in black America. This collection is enough to give even the most casual reader pause to reflect and to ponder if the world described in these pages is the same one they encountered in their history books in high school. If not, then the history books are incomplete.

ARTHUR ASHE
January 1990

FOREWORD

The present study had its inception four years ago. Consultation with my adviser, Professor S. H. Nobbe, and Professor Vernon Loggins, who wrote *The Negro Author*, advanced the notion that the material on Negro fiction should be brought up to date. My approach to this subject has been one of detachment, for I have endeavored to dissociate myself from all personal bias. Impressionistic criticism may be valuable and does have a function, but in a work of this nature, logical and seasoned scholarship takes precedence over opinionated discussions. It has been my purpose throughout to marshall evidence which proves the thesis rather than to generalize subjectively. As David Daiches points out in *Study of Literature*, one is always handicapped by inherent dangers of contemporary subjects. I may very well have become a victim of contemporaneity. Such was not my objective, because I have tried always to treat the material fully but with scholarly soberness.

I am especially grateful to Professor O. J. Campbell, Executive Officer of the English Department, Columbia University, who manifested an interest in my work. His observant eye has witnessed perceptible changes in the status of the Negro, yet his innate sense of justice has caused him to acquiesce in favor of the Negro's improved status.

I am grateful to Professor S. H. Nobbe, Professor Mark Van Doren, and Professor Dorothy Brewster who disciplined and pruned me of my excesses. I am grateful to Professor Alan Walker Read whose cordial receptivity of me as a student was gratifying indeed, and his suggestions helpful. I am grateful to Dr. Stewart C. Easton, Dr. Joseph Duncan, Dr. John Jacobs, and Mr. Burt Coleman of United Nations who read the manuscript at various stages and made pertinent suggestions. I am grateful to Syedsatid Hosain.

I am grateful also to Mr. Justin Pearson and Mr. John Brunner for suggestions, and Mr. Larry Harter checked the chapter, "Reputations," for errors in quotations and bibliography.

I am grateful to Mr. George Small, Counselor, Furnald Hall, and to Mr. Ben Jerman who made the facilities of Furnald Hall and personal property available to me. I am grateful to Mr. Jack Falcon for financial assistance.

The members of the staff of the New York Public Library, Schomberg collection, were most cordial and helpful, especially Miss Jean Blackwell, Curator.

And to the many students at Columbia University, with whom I held interminable discussions of this subject, I express my gratitude.

CARL MILTON HUGHES

Columbia University
June, 1953

ACKNOWLEDGMENTS

For permission to quote from copyrighted materials, I am indebted to the following:

American Book Company, For permission to quote from *History of American Letters,* by Walter Taylor (Copyright 1936)

Appleton, Century, Crofts Inc., For permission to quote from *Knock on Any Door,* by Willard Motley (Copyright 1947)

Basil Blackwell and Mott Ltd., For permission to quote from *Biographia Literaria,* by Samuel Taylor Coleridge (Copyright 1940)

Columbia University Press, For permission to quote from *What's in a Novel,* by Helen Haines (Copyright 1942)
The Negro Author, by Vernon Loggins (Copyright 1931)

Creative Age, For permission to quote from *God is for White Folks,* by Will Thomas (Copyright 1947)

The Dial Press Inc., For permission to quote from *Floodtide,* by Frank Yerby (Copyright 1950)

Dorrance and Company Inc., For permission to quote from *Flour Is Dusty,* by Curtis Lucas (Copyright 1943)

Doubleday and Company Inc., For permission to quote from *Blood on the Forge,* by William Attaway (Copyright 1941)
If He Hollers Let Him Go, by Chester B. Himes (Copyright 1946)

E. P. Dutton and Company Inc., For permission to quote from *The Confident Years: 1885-1915,* by Van Wyck Brooks (Copyright 1951)
Sartar Resartus, by Thomas Carlyle, *Everyman's Library* (Copyright 1948)
Alien Land, by Willard Savoy (Copyright 1948)

Farrar, Straus, and Young, Inc., For permission to quote from *Anger at Innocence,* by William Smith (Copyright 1950)
Last of the Conquerors, by William Smith (Copyright 1948)

Viking Press, Inc., For permission to quote from *The Portable Blake*, selections and arrangement, with introduction, by Alfred Kazin (Copyright 1946)

The American Democracy, by Harold Laski (Copyright 1948)

Yale University Press, For permission to quote from *An Essay on Man*, by Ernest Cassirer (Copyright 1944)

Ziff-Davis Publishing Company, For permission to quote from *Third Ward Newark*, by Curtis Lucas (Copyright 1943)

CONTENTS

THE NEGRO NOVELIST

INTRODUCTION

May we not say, however, that the hour of
Spiritual Enfranchisement is even this:
When your ideal world, wherein the whole
man has been dimly struggling and
inexpressibly languishing to work, becomes
revealed and thrown open; and you discover,
with amazement enough, like the Lothario in
Wilhelm Meister, that your "America is
here or nowhere?"

Sartor Resartus, Carlyle

This book examines novels written by Negro authors during
the decade 1940-1950. Two assumptions must be made
at the outset. First, there is one main stream of American
literature. Secondly, various ethnic groups like tributaries
flowing into a large river contribute to the main stream of
American belles lettres. Out of this amalgam which is cos-
mopolitan in character emerges our national literature. Indeed, the fusion of diversified nationalities into a common
mold which reflects a democratic society gives American
literature its distinctive flavor.

The present study is a specialized subject, and as such has certain limitations. Ostensibly, selectivity may very well appear to be only sociological content rather than literary criticism. Such is not the case, for the interest lies primarily in an analysis of the novel rather than in the Negro by social definition.[1] The working principle involved advances the method of writing of Negro novelists in the same manner that a writer uses when discussing Theodore Dreiser. In this instance attention focused on the fact of his German origin serves merely as a biographical detail.[2] The really significant aspect of Dreiser, man and author, is his naturalistic method of writing as revealed in *An American Tragedy, Sister Carrie,* and other of his works. In the same way the fact that a novelist is a Negro only illuminates the content of a novel when it appears manifestly. Biographical data can not be completely separated from particular novels. On the other hand, it need not be the central point unless, of course, it is an autobiographical novel.

The creative imagination of any writer reveals salient features of the culture which nurtured it. As a consequence novels which utilize materials within the cultural pattern disclose similarities of technique and general execution. Novels by Negro authors do not necessarily become excerpts of Negro life in the commonly accepted connotation of the word Negro. Usually, the underprivileged hero becomes a detested segment of the population. The Negro in America proves no exception to this general rule. Because of the stigma attached to the word Negro and the insistence upon the content of the

---

[1] Gunnar Myrdal, *An American Dilemma,* pp. 114-115. "The definition of the 'Negro race' is thus a social and conventional, not a biological concept. The social definition and not the biological facts actually determines the status of an individual and his place in interracial relations. . . . In modern biological or ethnological research 'race' as a scientific concept has lost sharpness of meaning, and the term is disappearing in sober writings."

[2] F. O. Matthiessen, *Theodore Dreiser,* p. 26.

Negro novel as sociology, books by Negro authors receive severe critical judgment.

Investigation of the novels shows that biographical material appears frequently. When it does, the novel has that peculiar coloring which literary critics designate a Negro cast. The implication is that the content of the novel deviates from the notion of generally accepted white norms. Emphasis upon the seamy side of life becomes unpalatable. Undeniably, this side of life diverges from known and acceptable white patterns of standardized living. Even in this milieu, the Negro affords an engaging phenomenon for fictional purposes. Dr. W. E. B. Du Bois, "prophetic historian of his people," [3] before midcentury mused eloquently that "one must remember that it would be inconceivable to have a literature, even that written by white men, and not have the Negro as a subject. For he injected a spiritual quality into American life." [4]

Negro authors, rather than the American concept of Negroes, may be viewed to advantage in the novels. Here is the craftsman seriously at work in a medium which he knows. The art of telling a story well has not eluded the Negro writer. In fact, it has always been characteristic of some Negroes. Whether a Negro relates incidents of ribaldry and earthiness because of impoverishment or isolation or whether he subscribes to urbanity with its attendant sophistication, there seems to emanate always from a certain type of Negro with the least provocation a spritely story. To sustain interest humor combines generally with this narrative gift. Negro novelists continue the tradition of the fable with a point. If the Negro writer has substituted a more grim and shocking realism, it is because humor fails to serve his purpose of advancement. The Negro author writes predomi-

---

[3] Ludwig Lewisohn, *Expression in America,* p. 355.
[4] W. E. B. Du Bois, *The Souls of Black Folk,* p. 293.

nantly the novel of purpose, and the critics, for the most part, assign him this category.

The *New Negro* insists that assimilation of the American way has become fait accompli. Irrepressible high spirits of other periods have been supplanted by frustrations of the Atomic Age. Negro characters appear who are the exact antithesis of prevalent concepts of Negroes and their behavior. The novelists who depict such characters echo the challenging sentiments of Alain Locke who wrote that the "intelligent Negro is resolved not to make discrimination an extenuation for his shortcomings in performance, individual or collective. He holds himself at par neither inflated by sentimental allowances nor depreciated by current social discounts." [5]

In retrospection the forties proved to be a productive period for Negro novelists. Actually, critical reception favored an increasingly large number of novels because of their high literary merit. This book, through critical analysis, develops the thesis that Negro novelists of the forties broadened their perspective. Less exclusively preoccupied with racial themes, they grappled with the problems of mankind in American society. As a consequence, Negro novelists attempt to illustrate, to interpret, and to understand life more fully. Their literary products contain an element of protest when they present a realistic depiction of the Negro world with its limitations. This tendency is paralleled by another which is far more inclusive than a single racial preoccupation. With this step taken the Negro author illustrates the two parallel tendencies which characterize the Negro writings of the forties. This tendency marks a break with naturalism and the accompanying philosophy of determinism or the mechanistic theory of life. It does not exclude realistic writing. Documented novels by Negro novelists have been rather

---

[5] Alain Locke, *The New Negro*, p. 6.

consistently referred to as propaganda. In the sense that "all literature propagates ideas," [6] this is admittedly true, but in the sense of the acceptance of a specialized doctrine contrary to our basic institutions, this is fallacious. Since uncertainties describe the forties, Helen Haines' observation gains in validity: "For the element of propaganda that is infused in the fiction of the last decade is primarily sign and expression of the turmoil of the period itself with its changing, intensifying social consciousness and its deepening conflict of political dogma." [7]

By taking up the cudgel for reform, the Negro novelists do not violate their medium. On the contrary, they align themselves with tradition, for social issues have been material for great works of literature. Literature, in general, and the novel in particular, which does not have substance and narrative power fails. Indeed, "intense social awareness" [8] characterizes the Negro novel of purpose during the forties. Thus, propaganda which does not stray from socially approved values within society is a part of literature. Because "literature is a social institution." [9]

The phenomenon known as the Negro world supplies source material for some Negro novelists. In recreating a world which approximates closely reality, they display penetrating insight into the structure of society. To present this material effectively is tantamount to translating actual, human, and personal experience to the level of literature. The Negro novelist enables the reader to understand immediately the difference between living under limitations imposed from without and superimposed handicaps arising from within. This blatant set of inequities has parallel cases in the historical past of countries subscribing to western civilization. The im-

---

[6] Mark Van Doren, *The Private Reader*, p. 32.
[7] Helen Haines, *What's in a Novel*, p. 84.
[8] Lionel Trilling, *The Liberal Imagination*, p. 214.
[9] David Daiches, *Literature and Society*, p. 269.

mediacy of the situation demands restraint of the writer. As a matter of fact, the life which he depicts taxes the ingenuity of the serious Negro writer because he must avoid the pitfall of emotionality. His language must fit the case. At the same time he has for his purpose to select and to organize highly charged material and to present it in such a way to attract an audience. He advances the notion that one man is ultimately without any advantage over another, but the advantage of power is always with one of the two persons involved. It becomes a case where Edward Gholson is incisive when he observes: "Logic forbids the Negro from entertaining any fantastic illusion about the eradication of prevalent injustices." [10]

Thus, the Negro novelist takes into account conditions of the inhabitants of the Negro world. For the most part the Negro role and status are indefinable. Assimiliation by the dominant group has not occurred, and subtle, often vicious, barriers prevent the facilitation of the process. The Negro can not escape racial self-consciousness and remains "within himself an ethnic." [11] Within society yet outside its full areas of participation, this enigma of life affords the necessary emotional conflict for the dramatic content of the novel. Indeed, the nature of the medium with its flexibility permits the Negro to write of life with flourishes and embellishments. By so doing he placates the conscience of white America. Paradoxically enough, knowledge that the dominant group may or may not have a national guilt feeling about the situation but has a vested interest which prevents alleviation of it makes the novel with Negro authors an instrument of criticism. Thus, the Negro novelist as critic of American society is in keeping with Freud's thesis that "we may expect

---

[10] Edward Gholson, *The Negro Looks into the South*, p. 104.

[11] David Reisman, *The Lonely Crowd*, pp. 334-335. (Reisman defines this situation as the monolithic process of life.)

in the course of time changes will be carried out in our civilization so that it becomes more satisfying to our needs and no longer open to reproaches we have made against it." [12]

Freud continues with an indictment of America which seems an untenable position, for the reason for the Negro novelist's attack upon American society is that he believes change is both possible and inherent in the democratic process. Furthermore, he agrees with Cassirer who expresses it more adroitly in this excerpt:

Business of Utopia is to make room for the possible as opposed to a passive acquiescence in the present actual state of affairs. It is symbolic thought which overcomes the natural inertia of man and endows him with a new ability, the ability constantly to reshape his human universe. [13]

Society bears the paramount responsibility for the development of literature because it is by definition concerned with the social process. Evidently close to society, literature comments upon it, ferrets out intrinsic weakness, and in a measure continues its traditions. The point of any fiction which is taken from a social milieu is to approximate reality, and in the process such fiction becomes part of the significant experience of mankind. It becomes revelatory of insights into the social order and into man who seeks to understand himself and society. This transformation of the familiar into a satisfying literary work becomes the function of the novelist in society. Aesthetics are not thrown overboard. As a matter of fact, the value of literature depends upon the craftsman's narrative gift and creativity. The novelist, using material of society, analyzes, objectifies, and presents. He may very well

---

[12] Sigmund Freud, *Civilization and Its Discontents,* pp. 92-93.
[13] Ernest Cassirer, *Essay on Man,* p. 61.

pose a moral question and demand reform. It is only through implication that the question of morality, that is to say, the goodness or badness of the situation in the novel strikes its mark.

Mumford Jones extends with consummate skill the idea in his definition:

> Literature . . . is not just a mirror reflecting social trends and economic predilections. It is not a faithful but amateurish replica of philosophical ideas only. These may influence it and furnish some part of its substance, but literary history is also a study of the relation of the forms of art to the development of sensibility in that portion of society which responds in a given epoch to literary appeals. The writer is neither wholly the embodiment of a primitive, irrational, creative urge, nor wholly the half-conscious product of sociological and economic determinants. His appeal is of course to thought and feeling, but his emotive direction like his emotional apperception is a part of the sensibility of his time, and his intellectual energy is not confined to the ideational content of what he writes but is also expended upon the conscious manipulation of form for the sake of aesthetic freshness.[14]

Terminology which will appear in this book must be defined. Negro novelists have employed naturalism and realism as literary forms. There are a number of definitions given by scholars.[15] In this book, however, naturalism means that art of writing which disdains literary graces and purports to tell the truth about life as it is revealed by science. In the collection of detailed evidence, there is methodical documentation of such matters as heredity and environment.[16] It takes in the underprivileged and dispossessed classes of society.

---

[14] Mumford Jones, *Ideas in America,* p. 42.

[15] Vernon Parrington, *Main Currents in American Thought,* p. 427.

[16] F. O. Matthiessen, *American Renaissance,* pp. i-xiv.

Often there is concern with the revolting aspects of life, and the authors use abundant psychological detail.

Realism, on the other hand, is to be understood as a general tendency or purpose of conveying to the reader a strong sense of things actual in experience and within the range of average life. There is obviously a correspondence between the two. But realism is the more inclusive literary form.

Naturalism in dealing with the observable facts of society which provides a setting in the case of the Negro points up the conflicts on account of racial differences. In a larger sense this type of writing becomes a part of a philosophy which conceives of man in a mechanistic framework, and his life is determined. He meets the inevitable frustration because of environment and heredity. On the surface this would seem to be the real basis from which all Negro novelist's portrayals of American Negro life must stem. But there enters the picture another set of complexes which are predominantly sociological, for such conditions as inequalities, injustices, and general suppression should be attributed to environmental factors and are only sociological in implication. Since the basic philosophy of naturalism assumes that man has no free will either external or internal, "belief in free will in the abstract" [17] only is an admitted fact by the naturalist. The philosophy underlying the American experiment in democracy is out of harmony with determinism and its mechanistic concept of man. Intelligent choice is the activity of free man whether he exercises it or not. Rationality is assumed, and irrationality is frowned upon. Furthermore, there is a pervading optimism, moralism, and a certain amount of individualism in the "American temper." [18] Since this is true, the Negro author, making no attempt to formulate a new

[17] Lars Ahnebrink, *The Beginning of Naturalism in American Fiction*, pp. 184-185.

[18] Vernon Parrington, *Main Currents in American Thought*, pp. 325-327.

philosophy, employs a naturalistic thesis rather than a brand of naturalistic philosophy. The Negro author subscribes to the type of naturalism which shows the influence of Theodore Dreiser rather than the great French writer, Emile Zola.[19] There is one aspect of life which is at variance with naturalistic philosophy, and that is religion. The Negro has accepted the ethical code of Jesus Christ, and he is, for the most part, under the influence of the church as propounded by followers of Wesley, Calvin, Luther, and the Church of England, or the Church at Rome.[20]

But there are numerous factors in the environment which operate against the Negro, and as such must be carefully documented and projected in narrative form for the sake of advocating change. Negro novelists stress the role of the "underprivileged" [21] and the dispossessed Negro inhabitant of America. There is an indictment of society in the novel of protest because the society in which the Negro lives permits vice and corruption to undermine basic personality growth. Environmental factors pave the way for the demoralization of the character of many Negroes. Here, the didactic element comes out. In a large sense the human spectacle so helpless before heredity and environmental forces evokes sympathy.

Negro novelists, anticipating sympathetic vogue books and using a naturalistic thesis, grapple with social problems. These problems arise from wrongs in American society which Negro novelists consider too urgent to by-pass. The position of the minorities in American society is often precarious. Most of the Negro novelists are imbued with the idea of American democracy. They believe earnestly that the ideals promulgated by the system may be attained. Convinced that the change is possible, the Negro authors underscore their com-

---

[19] Alfred Kazin, *On Native Grounds,* pp. 474-80.
[20] Mary Scally, *Negro Catholic Writers,* pp. 37-42.
[21] Helen Haines, *What's in a Novel,* p. 84.

mentary and protest against American injustice. This process becomes a relative question, that is to say, one of degree because in only a few instances is the assimilative process in operation. Faith in the American way, however, assumes almost spiritual proportions. For the American Negro believes with Mumford Jones that "Americans desire a world in which men shall have something like a fair share of mortal goods and a fair chance at immortal ones." [22]

Since the Negro novelist's output of the forties is necessarily the serious novel of purpose when he deals with racial themes, there appears and reappears protest against the Negro's role of subordination. On the other hand, there are novels which do not protest at all. By and large, they indicate an adjustment to the American way of life by Negroes in which there is a separateness in matters of race observed religiously. There comes from such a work resignation to the most elementary necessities of life. These works are objectionable to some Negroes because resignation to the status quo is out of harmony with concern for political and economic issues which are the most important elements in American life for the underprivileged Negro.

There emerge from works using naturalistic thesis by Negro writers vignettes of wealthy and poor people. The juxtaposition of the two has made almost an accepted fact of life that there must and will be these two segments in society. Along with this principle goes the fact that poor people have ceaselessly striven to improve, to become in fact a member of the wealthy group. At bottom the materialistic philosophy has invaded the consciousness of both groups. Conflicts remain between them. Often this situation alone has provided sufficient dramatic content for fictional purposes.

For practical purposes characters appearing in a work of

---

[22] Mumford Jones, *Ideas in America,* p. 72.

art may be rendered faithfully. Oppression in itself may or
may not move one to sympathy. In its abstract sense oppression may be reinforced with neutrality. It becomes another
aspect of sociology. But add human being to the situation in
which he is oppressed on account of "man's inhumanity to
man," and one begins to find room for sympathy and concern. Always forces are at work in society to oppress and
often to corrupt human beings. The serious writer, in a number of cases, helps to organize man's thinking on pertinent
social issues.[23]

This book adheres to a formal method of criticism.[24] The
point of departure is a combination of methods and proposes
to place Negro novels in a frame of reference which evaluates precisely their literary worth. To accomplish this purpose,
the author employs translation, interpretation, and evaluation.
The a priori assumption that literature is life with all of its
ramifications concerns us. All of life must not be lost in
ambiguity. The exact connotation here is life as reflected in
organized society, more particularized, organized life in the
American cultural pattern. Values common to the thought
generated in this society must be a component of critical
method. One is aware of constantly changing values in the
western world.

In general, American critical history continues to be realistic, and lifelike it ascribes to novels by Negro authors a
special place in the categories of criticism, or the author is
designated necessarily as a minor one.[25] In many cases
Negroes are omitted from critical studies which deal with
American literature. Such omissions imply a state of neglect

23 David Daiches, *Literature and Society,* pp. 262-267.

24 This method is based on the following sources: Stanley E. Hyman,
The Armed Vision, pp. 3-19; V. F. Calverton, *The Newer Spirit,* pp.
19-51; David Daiches, *Study of Literature,* pp. 71-84; T. S. Eliot,
Criticism in America, p. 205; E. M. Forster, *Aspects of the Novel,* pp.
40-80.

25 H. Steele Commager, *The American Mind,* p. 250.

of this aspect of American literature which has not yet been found worthy of equally serious consideration. However, such a fair appraisal as the following is gratifying:

> But more important than either the Indian or the cowboy literature which has been recovered, and added to the native stock of our tradition, is the growth of Negro literature which has made a far greater contribution to American culture. The contributions of the Negro to American culture are as indigenous to our soil as the legendary cowboy or gold seeking frontiersman. In fact, I think, it can be said without exaggeration, that they constitute a large part of whatever claim America can make to originality in its cultural history. . . .[26]

The Negro novelist is entrenched in the literary world. Simultaneously, he must operate in isolation. He is accorded all of the privileges and rewards of the profession. On the one hand, he is acclaimed; on the other, he is defamed. He is, and he is not. But indestructibility throws a protective armor, as it were, about him. He in turn refurbishes his richly endowed imagination and creates. Vernon Loggins, who studied the Negro authors, caught critically this evident power and he wrote: "If his (Negro's) consciously produced literature shows nothing else, it shows tenacity of purpose." [27]

The Negro novelist perceives quite clearly that the ultimate test is creative ability which speaks the voice of humanity. Translation means, therefore, in this book to present a concise resumé of the content of the book or a paraphrase. Often illustrative quotations will be given in order to acquaint the reader better with the particular work and the author's technique. The thematic content of the novel will be given. Fables have their own charm and interest for the reader of fiction. The books by Negro novelists continue in a measure this literary tendency.

---

[26] V. F. Calverton, *Liberation of American Literature,* p. 438.
[27] Vernon Loggins, *The Negro Author,* p. 365.

Interpretation means in this book the relation the particular novel bears to society. This implies that the Negro novel is literature which expresses ideals, sympathies, and hopes of those who look forward to the conquest of poverty, ignorance, and inequality. A society which harbors such debilitating diseases may very well run the risk of seriously endangering its functional role. In a democratic society where there appear articulate writers who represent the underprivileged, a predominantly social literature will emerge. Such literature has as its major purpose the material and intellectual elevation of mankind. This is by no means new in the annals of literature. Indeed, throughout the ages popular social writers have enriched the literature of a particular society because they brought forward in the language of the people controversial issues.

Sociological interpretation and naturalistic fiction have concordance at several levels. In others they hardly take into account other philosophical questions or literary innovations designed to be purely artistic. By interpretation the novels which deal with racial themes are realistic. The very nature of the Negro's position in American society would hardly permit, except in rare cases, any other approach. So it is "literature brought closer to the life which men know, the plain, the true, the human." [28]

Evaluation means the assessment of judgment upon the novel in terms of criteria for an aesthetically satisfying piece of fiction. Certain definite properties belong to the medium.[29] Stress is not placed upon the mere mechanics of the novel but rather upon the accomplishment of the author with the form. The following questions form the matrix of the evaluating process: Does the author accomplish his purpose? Does a particular author in question have anything to say?

---

[28] F. O. Matthiessen, *American Renaissance,* p. 471.
[29] Edwin Muir, *The Structure of the Novel,* pp. 80-86.

How does he handle his material? What are his techniques? Why does this particular character succeed or fail? Does the author insist upon social commentary only, or does he transform his material into an artistic rendition? Is it aesthetically good or bad? In totality does the work possess literary value?

This study deals appropriately with parallel cases within the dominant group of writers in American literature. Indeed, the unmistakable influence of Americanism attests to the commonality of creative treatment. In creative expression the one way of life makes the "all" myth more than a popular political slogan. There is, as most anthropologists admit readily, a cultural one to one correspondence between the two groups. Negro novelists have not written in cultural isolation. Naturally, there are similarities with the other group of writers dealing with similar themes.

Thus, the critical method evolved is one in accordance with modern criticism. This stems from the combat with traditional criticism which seeks to explain only in terms of classical studies and classical techniques. Contemporaneity suggests a use of accumulative experience. Naturally, this should and does take into account basic principles which were evolved in antiquity. In another sense this means indubitably emphasizing aspects of society far removed from antiquity. Surely, modern criticism maintains the essence of classical thought, but it brings into focus a multitudinous array of dissimilar problems. Interpretation must account for this social phenomena and entirely different type of writer, for various interpretations are given works by the modern writer unknown to the ancients. Literature is a social institution and employs as its medium language which is a social creation. The common approach in modern criticism which failed to be of any consequence at all to earlier epochs is to the relation of literature and society. Hence, literary products may be viewed as social documents. Litera-

ture so used yields outlines of a particular society. Indeed,
such an approach fosters a more complete comprehension of
the novel as assumed pictures of social reality. Sociological
and economic aspects of a society are cogently pointed out
in documents. Features of a society and concepts within in it
may be per se fallacious. Reflection upon certain novels
reveals contradictory character of men and the world they
have ipso facto changed.

Modern tragedy is discussed in relation to the novels.
Negro novelists have succeeded in writing novels which subscribe to the principles of modern tragedy. Walter Taylor
labels this type of tragedy "naturalistic of which Dreiser's
work is exemplary," [32] but Annis Sandvos designates it the
"tragedy of the common man." [33] The present writer is content to use the term modern tragedy, and it means insignificant men in terms of social strata who are frustrated, unable
to cope with life because of circumstances beyond their
control, and they are unhappy. These men are placed in a
society which creates desires but fails to provide the means
by which they may gratify them. They are circumscribed by
automatic mechanisms which are quite oblivious to the sufferings of mere, puny, and blundering man. Obviously, man
is helpless in such a situation before the overwhelming and
disintegrating forces which conspire against him. Thus, modern tragedy "assumes the insignificance of man" [34] rather
than his importance. As a consequence of this position, it
portrays the depressing and bleak aspects of man in his low
position in the scheme of life.

Modern tragedy differs from classical tragedy both in the
Greek and Shakespearean sense, for both deal with the great
and powerful of the earth. In such a social framework, great-

---

[32] Walter Taylor, *History of American Letters,* pp. 373-375.
[33] Annis Sandvos, *Flight from Aristotle,* p. 328.
[34] Taylor, *op. cit., p.* 374.

ness of human nature is portrayed, and man's importance in the universe is not challenged but accepted as a primary premise. These men, in keeping with their rank in society, expressed lofty ideals, powerful emotions, and grand passions. Their sufferings because of fate or some inherent weakness in the moral order evoke sympathy. One is stimulated from the reading of classical tragedy rather than depressed. There comes from such a tragedy that feeling that man still possesses strength of soul which may contend with an intervening fate. The Nemesis which pursues a Shakespearean character stems from spiritual torment, and one feels pity and terror, for by identification this fate may very well be personal for any lofty soul. Universal emotions of any man are expressed in both classical and Shakespearean tragedy. In a sense the fearful close of such a tragedy gives the spectator real elevation of mind and a sense of the nobility of mankind.

Modern tragedy does contain elements which call forth pity from the spectator, but it is an austere pity and one does not feel that he is nearer to the ultimate meaning of life. But one does discern easily that here is a mass of humanity under the control of forces which need not be. This calls for reflection upon the order and the particular manipulation man may give to his social structure to alleviate these sickeningly disintegrating conditions rather than "profound soul searching" or indulging in "sophisticated passion." [35]

Even though sophisticated passion is not generally ascribed to Negro novels, they had their historical origin in tragedy. William Wells Brown's novel, *Clotel; or, The President's Daughter: a Narrative of Slave Life in the United States,* appeared in London in 1853. Conditions of life for the Negro slave during the pre-Civil War days were tragic and sordid indeed. In a measure they continue so today. The heroine

---

[35] O. J. Campbell, *Living Shakespeare,* pp. 52-53.

Clotel meets a tragic end. American publication of this first serious attempt by a Negro novelist was delayed until 1864 despite the enthusiastic reception of it by Abolitionists. His second published novel in America was *My Southern Home* which appeared in 1880. Frances Harper wrote *Iola Leroy or, Shadows Uplifted* (1893), and Walter Stowers' *The Appointed* followed in 1894. Paul L. Dunbar, internationally acclaimed Negro poet, published his first novel, *The Uncalled,* in 1898. Charles W. Chesnutt's first fiction, *The Conjure Woman* (1899), marks the end of the output of Negro fiction writers of the nineteenth century.

At the beginning of the century, there was a group of Negro writers, guided by a sense of reform and protest based on moral compunctions, who wrote competent novels. Of this group works by Chesnutt express the aspirations of the Negro and his desires for integration. *The House Behind the Cedars* (1900), *The Marrow of Tradition* (1901), a treatment of the miscegnation theme also, and *The Colonel's Dream* (1905), a study in race relationships, complete his canon of novels.[36] Paul L. Dunbar added to the field of literature *The Love of Landry* (1900), *The Fanatics* (1901), both dealing with his life among white friends; *The Sport of the Gods* (1902) ushers in his protest against conditions imposed upon Negroes. Sutton E. Griggs, overwhelmed by the injustices inflicted upon Negroes, sacrificed art in his vehement protest novels: *Overshadowed* (1901) plunges into the problem of race; *Unfettered* (1902) is a variation of the same topic; *The Hindered Hand* (1905) is a bloody, bloody book with scenes of almost indescribable horror; while *Pointing the Way* (1908), as the title suggests, is his proposed solution of the Negro problem. Pauline Hopkins, in the tradition of the late nineties, produced her pleas in *Contending Forces*

---
[36] Helen M. Chesnutt, *Charles W. Chesnutt,* p. 147.

(1900). E. A. Johnson's *Light Ahead for the Negro* (1904) strikes an optimistic note in his analysis. John S. Durham turned his attention to the persecution of Negroes in Haiti in his work, *Diane: Priestess of Haiti* (1902). W. E. B. Du Bois, in his novel of purpose injects elements of the muckraking procedure of highly commendable merit. The plight of the Negro in the hand of the cotton belt octopus left many desiring immediate reform. *The Quest of the Silver Fleece* (1911) is the title of this effective novel.

G. Langhorne Pryor's *Neither Bond nor Free* (1902), as the title suggests, is an attack upon social conditions as they affect the Negro, while J. W. Grant in *Out of the Darkness or Diabolism and Destiny* (1909) strikes at the core of the social order. Robert L. Waring gives the Negro point of view in *As We See It* (1910), and Yorke Jones in *The Climbers: A Story of Sun-Kissed Sweethearts* (1912) follows the same approach. Oscar Mischeaux in *Conquest: The Story of a Negro Pioneer* (1913), his first novel, charts his course of action for Negroes. James Weldon Johnson's *The Autobiography of an Ex-Coloured Man* (1912) is the singular achievement of the protest literature of the period. He focused attention upon the problem of miscegenation and the attendant consequences of being a Negro in America. Actually, the autobiography had profound repercussions in the literature of the twenties and thirties known as the Negro Renaissance.

Race continued to be uppermost in the minds of the authors, but the emphasis shifted notably from the lynch motif to a glorification of black. Black as a color for its own sake is the watchword. Open rebellion against white standards and the initiation of an equally closed system based completely on the color black formulate a new set of regulations and properties. In one master stroke American weaknesses, foibles, hypocrises and irrationalities over race is mirrored. The work is one of the most significant contributions of the race theme in all of its moods in American literature.

The Forged Note (1915) by Oscar Mischeaux reviews evils of the Negro's existence. William M. Ashby's *Redder Blood* (1915) discusses miscegenation, while F. Grant Gilmore in *The Problem: A Military Novel* (1915) wrote one of the earlier war novels dealing with the Spanish-American War. Thomas Hamilton B. Walker wrote *J. Johnson: or The Unknown Man* (1915) which is largely biographical, and his *Bebbly: or The Victorious Preacher* (1910) dealt with Negro expression in religion. John E. Bruce in *The Awakening of Hezekiah Jones* (1916) presented a study in the Negro's political astuteness. George W. Ellis in *The Leopard's Claw* (1917) related events connected with the diamond industry in Africa. Oscar Mischeaux's *Homesteaders* (1917) again introduces the notion of emigrating to the less densely populated land in the Middle West. Sarah Lee Brown Fleming wrote *Hope's Highway* (1918) which piously resolved the race problem in religion. R. Archer Tracy in *The Sword of Nemisis* (1919) again attacked the race problem. Herman Dreer in *The Immediate Jewel of His Soul* (1919) followed the usual protest angle of Negro persecution in the United States, and Mary Ella Spenser, as the title *Resentment* (1920) indicates, develops the same theme. Otis Shackelford's *Lillian Simmons: or The Conflict of Sections* (1915) pointed to the vicious practice of segregation. William Pickens in *Vengeance of the Gods* (1922) invoked the God of justice to plead the Negro's cause, but he employed an ingenious trick which reversed the usual process. Joshua H. Jones in *By Sanction of the Law* (1924) described the flagrant practices of disobedience to the law in the American Republic where Negroes are involved. *Fire in the Flint* (1924) by Walter White discussed a Georgia riot and the injustices imposed upon the Negro. *There Is Confusion* (1924) by Jessie Fauset returned to the theme of passing which Walter White resumed in *Flight* (1926), giving credence to the all but white Negro's escape from Negro oppression to membership in the majority group.

W. E. B. Du Bois in his *Dark Princess* (1928) considered seriously the problem of union of the darker peoples of the world. In this probe into the international scene a new note is struck in political thinking. Rudolph Fisher in *The Walls of Jericho* (1928) exposed the fallacies of restricted covenants when a Negro moves into a white neighborhood. Nella Larsen in *Quicksand* (1928) discusses miscegenation. *Home to Harlem* (1928) by Claude McKay discussed World War I incidentally while glorifying Harlem despite economic barriers. Wallace Thurman in *The Blacker the Berry* (1929) wrote an avowed glorification of color piece. Nella Larsen complements her earlier work with the tragic grouping of her characters in *Passing* (1929). *Not Without Laughter* (1930) by Langston Hughes permitted the reader to view various strata of Negro life with economic sufficiency operating. Independence from the more subservient positions usually occupied by Negroes stand out. George Schuyler's *Black No More* (1931) offered one of the most scathing attacks upon American color phobia to be found in American literature. This rollicking satire gave the New Renaissance impetus with its incisive strokes. At the same time he attacks Negro leadership for its ineffectual role of vacillation. Jesse Fauset in *The Chinaberry Tree* (1931) guided the reader through the turmoil and final happiness of a fashionable Negro modiste. Arna Bontemps in his *God Sends Sunday* (1931) described the life of a Negro jockey. Countee Cullen's *One Way to Heaven* (1932) is a satire on middle-class Negro society and a study of the emotionalism of Negro religion with a perennial hypocrite as hero. Rudolph Fisher's *The*

Conjure Man Dies (1932) is a detective novel. *Infants of Spring* (1932) and *The Interne* (1932) by Wallace Thurman show the influence of Van Vechten's Harlem vogue and in his own fashion describes the lost generation of Negro artists. Claude McKay, with his *Banana Bottom* (1933), heads the list of important Negro writers. His tale gave a realistic picture of the island of Jamaica, glorifying black and the incidentally idyllic and pastoral quality of the life among the natives. Jesse Fauset in *Comedy: American Style* (1933) again presents the color line in a saga of white and black members of the same family. Their paths cross, and they recognize kinship. *Princess Malah* (1933) by John H. Hill documents a historical event in our glorious past in his discussion of George Washington. Zora Neale Hurston in *Jonah's Gourd Vine* (1934) gave an account of Negro life centered about the activities of a philandering minister. *Ollie Miss* (1935) by George W. Henderson is a simple novel depicting with clarity the life of sharecroppers in Alabama. O'Wendell Shaw's *Greater Need Below* (1936) placed the Negro problem in the stream of literature while Arna Bontemps delved into the Negro's history by depicting the Virginia Insurrection of 1800 in his *Black Thunder* (1936). Waters E. Turpin's *O Canaan* (1939) described a family history through several generations in Maryland. George Lee's *River George* (1937) documented the economic strangle of the Negro. Zora Neale Hurston produced *Their Eyes Were Watching God* (1937), a novel of Negro life during one of the floods in Florida. Significantly she portrayed life in an all-Negro town. Mercedes Gilbert in *Aunt Sara's Wooden God* (1938) discussed the problem of color when a mother has both a half-white child and a full-blooded Negro child. The odds favored the Negro child finally, but the mother worshiped the mulatto. Waters E. Turpin in *O Canaan* continued his family chronicle started in *These Low Grounds* (1937). Arna Bontemps in *Drums at Dusk* (1939) made another excursion into history. In this novel he gave the background to Toussaint L'Ouverture's great deeds in San Domingo.

Actually, the decade 1940-1950 represented a return to the pattern set by Charles Chesnutt in his novel, *The Colonel's Dream* (1905), in which all of the characters are Southern whites in conflict with Northern whites. Earlier, Paul L. Dunbar, Negro poet, in his promising novel, *The Fanatics* (1901), delineates white characters. The earlier Attaway novel, *Let Me Breathe Thunder* (1939), is a rollicking tale of Mexicans and whites on the road.

The essential difference between the earlier works and the novels of the forties is the reception accorded the novels by the reading public and the favorable criticism that the recent Negro writers have received. Publishers lost money on Chesnutt's works, while Frank Yerby of the forties enjoys the distinction of having written consistently commercial successes.

PORTRAYALS OF BITTERNESS

The Negro holds firmly the reins of his four horses,
    the block swags underneath on its tied-over chain,
The Negro that drives the long dray of the stone yard,
    steady and tall he stands pois'd on one leg on the
    stringpiece,
His blue shirt exposes his ample neck and breast and
    loosens over his hip-band,
His glance is calm and commanding, he tosses
    the slouch of his hat away from his forehead,
The sun falls on his crispy hair and mustache, falls
    on the black of his polish'd and perfect limbs.
I behold the picturesque giant and love him, and
    I do not stop there,
I go with the team also.
                Song of Myself   Walt Whitman

This chapter deals with categories in which novels of racial themes belong. First, there are psychological novels. Foremost among the novels which fall in this category is Richard Wright's *Native Son*. By his projection of a racial thesis, he anticipates Chester Himes' two psychological studies, *If He Hollers Let Him Go* and *Lonely Crusade,* and Curtis Lucas' *Third Ward Newark.* The second category is the economic novel[1] in which the plight of the Negro is graphically drawn. Ann Petry's *The Street,* William Attaway's *Blood On The Forge,* and Carl Offord's *The White Face* are representative.

Preoccupation with racial themes has been characteristic of Negro novelists in America throughout the twentieth century. Indeed, this tendency entrenched itself so firmly among the authors and the reading public that any deviation from the pattern proved unacceptable. In fact, a work written by a Negro dealing with other aspects of American life that was not, strictly speaking, Negro life usually drew rejection slips from prospective publishers. Thus the principle evolved that Negro novelists can write successfully and convincingly only about Negroes. Charles W. Chesnutt began the utilization of the specialized conditions of the Negro in an all white environment as material for a novel.[2] Writing in the expressionistic trend of his time, Chesnutt used the race phenomenon in producing a true work of art, *The House behind the Cedars.* The novel describes vividly problems of life peculiar to the American scene. Here, race is pictured in sharp relief and bold contrast. Moreover, the ultimate tragedy of the heroine, Rowena, is precipitated on account of her racial identity. Since the publication of Chesnutt's novels, racial themes in works by Negro authors have flourished in America. Strictly speaking, in this type of novel, there is always a primary postulate that because of color or ethnic background, Negroes in particular are different from their white neighbors even though both groups follow the same cultural

---

[1] Harlan Hatcher, *Creating the Modern American Novel,* p. 149.
[2] Vernon Loggins, *The Negro Author,* p. 272.

pattern. Negro writers, among whom Chesnutt was a pioneer, explode effectively the inherent fallacy of such a position.

In the decade 1940-1950 Negro novelists, following Chesnutt's innovation, achieved notable success with racial themes. As a matter of fact, exactly forty years after Chesnutt's *The House behind the Cedars,* Richard Wright became the "apostle of race" [3] with the publication of his phenomenally successful novel, *Native Son.*[4] Wright delves into the question of race with bludgeoning intensity. Actually, there exudes from his work such tremendous passion and concern for the Negro that only the most calloused person can read the book without extreme irritation or feelings of guilt.

Dorothy Canfield Fisher, novelist, whose works such as *Seasoned Timber* and *Deepening Stream* have enjoyed popularity, wrote an introduction to *Native Son.* In her introduction Dorothy Fisher describes in detail the underlying causes of Bigger's attitude and his type of mind. Bigger, simultaneously with his indoctrination of the Negro's inferiority, is introduced to the glowing account of American ideals and what they entail. The picture of the American citizen is inspiring indeed; particularly, what the American citizen should be. Bigger is made to understand that America is unique in its fundamental concept of individual freedom. All people are theoretically permitted to enjoy the freedoms of America and to participate as active citizens. The ideal American citizen is so conditioned that he becomes independent, courageous, and happy. He is encouraged to work out his own destiny within the cultural pattern in which he lives. American dogma is that any man may achieve financial success, leisure, and power.[5] Bigger knows this and wants

---

[3] Alfred Kazin, *On Native Grounds,* p. 372.

[4] Richard Wright, *Native Son.*

[5] Granville Hicks, *The Great Tradition,* p. 164.

desperately to be a genuine American citizen. He knows, however, from bitter experience that he can not attain the ideal because he is a Negro. This same society which holds out such an attractive way of life denies self-realization to him. He asks gropingly, "why?"

The conflicting forces at work within this youthful mind baffle Bigger, central character in *Native Son,* and at last overwhelm him. The consequence of Bigger's state of mind is an incurable neurosis. This psychological state produces in Bigger a criminal whose atrocious crimes astound and horrify the reader. It is clear, from the author's point of view, that society is responsible for Bigger. The only crime that he commits actually is the crime of being.

Richard Wright, like Chesnutt in his *Marrow of Tradition,* develops a thesis in *Native Son.* In effect he points up the fact that a Negro, placed in a hostile, white environment which denies him self-realization, throws the burden of responsibility for his crimes of frustration and fear upon society. In order to drives home his thesis, Richard Wright insists painstakingly upon the understanding of the psychological and sociological factors underlying the action of the novel.[6] In developing his grim thesis, Wright shows that the Negro's environment provokes crime, and unless the Negro is granted self-realization, one like Bigger will murder whites in order to obtain it. Striking at the core of race relationships, Wright does prove his case. In practice, however, the reverse is the case; for it is the Negro who is lynched with impunity without redress or remorse as the novel indicates.

Bigger's terrifying behavior pattern results from a special attitude produced by environment. Bigger, in truth, is forced to play such an unconventional role. In reality Bigger is a victim of society.

Richard Wright in his article, "How Bigger Was Born," [7]

---

[6] David Daiches, *Partisan Review,* May-June 1940, pp. 244-245.

explains carefully those qualities of personality which crystal-
lize into a type like Bigger. In his varied experiences in
Mississippi, Wright became acquainted with three individual
Negroes who, even though unlettered, intuitively resented
the role that they were forced to play in the world. Fully
aware of the consequences of their acts, these Negroes dared
to take their lives in their own hands. They flouted defiantly
traditions of white supremacy in an effort to break the
stranglehold of oppression imposed by Mississippi whites in
control of affairs. This control manifested itself in denial of
opportunity to the three men. Each in his own way found it
necessary to commit a violent crime which resulted in his
death in order to enjoy real freedom in that precious moment
between death and eternity. Deeply embedded within Bigger
is the sincere and honest desire to participate as a human
being without the limitations or a set pattern of life which
the order forces him to pursue. Bigger is a composite of the
three men. He, like his prototype, is driven to crime by fears
and frustrations produced by society.

With Bigger there is always a disproportionate amount of
fear, an anxiety, which rests squarely upon his utter race
consciousness. As a Negro all of the ideals espoused by men
echoing the ethos of the American democratic republic must
be denied him or granted grudgingly with emphasis upon
the fact that he is a Negro. Bigger is defeated before he is
born. Brooding over his plight, he becomes a frightened and
bewildered misfit. This leads him in the end to become a
violent youth who must be eliminated by society.

The Negro problem in the contemporary scene compelled
Wright to make of Bigger Thomas a spokesman for the dispossessed, the underprivileged, and the persecuted millions
of Negroes who inhabit America. Thus, Wright in creating
the character, Bigger, in *Native Son* strikes openly at the

---

[7] Richard Wright, *Saturday Review of Literature,* June, 1940, pp. 1-3.

society which produced him. Such a Negro as Bigger does
not conform to the generally accepted notions of the solution
of the problem. Wright emphasizes the fact that even though
gradual forces to correct the unmitigated oppression operate
to some degree, and certain gains in favor of the Negro are
won, reactionary forces, however, counteract the progress by
raising new barriers. This dramatic indictment of American
society is in keeping with the "angry thirties" [8] which produced Wright and his contemporaries such as John Steinbeck
and James Farrell.

Bigger Thomas is the embodiment of a particular type of
neurotic Negro. The psychology involved reflects the inter-
action between human personality and his environment. The
origin of Bigger's neurosis is frustration based on fear. As a
child he has been nurtured in a cesspool of bigotry and often
violent, human relationships in Mississippi. From infancy he
has been taught at home and in contact with whites that he
is a Negro. At best he must consider himself a little less than
a dog. In a fight with whites, he receives an injury. His
parents admonish him earnestly not to fight back but to take
all punishment inflicted upon him by whites. Bigger's nature
rebels against such injustice. Removed to Chicago, he then
settles in a ghetto which is all that his family's economic
standing can afford. Here, the pattern of race relationships
changes but only relatively. Bigger is still excessively aware
of his race. Conditioning, new and raw experiences in Chicago, drive home the lesson already mastered that he is a
despised intruder or a merely tolerated Negro. He ponders
over his fate and becomes increasingly embittered and ultimately mad.

Bigger's mental condition has been produced by the treatment of the Negro by the whites for hundreds of years in
America. He is a "member of an oppressed race, living in the

---

[8] Alfred Kazin, *On Native Grounds,* p. 369.

midst of the oppressors," [9] yet cut off from them socially, and in Bigger's case economically because he is unemployed. His behavior pattern becomes antisocial in the face of such punishment. Thus, he stands in sullen helplessness. This state of mind explains how he is able to feel happiness in freely accepting responsibility for a crime that he commits accidentally.

Biographical data about the author helps to explain the novel, *Native Son*. Richard Wright's background in Mississippi consisted of numerous effronteries to his personal dignity. Furthermore, his childhood may be best described as one of poverty. Hunger and a generous dose of brutality round out the picture of his youthful misery. In a violently anti-Negro section of America where dying embers of a dead aristocracy are rekindled by fantastic stories, Wright experienced the worst in race relationships. Indeed, the consciousness of the area has never accepted the Negro as anything more than a brute. These details appears in Wright's autobiographical work, *Black Boy*.[10]

The formative years of a person's life are the most highly impressionable ones. Humiliating, degrading, and "emasculating treatment by whites" [11] crystallized in Wright's consciousness. The one persistent idea in his mind was to escape this wrath of Achilles. Sufficiently removed from the actual scene, he, nonetheless, bore the scars of his wounds. Knowing that they will endure forever, Wright resolved to relate this particular set of his personal experiences to the world. The only feasible plan was to create a fictional character that would reveal the yearnings of his tortured mind. Incidentally, he divined it would make dramatic reading. His case was not to be confined to this character alone. Millions of Negroes still undergo to a degree the same type of experience. For

---

[9] David Daiches, *Partisan Review*, May-June, 1940, pp. 244-245.

[10] Richard Wright, *Black Boy*, pp. 20-60.

[11] Wright, *op. cit.*, p. 89.

example, many Negroes are deprived of education, so redress remains unquestionably a farce since the law operates against amelioration of conditions. Transferring this personal set of experiences to an imaginative creation, Wright achieved his apostleship for the Negro race.

The charge, communist inspired work, must be answered. Wright, the creative artist, is the exact opposite of Wright, the man with left-wing political views. Before the present strained relations with Russia became a dominant force in American affairs, Communist party members were not condemned too harshly. A number of "intellectuals" flirted with the ideas of Karl Marx and the "Communist party had its vogue." [12] Now common knowledge is that such affiliations are inimical to our national interests. The American lend-lease and Russian World War II partnerships are passé.

Admittedly, Wright had connections with the Communist party. But, like James Farrell, that hardly means that their books are necessarily communistic nor inspired by another ideology. Wright's views were presented in *The God that Failed*[13] along with the eminent French novelist, Andre Gide, and others. This forthright statement is a repudiation of communism. Frequent allusion to the Communist party and communism in the novel serve only as a technical device. It is part of the schematic plan and belongs to the organic whole. A creative writer, possessing a fluid consciousness, writes his impressions of life. His professional writing may or may not be influenced by his private life or personal political beliefs. By labeling every straightforward criticism of the conduct of American affairs communistic, persons expose a symptom of the uncertainties of our Atomic Age.[14] It has become a defense mechanism, and an automatic formula

---

[12] Malcolm Cowley, *Exile's Return*, p. 294.
[13] Crossman, Richard, *The God that Failed*.
[14] Eldred Nelson, *Our Atomic World*, pp. 26-40.

for disqualifying an opponent. The truth of the matter is that Wright expressed the resentments of millions of inarticulate Negroes. The struggle for eradication of injustices and inequalities of the underprivileged Negroes is difficult and slow. It continues to be evolutionary gradualism. Steinbeck in his novel, *The Grapes of Wrath,* poses brilliantly the same question of the plight of the dispossessed whites. The point of Wright's psychological novel of purpose is to portray intensely and clearly the racial issue. He develops his novel around the shock technique which demands atrocities and violence. An imposing number of great writers from classical Greece to the twentieth century have done the same thing. The correct interpretation of this "significant" piece of fiction[15] is that a creative imagination drew on its inspiration. Moral indignation and the philosophical concepts underlying American democracy inspired *Native Son* and not communism. Wright's purpose becomes evident. His work is conceived "in intuition," [16] planned with calculated deliberateness, and executed with economy and dexterity. His design of work insists upon penetration of the mind of the indifferent and unsympathetic bigot. Extreme pictures of incidents, melodramatically presented, achieved his purpose.

The novel, *Native Son,* is sufficiently exciting and moving. It invites comparison with John Steinbeck's *The Grapes of Wrath.* Both novels grew out of the depression years and the accompanying hardships of economic dislocation, and both deal with the dispossessed and underprivileged segment in our American society. In each case there is crime and violence. And the type of people represented "gains in dignity and deserves sympathy in the end." [17] Environment causes an exodus of both families who seek a better life. It is from

---

[15] Kazin, *op. cit.,* pp. 382-387.
[16] Joseph Beach, *American Fiction 1920-1940,* p. 338.
[17] *Ibid.,* pp. 219-231.

Oklahoma to California for the Joads while the trek from
Mississippi to Illinois is a reality for the Thomases when
Native Son begins. At this point the similarities disappear,
and the individual artistry of both writers asserts itself.

Steinbeck and Wright have something "in common with
Erskine Caldwell who treats poor whites of the South."[18]
But they seem to be artists with more intense passion for
improvement of the situation rather than a projected description of them. In the case of Caldwell, there is merely an
objective portrayal of the situation, and one gets the feeling
that there is "more humor" [19] than genuine concern behind
the author's treatment. In direct contrast Wright's novel
shows a diametrically opposed point of view of Negro characterization.

The whole province of life is at the command of the
novelist.[20] Wright works within his range of selectivity because
a pressing social problem becomes his material. He selects
an underprivileged group of America's polyglot population.
Consequently, the matter becomes more pronounced because
of race, for the main character is different from the majority
group by social definition.[21] Race hatred and underprivileged
people are facts of American life. Wright exploits this theme
by the use of the psychological technique. By creating a
character whose hatred has become pathological, the author
has opportunity to point up widespread emotional responses
and characteristic actions of a maladjusted personality. Symbolism, another literary device, appears to advantage. The
title *Native Son* suggests ironically the contents, and this
means, in context of American society, that a member by
right of birth is a citizen of the country enjoying all of the
rights and privileges which go along with citizenship. As the

18 *Ibid.*
19 *Ibid.*
20 Henry James, *The Art of the Novel,* p. 42.
21 Gunnar Myrdal, *An American Dilemma,* p. 114.

story unfolds, the venomous irony and frustrating paradox in the title become unmistakably clear.

Native Son, as indicated, first of all belongs to the category of psychological novel of purpose. It protests strongly against conditions in which underprivileged Negroes live and discriminations they must confront in the struggle of life. It blends with that vast amount of novels which treat social problems commonly designated protest literature. It may be more descriptively appropriate to designate them novels with moral purpose because at bottom of their vehemence is a concern for the morality involved in the situation.

The novel of purpose may or may not follow a conventional pattern of narration. In the case in point, however, it does. There is a beginning line of action,[22] including episodes and incidents which mount to a climax, and finally there is a resolution of the problem. *Native Son,* stripped to its barest component parts, involves crime-flight-trapped-apprehension motif which is familiar enough in literature. It presents a Negro youth from Mississippi in an impoverished setting in Chicago. Dissatisfied with his conditions of poverty, he turns to petty crimes oriented in the Negro world. He lands a job with a wealthy, white family where he commits murder accidentally; then, flight, a premeditated murder, apprehension by the law whereby society exacts its death penalty complete the line of action. But it is the intensity and passion with which Wright portrays this old theme, and the manner he infuses new meaning and a different twist which shocks the reader and brings to the novel a freshness and vividness which less capable writers fail to achieve.

More detailed, Wright builds around this motif a moving drama.[23] It is the compelling story of a black man in white, American society. The plot outline is simple enough. The

---

[22] Edwin Muir, *The Structure of the Novel,* pp. 80-86.
[23] Richard Wright, *Native Son.*

Thomas family, Mrs. Thomas, Bigger, Buddy, and Vera
occupy a rat infested and dilapidated apartment on Indiana
Avenue in Chicago, Illinois. The father has been killed in
Mississippi. The day begins with the ringing of the alarm
clock, but before the family is able to complete dressing a
big rat appears and throws the household out of balance
temporarily. Bigger kills the rat, and the scanty meal follows.
Mrs. Thomas urges Bigger to accept the job offered him by
the relief officials. Accepting a quarter for bus fare from his
mother, Bigger joins his friends, Gus and Jack. They discuss
the robbery that they plan to stage in the afternoon. Meanwhile they go to a cheap movie. At the appointed hour Jack
does not appear, and the robbery does not occur. Bigger finds
Jack in Doc's pool room and deliberately starts a fight with
him in order to avoid disclosing his own fear.

Bigger reports to the Dalton home where he is overwhelmed by the lavishness and luxuriousness which he views
for the first time in his life. Questioned by his prospective
employers, Mr. and Mrs. Dalton, Bigger is frightened into
a state of panic. He communicates this fear[24] to Mr. and
Mrs. Dalton, while Mary's forward advance adds only to his
discomfiture and fear. His first assignment is to drive Mary
to school in the evening at eight. Mary at once enters into a
little conspiracy with Bigger. Instead of going to school, she
stops at an old, dingy building, and her Communist boy
friend, Jan, joins her. They decide to have dinner on the
South Side of Chicago. At dinner they question Bigger about
his past. Bessie, Bigger's lover, is enraged when she sees
Bigger with the whites.

Jan leaves Bigger and Mary. At home Mary is in a
drunken state. Bigger takes her to her room, but before he

---

[24] Ralph Ellison, "Richard Wright Blues," *Antioch Review,* Summer
1946, p. 652.

leaves, Mrs. Dalton enters the room. Bigger, who is fearful of the outcome of a compromising situation, accidentally kills Mary with a pillow which he uses to prevent her from speaking to her blind mother, Mrs. Dalton.

Bigger takes Mary's body to the basement and burns it in the furnace after hacking off her head. He is questioned about Mary's strange disappearance and shifts the blame to Jan. Britten follows Bigger to the furnace room and detects a bone in the ashes. Knowing that he is about to be discovered, Bigger flees to Bessie. She reluctantly becomes his accomplice, and they draft and send a ransom note. After a few days Bigger is discovered, and after murdering Bessie and disposing of her body by throwing it down the shaft, Bigger is trapped. He is held for murder and rape of Mary Dalton. Jan secures the services of Max, a communist lawyer, to defend him. Bigger is tried and sentenced to the electric chair. Now that he is about to die, it dawns upon him what life is really like. He takes full responsibility for the crime. He exults in the knowledge that his violent act means his freedom. Proudly and defiantly he meets his death.

Bigger reveals his personality and his exultation in death:

"Aw I reckon I believe in myself . . . I ain't got nothing else. I got to die. . . .

"Mr. Max, you go home. I'm all right. Sounds funny, Mr. Max, but when I think about what you say I kind of feel what I wanted. It makes me feel I was kind of right. . . .

"I ain't trying to forgive nobody and I ain't asking for nobody to forgive me. I ain't going to cry. They wouldn't let me live and I killed. Maybe it ain't fair to kill, and I reckon I really didn't want to kill. But when I think of why all the killing was, I begin to feel what I want, what I am. . . . What I killed for must've been good. . . . It must have been good! When a man kills, it's for something. . . . I didn't know I was really alive in this world until I felt things hard enough to kill for 'em."[25]

Wright's success with this psychological drama may be best viewed through characterization. Bigger, psychopath, is one of the most lucidly delineated characters in fiction of this decade.[26] Just what is so arresting about this character? In the first place he towers over every other character in practically every scene in which he appears. When he is not present, his spectre seems to hover about other persons. The focal point of interest does not shift for one moment from him. Human relationships in the novel center about Bigger and his reactions to various situations. In the opening scene he enters the stage of the drama as a sullen and impertinent young man. He silences Vera and knows that he is Buddy's hero. He senses the inadequacy of his mother's religiosity and is bored with it.

With his friends he is a recognized leader, and Jack and Gus accompany him willingly in petty crimes. He has just that essential quality of being different to capture the imagination of the other fellow. He is utterly self-conscious about his race even though he accepts his blackness as a fact of life. He is embittered only because he can not effect self-realization and is disgruntled over the whole business of living as he knows it.

In two more situations Bigger shows his fear. After suggesting the robbery, he can not execute the plan. Out of fear and his sense of leadership, Bigger must bolster his ego with a fight. Inwardly, he knows that Jack's failure to appear on the scene is a relief to his own tension. In his bullying fight Bigger easily overcomes Jack and cuts Doc's pool table. Even

---

[25] Wright, *op. cit.,* p. 358.

[26] Milton Rugoff, *N. Y. Herald Tribune,* March 3, 1940; Clifton Fadiman, *New Yorker,* March 2, 1940, pp. 60-61.

then, he knows that it is fear which compels him to bully and destroy.

In the presence of whites, he is suspicious and frightened. He loathes whites, and with the Daltons, Bigger is an inarticulate, nervous black man. To the perceptive Mrs. Dalton this lack of control communicates itself. In fact it elicits sympathy from her. Mary, who is a symbol of death, provokes fear because she recalls violence, so her friendly gestures are interpreted to presage trouble. Bigger, therefore, hates her intensely. In company with Jan and Mary his fear may be best seen. Here is that warped youth who is so conditioned that intimate relationship with whites drives him almost frantic. Here is the picture of a self-conscious, black man thinking about two whites. Bigger's mind races in this way.

> Maybe they did not despise him? But they made him feel his black skin by just standing there looking at him, one holding his hand and the other smiling. He felt he had no physical existence at all right then; he was something he hated, the badge of shame which he knew was attached to a black skin. It was a shadowy region, a No Man's Land, the ground that separated the white world from the black that he stood upon. He felt naked, transparent; he felt that this white man, having helped to put him down, having helped to deform him, held him up now to look at him and be amused. At that moment he felt toward Mary and Jan a dumb, cold, and inarticulate hate.[27]

Obviously, Bigger as a character has all of the overt manifestations of a personality suffering from anxiety. This extreme degree to which he is affected is recognizable in the qualities of anxiety. First, there is an inordinate fear Gestalt within Bigger. His mind can not function because of this fear. He behaves instinctively without attempting to think, and there

---

[27] Wright, *op. cit.*, p. 58.

is the urge to violence as a means of release. He exhibits those bodily changes such as glandular secretions and the collapse when he is confronted with his deed. All of which are symptomatic of his personality deviation. He is self-alienated; a personality without meaningful existence and without an egocentric pattern as an integral part of his being. He suffers from frustration which brought on this mental condition. So, Bigger on one level is revealed to us in the impoverishment of his own personality deviation. On another level of interpretation, Bigger is an insolent and vindictive Negro youth. He is a rather extreme example of anxiety.[28] Bigger has the ability to keep himself locked in his private world. In matters of sex, he has a lover and considers such activity the stock equipment of a man.

Wright has flourishes of poetic brilliancy in such a passage. Despite himself, Bigger is lost in a moment of exhilaration.

> He felt two soft palms holding his face tenderly and the thought and image of the whole blind world which had made him ashamed and afraid fell away as he felt her as a fallow field beneath him stretching out under a cloudy sky waiting for rain, and he floated on a wild tide, rising and sinking with the ebb and flow of her blood, being willingly dragged into a warm night sea to rise renewed to the surface to face a world he hated and wanted to blot out of existence, clinging close to a fountain whose warm waters washed and cleaned his senses, cooled them, and made them strong and keen again to see and smell and touch and taste and hear, cleared them to end the tiredness and to reforge in him a new sense of time and space.[29]

Symbolism in a work of art has the advantage of lending itself to various interpretations. It may very well obscure or

---

[28] Rollo May, *The Meaning of Anxiety,* pp. 190-196.
[29] Wright, *op. cit.,* p. 115.

tend to give opaqueness to the work. Sometimes symbols have
a tendency to mar a work with obscurantism. In the case of
Wright's *Native Son,* the symbols have unmistakable clarity
of association. The first one is the rat. This animal is not a
very pleasant creature outside of psychological laboratories.
One nourished and grown fat on aged buildings and de-
cayed matter has added repulsiveness. Rats produce fear in
women, and the Thomases are no exception to this rule.
They know that rats will eat human flesh, and Bigger is
bitten in his first encounter with the rat. But he corners and
kills the rat with great satisfaction. This symbolizes Bigger's
own downfall later in the narrative. He is also cornered
and killed, for he is like a rat in a white man's maze of
civilization. Indeed, Bigger is put through the maze of
human experience like a rat only to be condemned because
he can not successfully get over the hurdles according to the
set pattern of the maze. In the end he is exterminated just
like a rat.

Another obvious symbol is the cross.[30] Instantly, one
relates to this symbol ignorance. Certainly, Bigger can not
qualify as a formally trained person. This lack of experience,
lack of education, lack of technical knowledge in the true
sense of the word, this lack of acceptance, and lack of racial
security become Bigger's cross of ignorance. The sum total is
staggering indeed in terms of personality criteria. More
pointed and universal in its application, the cross is a religious symbol. In our deep reverence of religion, this symbol
represents universal love, harmony, and the brotherhood of
man. This symbol enriches the lives of thousands of human
beings who look to the cross for pointing the way to eternal
salvation. Again, the cross denotes spiritual refurbishment,

---

[30] *New Republic,* August 12, 1946, pp. 176-180. ("The Negro is the
black cross in so far as he is the embodiment of the curse, the reminder
of guilt, the incarnation of the problem.")

light, and hope for the Christian believer. The pacifistic nature of the way of the cross has been the means of avoiding untimely deaths among Negroes and all races, for it throws out a restraining hand when passions are aroused.

Mrs. Thomas, Bigger's mother, is an example of a Negro woman enamored of the cross. It leaves her lifeless and devoid of positive action in a practical world, but it sustains and makes her inner spiritual life very rich indeed. Her whole approach to life is in terms of the cross, and truly for her the practical philosophy is to interpret life in terms of this symbol. Mrs. Thomas rightly believes that:

> Life is like a mountain railroad
> With an engineer that's brave
> We must make the run successful
> From the cradle to the grave . . .[31]

Again, in the deepest introspection which at times is a plea for guidance, she is fully cognizant of the rawness of life. She knows that she has embraced a faith which does not permit open fighting for life by her. Her attitude is acceptance of life with its inequities and injustices as the cross of this world. She wants to have deeply embedded in her heart Christianity, and she sings:

> Lord, I want to be a Christian
> In my heart, in my heart,
> Lord, I want to be a Christian
> In my heart, in my heart.[32]

Even Bigger succumbed to the purported balm of the soul before his personality became irretrievably warped on account of his totally thwarted ambitions. But the cross in American life means also persecution, vandalism, and lynching of Negroes.[33] It signifies that a band of lawless hoodlums

---

[31] Wright, *op. cit.*, p. 9.
[32] *Ibid.*, p. 30.
[33] Myrdal, *op. cit.*, pp. 559-562.

will superimpose their will upon unprotected Negroes. This will, in a number of instances, mean violent death just because they are Negroes. A flaming cross signalizes the burning intensity of white men's lust for power and the exercise of that power which is dangerous and menacing. It spreads death instead of eternal life, unmitigated torture instead of tranquility. Instead of the reassuring message of Jesus which says: "My peace I give you," it is an eruptive force of hate, anxiety,[34] and unbridled emotions running rampant with frenetic men gloating in violence, death, and the smell of burning human flesh. It is sadism at its wildest and most extreme form which derives joy from seeing exposed and mutilated bodies and flowing, human blood.

The cross of Jesus Christ symbolizes the supreme sacrifice which he made to atone for the sins of the world. Christian dogma thrills to the comforting idea that the sins of the world were taken away by this act of mercy, an act which sprang from a heart filled with love and compassion for mankind. The symbol of the cross, the same outward sign of the cross of Jesus, is the official one of the Ku Klux Klan. Their cross which is burning on top of a building in Chicago issues a call to lynch a black man.

Not a saviour in any sense of the word is this black man. But he is called a black monstrosity in the form of a man. The crowd designate him a "black ape";[35] the attorney calls him "a serpent, a lizard," [36] the mob abuses him violently. Love and compassion would be the last attribute to be ascribed to the crime. On the contrary, hatred and vindictiveness accompany and spur on the participants. Is this atonement for the sins of the world? It is far from it. This black man would die and burn in order to satisfy the sadistic urges of an outraged white mob. It is done because some white

---

[34] W. F. Cash, *The Mind of the South,* pp. 414-420.
[35] Wright, *op. cit.,* pp. 356-358.
[36] *Ibid.*

human nature will express its resentments of a black man's presence. Bigger realizes that the symbol he is wearing about his neck is identical in form with the Ku Klux Klan's symbol which can mean only a terrifying and horrible death for him. So, in rage he tears the cross from his neck and throws it as far as he can from him.

Two more obvious symbols appear in the novel, namely, the colors black and white. In art neither is classified as pure color. In the world that Bigger Thomas knows, the whole process of life hinges on these color designations. White human beings in America symbolize generally wealth and power. Black human beings equate poverty and misery in most cases. The whites are in the ascendancy while the blacks must be suppressed. Einstein's dictum: "Human beings who can bear children together can hardly be different from each other" [37] has never penetrated the forest of ignorance of Bigger's world nor is reason effective in the face of emotionality.

The crowning achievement in *Native Son* with symbols is the one black boy transformed into a symbol of over twelve million Negroes. Within the confines of the novel, this symbolic reference is more than plausible. It impresses itself upon the reader with pristine clearness. It takes along with it the gruesome idea that black men of necessity will be condemned before the bar of white justice because they are black; or to state the case differently, why would one expect justice when the laws are the exclusive privilege and draft work of white men generally?

Native Son, like most novels of purpose, is an author's commentary upon American society. It indicts America for its maltreatment of its underprivileged Negroes especially. It posits the dilemma of over twelve million Negroes in the United States. Life with this group of people on account of

---

[37] Earl Conrad, *Jim Crow America,* p. 147.

race is more difficult than it is with whites. His thesis, as David Daiches points out, will not exactly hold. Bigger's crimes are not what the Bigger Thomases of America are likely to be driven to do.[38] But Wright insists that unless American society changes its attitudes toward Negroes they will be driven to crimes such as Bigger commits. Although Daiches is most probably correct in his observation, Wright makes a decidedly caustic indictment of American society. David Cohn in an article in *Atlantic Monthly* could discern only bile and hatred and points with pride to his idea of an improved Negro race. Yet the official survey of the race problem appearing four years after *Native Son* indicates that Wright's crusading zeal was appropriate. Myrdal points out: "Negroes don't have a tenth of the things worth having in America. The Negro cannot be treated in isolation but he is a part of the complex of American problems in American civilization." [39]

Wright places in Max's defense for Bigger's life precisely what he feels that American society has done to Negroes like Bigger. The passage reads:

> The hate and fear which we have inspired in him (Bigger), woven by our civilization into the very structure of his consciousness, into his blood and bones, into the hourly functioning of his personality, have become the justification of his existence. . . . Every time he comes in contact with us, he kills! . . . a psychological reaction, embedded in his being. Every thought he thinks is potential murder. Excluded from, and unassimilated in our society, yet longing to gratify impulses akin to our own but denied the objects and channels evolved through long centuries for their socialized expression, every sunrise and sunset make him guilty of subversive actions. Every movement of his body is an unconscious protest. Every desire, every

---

[38] David Daiches, *Partisan Review,* May-June 1940, pp. 244-245.
[39] Myrdal, *op cit.,* p. 307.

dream, no matter how intimate or personal, is a plot or a conspiracy. Every hope is a plan for insurrection. Every glance of the eye is a threat. *His very existence is a crime against the state!* . . . He was impelled toward murder as much through the thirst for excitement, exultation, and elation as he was through fear![40]

In this novel Wright asserts that the Negro race and the Negro soul lay bare before the bar of white justice. The alternative of integration or overt violence resounds its reverberations in the minds of those who read this highly charged piece of fiction.

The core of Wright's novel is the insistence upon viewing the conflict between the two racial groups. The apparent discrepancy between Negroes and whites in the more tangible necessities of life and opportunities for realizing them disturbs our rational process. Wright asserts intrepidly that humanity need not suffer. The whole circumstance of social misery equates action. Recognition of the problem leads customarily to change in America. Acquiescence to the idea of change in favor of full equality of status for Negroes became an intellectual conviction years ago. Application of the principle or formulation of working techniques for making the idea a practical reality have yet to come.

Continuing his commentary, Wright asks for the two minimum essentials for a livable existence in America in positive terms. These have the commonality of aspirations of all people in America as this section indicates:

I say, Your Honor, give this boy his life. And in making this concession we uphold those two fundamental concepts of our civilization, those two basic concepts upon which we have built the mightiest nation in our history—personality and security—the conviction that the person is inviolate and that which sustains him is equally so.[41]

---

[40] Wright, *op. cit.*, pp. 335-336.
[41] Wright, *op. cit.*, p. 338.

Piercing the structure of society, and penetrating into the abysmal depths of consciousness, Wright establishes a sense of the tragic. Indeed it appears that his concern for the Negroes portrays the consciousness of the group through Bigger. This consciousness exposes a set of impulses and aspirations that is so fundamental until one must do either one of two things: agree with the premise and accept the change of full assimilation or become emotional at the author's temerity. Biological heritage should be the last thing to debar a person from the fullness of his American heritage. Wright's narrative power and his utter sincerity render it impossible to ignore this Negro consciousness.

There is stylistically a studied simplicity about Wright's technique. By concentrating upon fear and the psychological aspects of Bigger and his world, he gives form to his material with economy and speed. This novel realizes a full portrait of flesh and blood. By disciplined objectivity, the author permits Bigger to appear in several different states of mental torment.

Native Son is modern tragedy. Here is "the little man who can not find adjustment nor success in life." [42] This is the plight of the common man in any social order when he finds through no fault of his own that he is doomed. There is with Bigger a brooding sensitivity. His psychological reactions to life become portents of the ultimate tragedy that will befall him. Bigger wants to be a human being, to fly a plane, and to be happy. These are ordinary wishes of any youth. In the case of Bigger, these are denied him. He attempts to change his environment by adopting an attitude of contempt and cowardly bullying. He is frightened by his knowledge that this fear is almost uncontrollable. He is aware of the impossibility of self-realization. In his attempt to arrest the stifling forces which destroy him as a human being, he simply

---

[42] Annis Sandvos, "Flight from Aristotle," p. 328.

aggravates the situation, for he has with him this lurking fear of the inevitable set of frustrating events he will meet.

Environment is too overwhelming for Bigger. He commits a crime accidentally, then he disturbs our sense of propriety and rationality by committing another more fiendish crime. This is not the type of behavior of a youth who has control of himself or adjusted to the world. This is fear out of proportion to our norms, but society produced this youth with its warping influence. He has never been accepted as a human being. He can not succeed. He is not permitted to have the luxury of an ambition. Bigger has a tragic end because he resents this frustration, this sense of failure and defeat.

Wright's objectivity stamps him as an artist who is in full control of his medum. If he advances the premise of the injustices of the Negro, he in turn presents and clarifies the position of the majority group. Of course, Bigger must die, but somehow society does not avenge but defeats itself in Bigger's electrocution. He bequeaths a disturbing memory that society in taking its proscribed course and regular measure does not kill Bigger's spirit, and he triumphs in death. Wright shows his skill as a novelist by the movement that he gives the story. It has a dynamic quality,[43] and action proceeds with great rapidity. Indeed, it moves like the turbulent gushing of a great waterfall rather than the even flowing river. This is the prime reward of the shock technique. Once the avalanche begins there is no time nor means of damming the flood. No one is spared, and the probing into the depths of the recesses of a mutilated and warped personality has gripping and shocking force.

Wright's vigorous prose fits the case. He has a simplicity which fascinates and engages the reader. You know at all times what he is saying. It has gripping power and exciting quality which will not release the reader until he reaches the

[43] Arthur Pelham, *The Art of the Novel*, p. 216.

resolution of the plot. His approach is decidedly different from earlier writers because Wright permits no softening nor caressing of the infested sore which weighs so heavily about the Negro heart. Instead, he tears ruthlessly the scab from the wound and the rawness shows; the red, hot, human blood flows out.

Human values with Wright are important, and his insistent set, mentioned earlier, is equivalent to the American democratic promise. Around personality and security generates our ability to gain happiness and the fulfillment of our aspirations. They presuppose our self-realization through spiritual and materialistic acquisitions. In short, a life which admits of problems always, but one which accepts the common denominator of humanity more important than biological heritage. These values are analogous with those sought in western civilization everywhere. It is a reasonable position, and upon these values[44] man may really come into the fullness and richness of his being.

Native Son is really an extraordinarily disturbing book. This impact strikes first in the general organization, frame of violence, and the Negro problem because it is an American problem which affects ultimately most of the inhabitants of the country either directly or indirectly. The selection of a criminal rather than an ordinary Negro, the rejection of the platitudes of professional race workers, and an insistence upon the immediacy rather than gradualism shock one into an awareness of the urgency of the situation. The crimes perpetrated by this neurotic fiend[45] penetrate into our consciousness with a sense of horrifying reality. Bigger destroys our concept of reason. The realm of the psychopath is depressingly unpleasant. Having experienced what it means to be a

[44] "Changing Values in the Western World," *American Scholar,* Summer 1951, pp. 341-358.

[45] Erich Fromm, *Escape from Freedom,* pp. 137-139.

Negro almost a century after emancipation, Wright knows that anything less than unbelievable violence would not register with the reading public.

The book disturbed David Cohn to such an extent that he wrote an article in *Atlantic Monthly* in which he unleashed a scathing attack upon Wright as an individual and discredited *Native Son* as a work of art. The same sort of reaction, naturally, came from the *Southern Review* which will be discussed later in this book. In Cohn's attack there is the typical southern attitude and point of view presented. He begins by referring to the "headlong attitude of a Mississippi born Negro" [46] which deplores the fact that the conditioning of that state failed to crush the author's spirit. He mentions the fact that the two races are different and that the cultural pattern in America is predominantly Anglo-Saxon and will remain that way regardless of any suggestions that the new generations of Wrights might offer to the contrary. So far as Cohn is concerned, the Negro is and should be completely segregated from the whites. The final element in this vitriolic estimate of *Native Son* is the blunt statement that the Negro has all that he needs in America. Cohn refers to the fact that the Negro controls less than one percent of the nation's wealth and, he continues, "if the Negro suffers under handicaps both socially and economically conditions are improving." [47] Furthermore, the lesson of history teaches that the Negro like the Jew must have thousands of years of persecution before Anglo-Saxon America decides that he must be accorded the status of full-fledged American citizen.

Cohn's point of view is testimony of the effectiveness of the work, and it is also a tribute to the author's ingenuity because the calculated goal of the novel was realized. The novel is fraught with excitement. Bigger Thomas' hatred

[46] David Cohn, *Atlantic Monthly,* June, 1940, pp. 659-661.
[47] *Ibid.*

alone is enough to pierce thick-skinned, reactionary, white Americans. But there is an even more cutting aspect to the novel. Wright shows his knowledge of white psychology by placing the flower of American ideals—a white girl—in a most impossible situation. Death is not enough for her because Bigger hacks her head off and mutilates her body. Think of it! Anything more revolting could hardly be presented by a Negro author. Then, with less compunction, he murders Bessie with a brick as if she were a rat. All of this amounts to chaos which is Bigger's reaction to American life. Every fiber and nerve of Bigger is laid bare. The hideous picture of the working of a pathological mind is more than fascination for the morbid and abnormal in Wright's novel. It is the soul of a warped youth who would have gladly relinquished his mantle of oppression for one of the ordinary human being. Underneath Bigger's layer of callousness is the quickening sensitivity of the man who might have been. By extension he is twelve million black people in America acccording to Wright. These people suffer because they are members of an oppressed race existing in poverty for the most part in the land of the oppressors who thrive in wealth and power. Here is the situation to Wright when he elects to make Bigger a spokesman for the underprivileged American Negroes:

> Multiply Bigger twelve million times, allowing for environmental and temperamental variations, and for those Negroes who are completely under the influence of the church, and you have the psychology of the Negro people. But once you see them as whole, once your eyes leave the individual and encompass the mass, a new quality comes into the picture. Taken collectively, they are not simply twelve million people; in reality they constitute a separate nation, stunted, stripped, and held captive *within* this nation, devoid of political, social, economic, and property rights.[48]

---

[48] Wright, *op. cit.*, p. 333.

By detailing the psychological, sociological, and economic factors as they pertain to the Negro, Richard Wright anticipates most of the Negro novelists of the forties. Those serious novelists who deal with the race problem find in him a definite statement of the case of the Negro. His work so explicitly details the case of the Negro in his grievances, demands, and aspirations that most of the subsequent serious novels enlarge upon one or several elements contained in his work. For example, *Blood on the Forge,* by William Attaway, is an extension of the economic factors described in *Native Son.* Here, Attaway is concerned with the problem of the Negro, and he protests against the discriminatory practices encountered in the steel mills after World War I. Both novelists explain at length the emasculation of personality because of identification with the Negro race in America.[49] The two differ in the conception and thesis rendered. Chester Himes in his two psychological novels, *Lonely Crusade,* and *If He Hollers Let Him Go,* bears the imprint of Richard Wright's psychological probing. But Himes lacks Wright's intensity. Curtis Lucas in his *Third Ward Newark* gives a picture of a morbid mind of a neurotic girl in much the same style as Wright. This character is made to resent her status as a Negro woman without the protection of the law.

Ann Petry in her book, *The Street,* is concerned with a similar theme. In her statement her thesis is derived from unwholesome environments and the disastrous effects of them upon Negroes.

Chester Himes, in his two novels, *If He Hollers Let Him Go* and *Lonely Crusade,* shows the influence of Richard Wright and James Cain. Himes, like Cain, in *Butterfly,* who also wrote *Past All Dishonor* and *The Postman Always Rings Twice,* describes industrial conditions. There is a similarity as to style and the psychological presentation of characters.

---

[49] J. Saunders Redding, *On Being a Negro in America,* pp. 33-46.

Himes presents the theme of exploitation and discrimination in war industry as directed toward the Negro. In addition he gives the psychological reaction of a Negro to this situation which is to emphasize crass materialism. He develops these themes through the characterization of Bob Jones who is a psychological case study.

The slender story begins with Bob Jones, foreman, in Atlas Corporation during World War II. He is a maladjusted war worker for he permits whites "to eat on his brain." [50] First of all, Bob is anxious to succeed on the job and is self-conscious because he has never worked in an integrated situation before. Homer, Smitty, Conway, and Pigmeat, members of his crew, find life rough because of racial prejudices between whites and Negroes. An insignificant matter such as borrowing a tool brings out latent hostility. The Negro men resent white bigotry and the whites refuse to take orders from a Negro foreman. Bob is so self-conscious and unhappy over the situation that he has become a neurotic Negro. His mental condition as a consequence of his neurosis and anxiety is described in the following passage:

> I was even scared to tell anybody. If I'd gone to a psychiatrist he'd have had me put away. Living everyday scared, walled in, locked up, I didn't feel like fighting any more; I'd take the second thought before I hit a paddy now. I was tired of keeping ready to die every minute; it was too much strain. I had to fight hard enough each day just to keep on living. All I wanted was for the white folks to leave me alone; not to say anything to me; not even look at me. They could take the goddamned world and go to hell with it. [51]

Bob is a rather remarkable leader with ability, education, and material property which gives him an advantage. He

---

[50] Chester Himes, *If He Hollers Let Him Go,* p. 181.
[51] Himes, *op. cit.,* p. 5.

takes men to work and has a ready smile and chitchat for the crew. He has a harmless affair with his landlady, but he is in love with Alice Harrison, Negro socialite.

On the job, Madge, a breezy blonde from Texas, is attracted to him, but she holds her white skin as a barrier. At the same time she suggests familiarity by her appearance and walk. This negative appeal which Madge has for Bob comes from the fact that:

> She looked like a big overpainted strumpet with eyes as wild as Oklahoma. . . . So it wasn't that Madge was white; it was the way she used it. She had a sign up in front of her as big as Civic Center—Keep Away, Niggers, —I'm White! And without having to say one word she could keep all the white men in the world feeling they had to protect her from black rapists. That made her doubly dangerous because she thought about Negro men. I could tell that the first time I saw her. She wanted them to run after her. She expected it, demanded it as her due. I could imagine her teasing them with her body, showing her bare thighs and breasts. Then having them lynched for looking.[52]

Bob gambles with John Stoddart and others and wins, which causes a fight for John is a bad loser. John Stoddart, who is white, beats Bob which infuriates him. This sense of defeat brings on a psychological nightmare which is the delayed reaction of extreme race consciousness. Bob seeks revenge by plotting to murder John Stoddart, and he goes to his home in order to do it. But he realizes that his rather arbitrary design will solve no problem and desists.

Back at the plant, Bob is walking through the ramp in the building in order to reach his own crew when he encounters Madge who has been sleeping. The two individuals had indulged in sexual acrobatics the night before at Madge's small hotel. Nonetheless, when she hears the approaching

---

[52] *Ibid.*, pp. 150-152.

steps of white men, rather than be seen in a compromising situation with a Negro man she cries:

> Help! Help! My God, help me! Some white man, help me! I'm being raped![53]

The door is broken down, and horrified, Bob is beaten by the men. Rather than face a trumped up charge of rape, Bob accepts the alternative of the army which the owner of the plant offers him.

Social commentary here deals with a set of complexes indigenous to the American scene. In California where the integration of all workers in wartime industry became a necessity, Negroes fared badly enough to cause some observers to judge the experiment only partially successful. In another sense the fact of integration was a reality, but with it came psychological maladjustments as *If He Hollers Let Him Go* shows. The Fair Employment Practice Commission apparently made efforts to make the new experiment work. But the psychology of the worker in a number of instances defeated the program. This is due to the lack of understanding of people and unfamiliarity with each other.

Characterization of Bob Jones is the most notable achievement in *If He Hollers Let Him Go*. Educated Bob Jones is a psychological case study many steps removed from Bigger Thomas of *Native Son*. He is involved in some rather trying situations. The newness of it all, inability to effect disassociation from raw and telling childhood experiences, and failure to achieve financial success produce in him arrogance. This attitude will lead inevitably to emotional conflict. The type of job that Bob had wanted is now his, but his arrogant attitude persists which makes adjustment to his desirable situation nearly impossible. His response to a fellow white worker will hardly make for evenness in human relationship.

---

[53] *Ibid.*, p. 219.

Despite the fact that the white man challenges him, Bob's reply is:

> I smiled at him. "I don't want to fight you," I told him. "I want to kill you. But right now I'm saving you up."[54]

The most frustrating condition which Bob faces is the inability to use his power as foreman. The whites simply refuse to work with him. This is the result of conditioning which whites have had. It means that orders are to be given only by whites. Bob feels that this is an unjust and very presumptuous attitude on the part of the white workers, for he is the foreman. His girl explains the situation in an attempt to comfort him. She insists that his difficulty on his job as foreman is typical of Negroes in supervisory jobs with whites in subordinate positions. Her explanation reads:

> That is typical of most Negroes working in a supervisory capacity where whites and colored are employed. Many Negroes whom we think are in top positions are actually no more than figure heads and are much more frustrated than you. I can't give direct orders on my job either, although I am classified as a supervisor. Only suggestions. It almost drives me mad to see cases handled incorrectly and have no power to correct them.[55]

Lonely Crusade uses the same material for the development of a thesis similar to that of *If He Hollers Let Him Go*. Himes exhibits, nevertheless, a more advanced conception of his medium. He uses the steel cage technique, that is to say, the Negro is in a steel cage on the economic level with whites in control of the wealth. Himes is consistent, and his themes deal with materialism and communism. He develops the angle of materialism around the character, Lee Gordon, who advances the notion that Negro personality will be destroyed in the realistic world of practical affairs. The Negro, there-

---

[54] *Ibid.*, p. 155.
[55] *Ibid.*, p. 204.

fore, must hate everyone and everything in order to survive or to achieve individuality, along with material property, in a highly competitive economic market. This means that Lee Gordon is a person who hates Jews, Communists, white women, and other Negroes. Obviously, this offers no solution to the problem of living in America to Negroes or whites. But it does show a comprehensive awareness of the tormented and twisted personality of the Negro like Lee Gordon.

The plot opens with Lee Gordon, union organizer, in a Comstock plant in California. His position as organizer places him in a vulnerable position for the activities of the Communist party. On the job, Joe Ptak, manager, briefs him on the organizing tactics of the Communist party, pointing out the dangers to be recognized immediately.

Lee has a remarkably stable home life for he has been married to Ruth, a patient lover and helpmate, for eight years. She is employed by Western Talkies as a secretary. Lee's brooding race consciousness makes him anxious to succeed because of the haunting memory of past failures. At times Lee's brooding assaults reasoning process and stresses morbidity when he informs us:

> There had been that deep fascination, that tongueless call of suicide, offering not the anodyne of death, but the decadent, rotten sense of freedom that comes with being absolved of the responsibility of trying any longer to be a man in a world that will not accept you as such.[56]

On the job Lee signs up John Ellsworth and accepts his invitation to a party given by the Communists where he meets Jackie. This casual meeting leads to an illicit love affair. Luther, a burly Negro Communist who is married to Mollie, a white Communist, knows the art of subterfuge and plays the role of the humble Negro to the lordly white in order to acquire money. Through Jackie, Lee becomes in-

---

[56] Chester Himes, *Lonely Crusade*, p. 48.

volved in the Communist party. Indeed, he is so infatuated with her he forsakes Ruth, his wife. When Hugh Johnson, the official spokesman, who is a large, educated, black man, tells Maud Hammerstein, a Jew, that she is to dismiss a member, Jackie is apprehensive. Although Jackie does not know it, this is purely a disciplinary measure in order to keep the party under-control. At the meeting Jackie is voted out of the party, and Lee dares to defend her.

Meanwhile Lee accompanies Luther who murders Paul over a financial deal. Lee is sickened by the sight of such brutality, yet he accompanies Luther to his apartment where he silences nymphomanic, Mollie. Lee finally leaves Luther and comes to this conclusion:

> Lee Gordon reached a conclusion sitting there: that the one rigid rule in human behavior was to be for yourself and to hell with everyone else; that within human beings, himself included, were propensities for every evil, each waiting its moment of fulfillment; that honor never was and never would be for the Negro, and integrity was only for a fool; that from then on he would believe in the almighty dollar, the cowardice of Negroes, and the hypocrisy of whites, and he would never go wrong.[57]

Lee goes to Jackie instead of Ruth, and manlike when he is in love, relates the incident of the murder to Jackie. He pleads with her to marry him, but Jackie candidly refuses his offer of marriage insisting that she can not take advantage of a Negro woman. This brings out her real attitude toward him. It is an attitude of utter contempt and disdain, for, after all, she is white:

> She could not tell him that now in her mind, in the whiteness of her soul, she was repelled by the very blackness of the skin that . . . first attracted her. So she continued to similate this sympathy for Ruth. . . . "I can't

---

[57] *Ibid.*, p. 238.

do that to a Negro woman, Lee. I'm white, Lee—white!
—Can't you understand? I'm a white woman and could
not hurt a Negro woman so." [58]

Following this dramatic refusal, Jackie turns informer
on Lee, and before he knows what has happened policemen
are at the apartment. The union and Mr. Foster, owner of
the plant, reconsider his case, and Lee is retained on the job.
Lee emerges a full-blown character who attacks his job by
relieving the fainting Joe of the union banner, and he
marches proudly down the street.

Bob Jones and Lee Gordon have similar characteristics.
Both men suffer from frustrations which they experience as
a result of membership in the Negro race in America.[59] The
two men exhibit a consuming sensitivity, and both are college
trained. Particularly revealing is the brooding that both men
engage in intermittently. It must be emphasized that Lee of
Lonely Crusade like Bob Jones of *If He Hollers Let Him Go*
is able to recognize the difficulties which he faces in American
life and to articulate his grievances. As a thinker, he is
totally confused. He is the picture of a sensitive Negro re-
acting to discriminatory practices in the Comstock Atlas
Defense plant. He is anti-Semitic, anti-white, and anti-
Communist; in some cases he is anti-Negro also. The obvious
lesson to be derived from this portrait is that in a different
world "Lee Gordon's frustrations would not exist." He would
have an opportunity to effect proper adjustments to the social
order without the restrictions of race.

Himes covers many issues in this novel. The first condition
of society that he is concerned with is the operation of the
Fair Employment Practices in the United States as it affects
the Negro. With such a consideration he develops his theme
with a condition in society as background material. Himes

---

[58] *Ibid.*, p. 302.
[59] Abram Kardiner, *The Mark of Oppression*, p. 77.

selects that highly potent period when the nation was threatened by the aggressive forces of Nazism.

During World War II the nation was disrupted. Persons working in war industry had to adjust and readjust their habits of life to the exigencies of the times. In the war plant Lee found opposition to his role as organizer of labor. War did not change the existing prejudices of whites against the Negro.[60] Himes' experience with this condition in American society forms the basis of his indictment.

The Communist party with its intricate system attempts to usurp the power of the labor union. Here, Himes documents carefully. His attack upon the Communist party is raw and vitriolic. He rejects the party because of his experience with it. The Communist party is anything but an attractive organization. Himes permits his central character, Lee, to discover that the Communist party is composed of one of the most foul groups of political agitators and power hungry mobsters in the world. The party persecution tactics disgust Lee.

The question of the relationship between Negro and Jew comes out in this novel. In the exchange between the races, Lee is almost broken. He becomes disillusioned because in the guise of friendship Jews practice the same condescension that whites are prone to assume when they deal with Negroes. Lee detects the weak elements in the intellectual Jew's argument. Jews, according to Lee, talk of equality of races and proffer friendliness only to exploit the Negro and to combine with stronger white forces in order to coerce and suppress the Negro. The view may very well have some foundation, but this author feels that there is another side to the question. But Himes' forte is the psychological novel, and his projected narrative and characterizations are convincingly done.

Third Ward Newark, Curtis Lucas' second novel, is the

---

[60] Harold Laski, *The American Democracy,* p. 362.

story of Wonnie, a Negro girl, who develops an incurable neurosis. A harrowing experience of childhood causes this mental state.[61] The thematic structure consists of three issues which reflect the Negro problem. First, there is the economic situation with its discriminatory practices. Secondly, inadequate housing for Negroes is a concern of the characters. Thirdly, destruction of human personality by rape and violence makes of Wonnie a tragic figure.

The plot outline is simple and begins in Newark, New Jersey, when Wonnie is an unprotected girl of twelve years of age living with her Aunt Sarah and sister, Hattie. Aunt Sarah works for a meager twelve dollars a week, yet she maintains a home for the two girls. She dies suddenly, and Hattie must assume the responsibility for Wonnie and herself. The problem of maintaining the home becomes too much for her. She earns only eight dollars a week. She has a beautiful face and attracts men easily, so she becomes a prostitute. All goes well for a while until she is apprehended and sent to prison. Wonnie becomes a ward of the state.

Mildred, a girl fifteen years of age, befriends Wonnie at the state farm, and they decide to escape. They succeed, but Mildred becomes a simulated prostitute, that is to say, she accepts money from men with the promise of sexual favors. On the streets at midnight, Ernie and Walker, two white men, force them to accompany them to a deserted field near a river on the outskirts of Newark. Mildred and Wonnie are raped, and in the struggle Ernie kills Mildred and throws her body into the river. Wonnie is left derobed to die.

Wonnie does not die, however, and is sent to college as a result of a fund that Ernie established during the election after Wonnie's body is discovered still alive. Having had four years of formal training, Wonnie returns to Newark. Her first act is to go to the authorities in Newark and charge

---

[61] Karen Horney, *The Neurotic Personality of Our Times*, p. 20.

Ernie with murder and rape. Her charge is dismissed on the
ground that there is not sufficient evidence. This brusque
dismissal becomes a revenge fixation with Wonnie.

Reunited with Hattie, Wonnie begins a life in the Negro
world. She meets, loves, and marries Joe, but she can not rid
herself of her obsession for revenge and feeling of cheapness.
In Ernie's bar a riot breaks out, and he murders her. Joe,
arriving on the scene too late, fights with Ernie who, after
the idea settles in his mind that he will have to face a charge
of murder, commits suicide.

The social commentary that this novel makes is in keeping
with the themes that it develops. When the book opens the
economic situation in Newark is like this:

> Times were hard all over Newark then, but they were
> hardest in Third Ward. There were some jobs, but the
> white men got first call on them, and there were not
> enough to go around. Colored men and women devised
> their own ways of making a living. Some of the men took
> the jobs that the white men did not want, while others
> scuffled and robbed and stole and pimped. Some colored
> women took domestic jobs or worked in the laundries.
> Others went up on Broome Street and sold their bodies.
> They all got along somehow.[62]

The second theme is that of inadequate housing for
Negroes. Newark, like most large cities, has definite sections
for Negroes, and any attempts to live in better quarters are
usually met with resistance by whites. As a consequence,
many undesirable features are present in the old buildings
Negroes are permitted to occupy.

Wonnie and Joe work in the shipyard where they are
friendly with Mary, who is sympathetic to Negroes. In discussing the very inadequate housing facilities, Mary informs
Wonnie that there is a vacancy in her building. She is agree-

---

[62] Curtis Lucas, *Third Ward Newark*, p. 6.

able to the idea of having Wonnie and Joe occupy the apartment building in which she lives. In fact, she insists that they apply for the vacant apartment. But when Joe and Wonnie apply for the apartment the shallowness of a less genuine white friend than Mary greets them. Such a passage illustrates clearly the position:

> But when Mary [white] took her to the superintendent, the man balked. Sure, he knew how it was with the colored people, and he would like to let her and Joe have the apartment. But he just didn't dare. Where Mary wouldn't mind, other tenants would object. "I know it's wrong," the man said patiently. "I'm for the colored people. I belong to the NAACP, and I help support the Urban League. But this one thing I can't do. I can't let you have the apartment."[63]

The final theme, and most significant in terms of personality and characterization in the novel, is the effect of rape upon Wonnie. This explosive American theme is discussed in this novel in reverse. Usually, Negro men charged with rape of white girls in certain sections of the country are lynched. The situation reversed, the charge becomes an effrontery of law and order among whites, for such action is not precisely considered criminal. The Negro woman does not have such an exalted status, nor is she held in high esteem. This knowledge becomes for Wonnie an obsession and the basis for her anxiety. She expresses herself in extreme hatred on the one hand and mental torment on the other.

William Attaway's *Blood on the Forge* anticipates *Lonely Crusade* and *If He Hollers Let Him Go* by Chester Himes in the naturalistic thesis presented and in many ways so does Carl Offord's *The White Face*. The thesis in *Blood on the Forge* is that Negroes are objects of discrimination and injustice on the labor market, especially when they offer "com-

---

[63] Lucas, *op. cit.*, p. 195.

petition to white men." [64] Attaway develops this thesis around
economic conditions in the steel mills of Pennsylvania after
World War I when Negroes were brought from the South
for scab labor purposes.

The plot outline is simple but filled with many possibilities
of which Attaway takes full advantage. The opening scene
of *Blood on the Forge* is a sharecropping farm in Kentucky.
The world that Attaway creates and the shanty which he
describes make the Lesters of *Tobacco Road* by Erskine
Caldwell appear occupants of a hospitable and comfortable
home by comparison. The principal characters, Big Matt,
Chinatown, Melody, and Big Matt's wife, endure poverty
and squalor in a miserable shanty. This family belongs to
the class of substandard workers comparable with those under
feudalism during the Middle Ages. Under such a system the
human personality of the Negro workers is ignored completely. Here in an elemental existence, the three brothers live
together. Despite the impoverished condition of the farm,
the men are healthy and strong. Big Matt, leader of the
trio, is a powerfuly developed, huge, black man. Chinatown,
smaller in stature but equally well-built, is slightly larger
than the musically talented Melody. These three brothers
share a deep-rooted attachment for each other. This affection
is born from mutual understanding and common suffering.
Each has a different expression for the same frustration
which is self-realization as a human being. Big Matt wants
to preach and holds the primordial theory of having a boy
child as the only means of self-perpetuation. He daydreams
of preaching, reading his Bible in his spare time. He approaches the mystic's world while Chinatown wants the
brightness of this world to come into his being. Taking his
cue from the sun, he has a gold tooth which is his one prized
possession. Melody plays haunting strains on his guitar. Thus,

[64] William Attaway, *Blood on the Forge,* p. 167.

these sharecropper dreamers in their private worlds present dissatisfied men who want to escape from their present life. Externally, however, they exhibit a solid demeanor which sustains them.

A fight between the white straw boss, Smothers, and Big Matt ends with Big Matt victorious. As a consequence, the three men make a hasty flight from Kentucky to the steel mills of Pennsylvania. The men realize that they can not have a satisfactory adjustment[65] of money matters which pertain to the yearly crop now that Big Matt has beaten Smothers. For the trip to Pennsylvania, the men are crated up in boxcars like cattle. One hell is exchanged for another, but the difference is more revealing and damaging in Pittsburgh because of the higher demands made upon the men. Living conditions are bad, and the hard work in the furnace rooms of the mills overwhelms the brothers and saps their abundant vitality. Furthermore, Big Matt and his brothers are the victims of unsatisfactory labor union strategy, for they are employed to break a strike rather than to become members of the union. Big Matt is given the official role of strikebreaker deputy. In the labor battle which follows, Big Matt loses his life, and Chinatown and Melody are left blind and mutilated.

The social commentary in this novel is one of economics. Job security is all important in America. From the beginning these men are made to suffer hardships on account of their race.

"The social criticism is as searching as any to be found in contemporary literature" [66] is the opinion of Drake De Kay of the *New York Times Book Review*. Attaway follows the conventional approach which is essentially documentation of

[65] Myrdal, *op. cit.*, p. 559. ("Any white man can strike or beat a Negro, steal or destroy his property, cheat him in a transaction. . . .")

[66] Drake De Kay, *The New York Times Book Review*, August 24, 1941, p. 18.

evils inherent in the social order with particular reference to the Negro. Usually, flagrant injustices, discriminatory practices, and oppression compose the framework of such a novel. The danger that a Negro writer has to avoid is being too reportorial and documentary. There is, of course, no room for sentimentality because this is the grim business of projecting incidents of real life truthfully yet with narrative skill. Again, the Negro author has to prevent himself from becoming tractish in his fervor for advocating change rather than remaining purely objective. Attaway achieves success in *Blood on the Forge.*

On the farm in Kentucky, the men have nothing at all to do with decisions as to financial matters or just how the farm should be operated. They have insufficient food. Big Matt's wife cannot nurture a baby, she is so undernourished. Race relationships between whites and blacks are distinguished by the complete emasculation of Negro personality.

In Pennsylvania the steel mill is worse than the farm. Here, the men encounter open hostility. The adjustment of the sharecropper to the industrialized East is difficult. The living conditions are unsuitable, for the men occupy a pill box for an apartment. Working conditions become a battle against roaring, deadly hot furnaces of molten steel which proves paralyzing to the men. The hours which are required of them tax their endurance. In the battle against steel, each time the men lose to the overwhelming heat, grime, and stifling odor from the gigantic steel ovens.

Overpowering as it is, steel is not enough. The men have to contend with racial conflict. Fearful of their jobs, Slavs, Italians, Poles, and other whites resent the presence of the black men. In this connection the friction brought on by the failure of the union to mobilize the Negro workers properly demonstrates racial hatred in no uncertain terms. Indeed, the conflict becomes a race riot. Scabs are hated by organized

labor and rightly so. In the battle which rages as a consequence of this situation, Big Matt finally asserts himself;
his personality becomes realized. In the gruesome business of
killing white men, Big Matt strikes with vengeance. He can
not forget his past experiences in Kentucky nor his Mexican
mistress calling him "peon" or "black." As a result he behaves
as if he were solving the whole race problem when he releases
recklessly his almost superhuman strength. One observer says:
"He was game, all right, but crazier'n hell . . . they're fightin'
the race war 'stead of a labor strike." [67] Of course Big Matt
Moss, the fighting "black Irishman," dies in the labor battle.
In that evanescent moment between hell and destruction,
Matt achieves self-realization in a violent death. Characterizations in this novel approximate invariably reality. One gets
the feeling that he has seen one or all three Negro men.

Modern tragedy takes into account the failures and frustrations of the life of the ordinary man in highly industrialized civilization. The machine robs man of that sense of
immanence that he had in less highly developed epochs.
Blood on the Forge shows little man meeting and experi-
encing tragedy in an industrialized setting. Human beings
in society need not suffer such defeats and frustrations. But
what should be, rarely if ever, is in accord with what is.
Melody is almost a mystic, and from his private other
worldly plane he can best explain his tragic ending. First of
all, he gets a warning:

> This warning was for something much worse. Perhaps
> the monster had gotten tired of an occasional victim.
> Perhaps he was about to break his chains. He would
> destroy masses of men, flesh, bones and blood, leaving
> only names to bury. Fear of that drove everything else
> out of a man.[68]

[67] Attaway, *op. cit.*, p. 275.
[68] *Ibid.*, p. 184.

This warning is followed by a consuming bitterness:

> A bitterness toward all things white hit him like a hot
> iron. Then he knew. There was a riding boss—Big Matt.
> Big Matt Moss from the red hills was the riding boss.
> For the first time in his life he laughed aloud. Laughing
> crazily, he held the man by the neck.[69]

Then Melody's warning becomes more than an ordinary sign,
for it approaches death:

> Like a reflection in disturbed water, the face of the young
> Slav came into vision. He looked at that face from a
> great distance. It would only be a moment before he
> must crash to the ground. His eyes were objective. He
> had all of the objectivity of a man who is closer to death
> than life. From that dark place he looked back at the
> world.[70]

Big Matt's death is a psychological dream but his inevitable
tragedy is realized:

> Big Matt looked at the mills, and big feelings were lifting
> him high in the air. He was big as God Almighty. The
> sun was down, or his head would have thrown a shadow
> to shade the river front. He could have spit and quenched
> a blast furnace. Big Matt's eyes were big as half moons.
> They stretched and their full size showed white all around
> black pin points.[71]

The White Face by Carl Offord invites comparison with
Bucklin Moon's *Darker Brother* for both novels describe life
in Harlem with sympathetic understanding. The similarity
ends at this point, but the contrast is even more provocative.
Moon succeeds in stressing the human qualities of the Negro
while Offord concentrates on the working of Harlem's political and social underworld. He brings race antagonisms into

---

69 *Ibid.*, p. 271.
70 *Ibid.*, p. 273.
71 *Ibid.*, p. 272.

the narrative. In his discussion of a growing anti-Semitic feeling in Harlem among Negroes, he is expressing the same attitude Himes offers in his *Lonely Crusade*. Like Attaway's *Blood on the Forge*, *The White Face* depicts the hazards and conflicts involved when sharecroppers from the South come East. Adjustment proves difficult, and since political issues must be faced, very often the newly arrived Negro can not make proper decisions. Offord gives documentary evidence of dissenting groups and various political movements underway in Harlem during World War II years.

Carl Offord's novel tells the story of Nella and Chris. These two sharecroppers flee from a farm of peonage in Georgia[72] because Chris fights with a white man and believes that he has killed him. When Nella and Chris arrive in New York, they find open hostility from their relatives. Chris can not find employment and rarely leaves the apartment except at night because he is afraid of apprehension. Nella, on the other hand, secures employment with a Jewish family.

Fascist agitators make speeches, and Chris listening to them at night becomes confused in the shifting position various agents take on political issues. Chris foolishly gets the idea that Nella is going to betray him, and he feels that he must kill her. He goes to the place where she works, and a fire starts in the building. Chris is held by the authorities charged with arson.

Nella succeeds in getting him freed of charges, since the white man did not die in Georgia, and the fire was caused accidentally. Instead of appreciation, Chris' hatred grows and when she visits him at the prison he insults her. In his fury he makes an attempt to take the guard's pistol and is shot. Nella realizes that the dead form in front of her is her husband, but she feels no pain nor sorrow.

---

[72] Carl Offord, *The White Face,* p. 19.

Chris is a completely different man from the one in this situation in the beginning of the narrative:

> He saw the whip descending, tried to jump back. The hot, singing wind of it brushed his face. The blow landed across the same shoulder: stinging with fire. Again the whip was slashing, but in that instant the abuses of his entire life came together in a crashing fury and he rushed in blindly, whaming his big fist into the fat, paunchy belly. Mr. Harris grunted and sank to the floor. Chris stood over him, panic-stricken, staring. For a moment he couldn't move, then suddenly the urge to flee broke upon him. He leaped to the desk, snatched up a handful of bills and rushed out.[73]

Perhaps Nella remembered the harshness of her life which consisted of a situation devoid of comforts for it meant that: "We are just eating and paying bills." [74]

Ann Petry's *The Street* is a straightforward novel with a naturalistic thesis. Petry postulates the premise that environment exerts a tremendous influence upon the course of an individual's life. In an unwholesome environment a Negro is doomed to meet disaster in America. The thesis is common to writers who subscribe to naturalism in fiction. Ann Petry, however, brings to the theme a refreshing technique[75] which gives her stature of a mature and serious writer of fiction. In following the lead of Wright, Attaway, and earlier Hurston, Ann Petry joins the ranks of the Negro writers who discuss some aspects of the Negro problem. Her work has considerable technical advance over the pioneering novels on racial themes, but the issue remains the same.

To present her case Petry creates a world which contains all of the elements of bitterness and eventual destruction on

----

[73] Offord, *op. cit.*, p. 20.

[74] *Ibid.*, p. 83.

[75] Paul Bixler, *Antioch Review*, Summer 1946, pp. 269-273. ("No more forthright attempt at naturalism has appeared recently in our fiction —Zolaistic detail and an economic determinism reminiscent of Flaubert.")

account of race relationships in America. Immediately the reader is introduced to a symbol of foreboding disaster and destruction. It is the street. A whirlwind blows angrily bits of filth and refuse from opening doors into the street with unabated fury. The powerful wind with its sweeping fury almost takes the pedestrian bodily from the street. This is 116th Street and Seventh Avenue, New York City, where thousands of Negroes live in abominable apartments. Their common virtues are filth, dirt, and stench.

The heroine, Lutie Johnson, appears in this setting, blown about by the whirlwind in the street. Lutie Johnson is a beautiful, intelligent, and uncompromising Negro girl who attacks energetically the problem of living.

Her story really begins in the depression years when she and her husband, Jim Johnson, were unemployed and living in Jamaica. Upon the recommendation of Mrs. Pissini, Italian shopkeeper, Lutie lands a job with the wealthy Chandlers in Connecticut.

The Chandlers are a miserable group, since Mr. Chandler drinks excessively, and Mrs. Chandler has a love affair with a friend of the family. Her friends hold Lutie in low esteem, and she hears them discuss her in this way:

> Sure, she's a wonderful cook, but I wouldn't have any good-looking colored wench in my house. Not with John. You know they're always making passes at men. Especially white men. And then—Now I wonder. . . .[76]

The idea of such a notion shocks Lutie, for she has been trained in the puritanical concepts of morality and virtue by her grandmother. She reacts to this revolting statement which is so far removed from her principles:

> It didn't make her angry at first. Just contemptuous. They didn't know she had a big handsome husband of her own; that she didn't want any of their thin un-

---

[76] Ann Petry, *The Street*, pp. 40-41.

happy husbands. But she wondered why they all had the idea that colored girls were whores.[77]

The servant quarters, not to mention the opulence of the house proper, impress Lutie. She would like to own a home like the domestic quarters in order that Bub, her little boy, could thrive and develop into respectable manhood.

Since Lutie does not return home weekly, her husband brings another woman into their home to live with him. Returning home unexpectedly, Lutie finds them having breakfast bought with the money she sent for Bub. Automatically, she resolves their relationship. This background explains Lutie's presence on the street as the book opens.

Lutie's effort to maintain herself and Bub by working hard and honestly are thwarted. She tries for the Civil Service and is placed on a waiting list. Singing with Boots proves to be a dead end. Mrs. Hedges offers a preposterous and insulting solution:

> "Dearie, I been thinkin'—" Mrs. Hedges' voice halted her. Mrs. Hedges studied her from head to foot with a calculating eye. "If you ever want to make a little extra money, why, you let me know. A nice white gentleman I met lately—." Lutie walked up the street without answering. Mrs. Hedges' voice followed her, "Just let me know, dearie." Sure, Lutie thought, as she walked on, if you live on this damn street you're supposed to want to earn a little extra money sleeping around nights. With nice white gentlemen.[78]

Lutie rejects white men on principle. Because of this attitude, she refuses to consider an affair with them either for love or money.

The superintendent in the building in which she lives is a sex degenerate who upon sight builds an overwhelming

---

[77] Petry, *op. cit.*
[78] Petry, *Ibid.*, p. 84.

passion for Lutie. Mrs. Hedges rescues her from the clutches of the fiend. But revenge for his rejection leads Jones, the superintendent, to introduce Bub to crime. He rifles the mailboxes in the neighborhood and is apprehended. Seeking frantically for financial aid, Lutie visits Boots' fashionable 409 Edgecombe Avenue apartment, "Sugar Hill," home of some famous and wealthy Negroes. Junto, the white man who controls a section of Harlem with his business and houses, awaits her. He wants her body as a prostitute in exchange for the money. Lutie murders Boots and boards a train for Chicago. Bub will not have his chance because he will be sent to the reform school. "The street will get them sooner or later, for it sucked the humanity out of people, slowly, inevitably." [79]

Social commentary in this book has far-reaching implications in the matter of environment. In the first place the general housing conditions of the Negro families in this section of Harlem are depressing and inadequate. A mother who attempts to make her own independent living with a growing boy left to the street has a difficult task. Lutie is fully aware of her responsibility as a mother. She is handicapped by the absence of a husband who is dependable. She has to steer a broken home against overwhelming odds. The primary factor here is the economic struggle that she has to make. Lutie has ability and knowledge, but she can not secure job nor opportunity to fend for herself and Bub. Race enters the picture and looms as the portent of doom. If she were not a Negro, she would be able "to find a good job" [80] and events would take a different turn. Race relationships in this novel are not strained in the ordinary sense so that the

[79] *Ibid.*, p. 176.

[80] Myrdal, *op. cit.*, p. 391. ("The vicious circle of job restrictions, poverty, and all that follows with it tends to fix the tradition that Negroes should be kept out of good jobs and held down in unskilled, dirty, hot or otherwise undesirable work.")

emphasis upon sensationalism destroys the protest. It is far more realistic, for there emerges a slickness which presupposes that there will be dualism. Segregation, low incomes for Negroes, and a crushing defeat for respectable Negro women appear as a matter of course. The book seems to say with straightforward frankness that this is the way it is. The Negro world painted in the novel has gripes against the system which denies to Negroes a job. Petry parodies situations considered good enough for Negroes on the economic level. For example, the job of a pullman porter stifles the personalities of the men. Education is important, but white teachers would rather not teach Negro children. They simply are not as bright as whites according to their point of view. Patriotism is challenged because of the segregated army which mocks democracy. Then those Negroes who do share the country's prosperity adopt readily the cynical attitudes of the whites. Boots, who becomes disgruntled over affairs, is as sophisticated and heartless as Junto, his mentor and employer.

Lutie has a set of values that are compatible with our accepted notions of respectability. In this attitude she is unshakable and uncompromising. A weaker person would have accepted much earlier the offer of easy money since it at least would have solved the problem of financial security for the immediate future. Hattie, a character in *Third Ward* who is attractive, does not even attempt to struggle. When she is aware of her powers, she yields and is destroyed in the process. The stranglehold of the environment will eventually ensnare her, Lutie fears. Yet her grandmother's words always come to her when she is approached by a white man:

> Lutie, baby, don't you never let no white man put his hands on you. They ain't never willin' to let a black woman alone. Seems like they all got a itch and a urge

> to sleep with 'em. Don't you never let any of 'em touch you.[81]

If her father could have helped her with Bub, the load would have been lighter. He is a drunken sot whose mistress has no knowledge of the proper way of caring for children. The mistress gives Bub, then a little boy of six, gin to drink. This is a circumstance of Lutie's environment which hemmed her in. It constantly pushed her back. Mrs. Hedges and Junto had sacrificed principles long ago, and the result was wealth. They maintain conditions by owning buildings and fostering vice similar to that found in *The Street*. Their delight now is the exploitation of the clean and pure who happened to come on the street.

Lutie advocates in this struggle for existence a free, capitalistic society in which the Negro no less than whites can gain as much as he desires or is capable of gaining. There is obviously class and caste consciousness among Negroes as among whites. Lutie knows the evils of her world would be eliminated with sufficient wealth. Lutie is sensible and realizes that the mere possession of money does not insure happiness, but undeniably, money places a metallic coating on suffering in America. She is tremendously impressed with Chandler's enthusiasm for money when he says:

> Richest damn country in the world.—Always be new markets. If not here, South America, Africa, India— Everywhere and anywhere. Hell! make it while you're young. Anyone can do it—Outsmart the next guy. Think up something before anyone else does. Retire at forty.[82]

American crass materialism has its attractive side, and Lutie discovers that with the Chandlers the bitch goddess success means money. Lutie has the idea that people stressed

---

[81] Petry, *op. cit.*, p. 45.
[82] *Ibid.*, pp. 40-43.

far more important concepts of success as, for instance, the humanitarian impulse, or life of service, or political aspirations, but Chandler's remark dispels the idea:

> No. They didn't want their children to be president or diplomats or anything like that. What they wanted was to be rich—"filthy" rich as Mr. Chandler called it.[83]

Lutie discusses values continuously because she wishes to abide consistently by her principles. Her values must serve her purpose in life and have a salutary effect upon her restless mind. Respectability is important to her, for she repudiates her father and his free and easy life of drunkenness. She considers her husband the scum of the earth when he takes her money and keeps another woman in their apartment. Lutie wants security and this means the material possessions of this life for her and Bub are important too:

> . . . she didn't lose her belief in the desirability of having money, though she saw that mere possession of it wouldn't necessarily guarantee happiness.[84]

Petry makes Lutie express a feminine point of view which shows the danger of making generalizations about a race. The attitude that Negro men are not men but ethnics and that Negro women are wenches is a presumptious error. Lutie as a characterization negates emphatically the idea. She equates morality to the level of sex selection. In fact, her principles, too puritanical perhaps, are so deeply embedded in her consciousness that romantic love with a Negro man is the only type for her until her ultimate destruction results. Living among vice yet essaying to surmount the seemingly innumerable obstacles, Lutie wages a losing battle. She insists on swimming upstream against the currents. Her indomitable will helps her, and she could reach her destination if the

---

[83] *Ibid.*
[84] *Ibid.*, p. 49.

external forces had not combined to overpower her. In her course she will not permit society to make a prostitute of her in order to gain material comforts. White men are repulsive to proud Negro women while others, according to *The Street* indulge in illicit affairs without compunction.

As to technique, Petry to an eminent degree embellishes her novel with sustained atmosphere. Her narrative powers are most fruitful in a realistic descriptive passage. Her prose has shining brilliance and simplicity in such a section from the opening chapter where she paints her word picture this way:

> It (wind) did everything it could to discourage the people walking along the street. It found all the dirt and dust and grime on the sidewalk and lifted it up so that the dirt got into their noses, making it difficult to breathe; the dust got into their eyes and blinded them; and the grit stung their skins. It wrapped newspaper around their feet entangling them until the people cursed deep in their throats, stamped their feet, kicked at the paper. The wind blew it back again and again until they were forced to stoop and dislodge the paper with their hands. And then the wind grabbed their hats, pried their scarves from around their necks, stuck its fingers inside their coat collars, blew their coats away from their bodies.[85]

By contrast Petry develops her thesis. It is by alternating pictures of the two worlds that is the white world and the black world of the street that she secures desired effect. Her presentation has an utter, realistic impact because she shows that in both worlds problems arise, but the one has the advantage over the other in abundance as pitted against poverty. In the white world adversity is merely an intellectual idea because wealth puts a metallic covering on emotions, and material properties are taken as a matter of course. On the

---

[85] *Ibid.*, p. 2.

other hand, the Negro world that Lutie knows is one of poverty. People here can not climb above nor to the level of adequate essentials.

Mrs. Palmer's Honey by Fannie Cook, a white novelist, involves a Negro heroine similar to Ann Petry's Lutie Johnson in *The Street*. The two novels have in common an unwholesome environment and its effect upon a Negro woman's attempt to advance and progress in life. Lutie is stronger of the two. For the cause of the Negro, Lutie's character is inspirational[86] while the heroine in *Mrs. Palmer's Honey* serves essentially as a foil to the more significant aspects of political life so far as the author is concerned. She permits her heroine to succeed as a labor leader.

Ann Petry's *The Street* adheres more closely to the requirements of American naturalistic fiction than *Native Son*. The reason is that the religious element does not enter at all, nor does the author attach any psychological morbidity or other mental state to Lutie. She is determined by forces within the social framework. Her exercise of volition is made an infantile affair because of repeated frustrations. She is maneuvered on every turn by environment. The fact that she is bound by her decision to be a morally pure woman in accordance with her standards shows how ineffectual such a position is against relentless forces of environment. These forces disintegrate human personality. In the first place the street itself has a negative influence when it is in a dilapidated neighborhood. Her economic background will not permit her to take an apartment in a better one. The apartments in the building are unsuitable for homes. Along with this there is vice in the truly naturalistic tradition.

The Street gives a very graphic picture of what this type of environment means with its criminal effects on Negroes or any other inhabitant:

---

[86] Lucy Lee Clemons, *Phylon*, Jan., 1946, p. 96.

It was a bad street. And then she thought about the other streets. It wasn't just this street . . . she was afraid of or that was bad. It was any street where people were packed together like sardines in a can. And it wasn't just this city. It was any city where they set up a line and say black folks stay on this side and white folks on this side, so that the black folks were crammed on top of each other—jammed and packed and forced into the smallest possible space until they were completely cut off from light and air.[87]

Juxtaposition of images is effective with Petry. She gives the emollient picture of womanly courage and the obdurate and blasé successful man. Beautiful flowers on a push cart appear in a littered street. Ineluctable desire of a Negro for success meets only the invidious denial by whites. Her presentation is starkly realistic, and she pushes home her urgent need of economic security. It is the lack of job opportunity which means that she is defeated and economically insecure. She indicts society for this condition, and by careful documentation of issues, *The Street* achieves its purpose. Where Wright indicts vehemently society through Bigger's hatred, Petry accomplishes the same through restraint. Where Wright registers a furious consciousness on the world, Petry impresses character, a character which indicts because of its existence. The difference between the two authors is essentially in point of reference. One is shooting at the target more emotionally than the other.

Decidedly convincing are the several characters in *The Street*.

Of course, Lutie is the most important, yet she offers no problem psychologically except the "symptomatic one of anxiety."[88] Her anxiety comes from frustration on the economic level, and beautiful and intelligent Lutie knows pre-

---

[87] Petry, *op. cit.*, p. 206.
[88] Rollo May, *The Meaning of Anxiety*, pp. 190-196.

cisely what she wants and what her chosen course of action must be. Her affectionate nature makes her a good mother.

Other fully realized characters in the novel are Mrs. Hedges, William Jones, superintendent of the apartment building, Bub, Lutie's son, and even Junto, the enterprising Jew. Jones, however, is worth noting a little more carefully. He is a lurking and sinister force which causes the ultimate downfall of Lutie. His sex obsession drives him insane. But Mrs. Hedges, "a mountain of a woman," is more than a foil for Jones.

Bub has childish fears and is easily influenced as most growing children are. So, Jones who is frustrated and irate because of his ungratified sex designs on Lutie, leads Bub easily into crime. This is the final act of the drama, for with Bub's apprehension Lutie walks on the stage of the final act of her tragedy. She is a tragic figure in her ineffectual battle against environment. By its insidious power Lutie is destroyed. For she is one of the many underprivileged women who dare to maintain dignity and character, yet find in life those frustrations, fears, and ultimate unhappiness the only reward for the effort. Her whole life has been one of disappointments and bitterness. Her marriage is a failure, her parents are disappointing, her beauty is not an asset, and happiness eludes her grasp. She stands before us the embodiment of modern tragedy.

It Was Not My World, by Jenkins Deaderick is not so much a novel as it is experiences very deliberately sensationalized. Deaderick makes an issue out of publication difficulties. In an explanatory note he attacks publishers for their resentment of "charged" material pertaining to Negroes. In the end he had to publish his own work. Admittedly, it has a set of horrifying experiences. But horror for the sake of horror fails to arouse our sympathy or our fears.

The author starts out with the presumptious statement that he has written a novel to end all novels. Such a bold stroke may very often be the intention of authors in a static society. In a dynamic society this position is much too precarious and untenable. Novels will be written despite the many classics familiar to lovers of good literature.

The theme, *It Was Not My World,* suggests that Mississippi is an unsuitable place for the Negro to live. Despite lynching, bigotry, and discrimination many Negroes survive in Mississippi. It is only with a penetrating eye for distillation that makes this material aesthetically satisfying in a novel. Out of this material must come a synthesis with characterizations and significant aspects of this situation in order to become fictional drama.

It Was Not My World has four episodes involving cardboard characters such as Colonel Knox and Hattie Mae. Into a situation of semislavery comes the college-trained author. A lynching occurs, and the political life proceeds as always.

Rebecca Barton writes of this type of novel this way:

> Direct articulation of the author's particular grievance through the mouths of his characters, implications of injustices through choice of setting or creation of atmosphere, consciousness of race, has resulted in the cruder probing from brooding spirit.[89]

With the publication of the *Last of the Conquerors,* by William Gardner Smith, racial themes enter the international scene. Ironically enough, the German people, whom the Negroes accepted as their sworn enemy as United States soldiers, welcomed the Negro as a conquering hero. Color lines did not exist, and the life among the conquered Nazis proved more congenial than life in Dawkins', the central character, American home. William Smith, a young author, draws characters who participate in every phase of German life. The love affairs which result from such intimacies have

---

[89] Rebecca Barton, *Race Consciousness and American Negro Literature,* p. 11.

more verisimilitude than similar situations in modern fiction
because of the spontaneity which characterizes the origin.

Race relationships between white and Negro troops were
strained in Europe because of the fraternization between
Negroes and Europeans. Conditioning and feelings of resentment caused many unnecessary bans and conflicts to exist
between fellow soldiers. Negro troops were placed under the
command of Southern white officers who not only were prejudiced but who sought opportunities to emasculate Negro personality in the name of the United States Army. This comes
out with full significance in the novel.

The novel develops the rather inflammatory theme that
life in conquered Germany was better for Negro troops than
life in America,[90] and in the conduct of affairs and life, color
is of no consequence to some Europeans.

The plot in Smith's *Last of the Conquerors* follows
the pattern of straightforward narrative. The reader is introduced to Hayes Dawkins, United States Negro soldier in the
army of occupation in Berlin. Like all American soldiers,
Dawkins hated Germans and had derived his distorted notions
of them as human beings from Adolf Hitler's *Mein Kampf*.
In Berlin his duty as a soldier required that he work with them
in an office. Working with them intimately and freely asso-
ciating with them, he becomes aware of their quality of
human beings which is decidedly different from what he had
been led to believe. Among the workers is a beautiful German
girl, Ilse, with whom Dawkins becomes friendly. Their friendship develops into a love affair. At the Canteen and in the
German homes, they discuss frankly the Negro's status in
America. To the Germans the Negroes represent the privileges of any American. They assume that the Negro's background is similar to the white soldier in every respect. Their

---

[90] *Catholic World,* October, 1948, p. 276.

colorful impression of American life is derived from American films shown in Berlin. Dawkins and his companions, through false pride, will not disillusion them but permit the Germans to keep their preconceived notions of American life.

Life in Berlin for the Negro soldier follows the pattern of the Germans. In their free time Hayes Dawkins and Ilse attend the opera and dine at the cafes. Suddenly, the men are transferred from the command of Captain Doyle to Widsdorf. Life is unnecessarily rugged and stifling because of the low character and prejudiced attitude of the Southern commander. In this United States Army prison for Negro soldiers, a first sergeant goes beserk and commits murder, barely missing the captain who motivates the crime. Dawkins witnesses the crime and his report of the affair in exact details to the colonel negates rather than confirms the captain's version of the story. To avoid court-martial proceedings, Dawkins returns to America, leaving behind his lover, Ilse, who had followed him from Berlin to Widsdorf.

Social commentary in this novel begins with the army of the United States. The caste system in the army provides a springboard for the usual exercise of discrimination and injustice to the Negro citizen.[91] The common knowledge that the Negro citizen has a vested interest in the country and serves proudly does not alter the army's attitude. As practiced in Widsdorf, if anything, Negro patriotism intensifies his status as a second-rate citizen. To be sure, the Negro must not forget; so a Negro-hating Southerner is placed in command. The novel discloses the fact that such an officer is a man of low calibre with little, real, military knowledge. Frequently, such men are guilty of abusing their position, of which Captain Smith in the novel is representative.

The theme of integration is discussed and shown to work

---

[91] Roi Ottley, *The Black Odyssey,* p. 189.

in a dictatorship with less self-consciousness and matter of factness than is ever achieved in America. The Negro soldiers are amazed to learn what it means really to be accepted as a human being. In German life, devoid of any visible barriers, Dawkins' home serves as an illuminating picture in contrast with his native Philadelphia where Dawkins lived in a ghetto area provided especially for Negroes. There are numerous places in Hayes' home town, as he presents in his stream of musings, that Negroes do not frequent because of known policy of discrimination. Custom sanctions omit Negroes, and in order to avoid embarrassment Negroes consider such places "off-limits." Dating white girls is frowned upon, so falling in love with one is impossible or unthinkable with Hayes Dawkins in Philadelphia. In Berlin, capital of Nazism with its publicized hatred of Jews, and contempt for every other nationality but Germans, all public places receive Hayes Dawkins as just another American soldier of the conquering army. He visits these places with his German girl friend. Together they hear and appreciate the great music on the German opera stage which includes *Die Meistersinger, Faust,* and others. They dine in cafes, visit other Germans, and more stimulating, they enjoy the electrifying passion of real love. Dawkin's case may be multiplied by as many Negroes as comprising his outfit. To men like Dawkins this is a shocking revelation. Actually, they learn for the first time in their lives[92] the meaning of freedom from their enemies. The old principle operates. The army captures the city, but the city captures the army.

Smith presents his case in several provocative scenes. It dawns suddenly upon Dawkins the significance of the life that he is living in Berlin. The following excerpt shows his use of the stream of consciousness technique in his reaction to the explosive theme of mixing between the two races:

[92] Charles Rolo, *Atlantic Monthly,* Oct. 1948, pp. 106-107.

I had lain on the beach many times, but never before with a white girl. A white girl. Here, away from the thought of differences for a while, it was odd how quickly I forgot it. It had lost importance. Everyone was blue or green or red. No one stared as we lay on the beach together, our skins contrasting but our hearts beating identically and both with noses in the center of our faces. Odd, it seemed to me, that here, in the land of hate, I should find this one all-important phase of democracy. And suddenly I felt bitter.[93]

So pronounced is the affection of the Negro soldiers for Berlin that not one of them wants to leave. Smith illustrates this graphically and dramatically in the presentation of the suicide of one of the soldiers and his lover. Another Negro fled to the Russian border. The soldiers discuss the issue from various angles. It is a question of making a decision after having carefully weighed the evidence. Free men want to arrive at a proper course of action through reason. One must know what it is that he is giving up in America and what the new country offers. In the discussion Homo, a fellow soldier, gives his decision to desert the United States:

I got it all figured out. See, about two months ago, I was in the Russian sector and this Russian officer approached me at the bar and bought me a drink. We sat down and started talking about things in general and after a while we got around to the race question in the States. This officer knew more than I did about it. He could name names and call dates, like the Scottsboro boys' case and the Philly PTC strike. He asked me why I didn't go to Russia to live. I told him no, I wasn't for that. He said that if I ever wanted anything I could come to him and he gave me the name of his company. So now I figure I might as well go into Russian sector of Berlin to live for a while.[94]

---

[93] William Gardner Smith, *Last of the Conquerors,* p. 44.
[94] *Ibid.,* p. 107.

The *Last of the Conquerors* is outstanding for the quality
of its style. Malcolm Cowley, editor and critic, found it comparable to the "early Hemingway"[95] and in rendition equally
good as any of the postwar novels. It is a simple, clear, and
restrained style. If anything the author with his lucidity is
guilty of understatement and oversimplification of the issues.
Nonetheless, it is a highly readable book, and the very restraint
of the cruel story which the book unfolds wields a shocking
impact. Writing of this type is an achievement when one considers the extreme youth of the author. The work was finished
before he was twenty. In this regard Smith is comparable
with Gore Vidal, author of *Judgment Paris,* who made his
literary debut about that age. The work is realistic and a
part of his war experience. Even though he did not participate in the battles of World War II, he did spend one year
with the army of occupation in Berlin. Smith is especially
powerful in his flashback which describes the housing conditions familiar to him in Philadelphia.

The discipline of the army with its especially brutal application to the Negro troops embitters the soldiers. Living conditions, although unnecessary, were of the most meager sort.
This contrasts with the quarters of the white soldiers who, a
few yards away, live in luxury by comparison. All of the
hardest details are given the Negro troops. Homo gives his
reaction to this injustice as a contributing factor to his desertion. In another country, perhaps, he could get the type of
job that he wants without any restrictions. Certainly, the
stigma of race would be removed. His companions defend the
United States and the scene goes like this:

> "Hell, Homo, you could do that in the States."
> "I know. But the feeling inside wouldn't be the same.
> Maybe I'm a queer guy. I don't know. I don't mind do-

---

[95] Malcolm Cowley, *New Republic,* Sept. 27, 1948, p. 33.

ing nothing as long as I got the right feeling about it inside of me. See, if I dig ditches over here it'll mean that there just ain't no other jobs of my type open—for nobody, white or colored. It won't be because of my skin. And if I know that, I feel okay inside. Then I'm all right. That sounds crazy, don't it? But it's the way I am."[96]

One Negro trooper feels that this is for him the means of self-realization, and he acts upon that conviction. It is apparently a very realistic position for the Negro soldier takes to the defense of the American way as Homo's buddy does. Yet individual happiness is a very personal and at best a transitory and illusive state.

As a work of art, the novel has more technical excellencies than faults. For some readers too much emphasis may very well be said to go to the love escapades of the soldiers rather than to the business at hand, which was to occupy a country of defeated Nazis. In his presentation Smith uses the method of understatement at the expense of clarity in some sections of the book. It seems again that there is an element of false pride among the Negro soldiers in their discussions with the Germans. It may have made for more honesty and integrity to admit that Hollywood versions of America are for the most part false and that Germans must know about the American race problem. But this is to cavil with a highly successful novel.

Felice Swados in her first novel, *House of Fury,* deals with life in a penal institution. Women in prison have a rather interesting place in fiction, for the author usually sentimentalizes about the horror of prisons. By so treating the subject, the author becomes generally the villain. *House of Fury,* as the title indicates, is no such tale. It develops two themes;

---

[96]Smith, *op. cit.,* p. 108.

namely, that discrimination against Negroes exists in prison life, and that stringent regulations give the authorities power which they abuse.[97] As a consequence, reform in prison administration is necessary.

House of Fury is reminiscent of *House of Refuge,* by Grace Leake. Both authors have the same theme and describe conditions found in houses of correction for teen-age girls. In the case of Leake, however, the scene is the South where conditions are not in conformity with our standards for such institutions. The book, therefore, invites an initially harsh criticism because of the deplorable conditions under which inmates live. Swados is more fortunate in matters of setting and living conditions for the girls.

The plot outline gives a straight line of action which involves several rounded characters of whom Jeff is the most highly realized. Having been committed to an institution not far from New York City, Jeff serves her sentence. But she is enamored of humanity in a sense, and remains as a monitor of the institution. She has mastered her trade and now feels that the girls will respond to her leadership because of her own prison record. She has additional sympathy for the girls as a consequence of her inside information from the administrative and inmate's position.

The day starts, as in all institutions, with the morning meal and work assignments. Here, in a large area with cottages for the girls, the racial issue comes into the picture. It is the policy of the institution to keep the white girls and the Negroes separated. In matters of work, this is a different story, for they all work together. One of the chores is work in the orchard. At work, Pal, a boisterous and indifferent Negro girl, shocks the other girls with her ribald stories of sex about white men and Negroes, too. She makes sex appear so earthy and at

---

[97] Harold Laski, *The American Democracy,* p. 469.

the same time disturbingly suggestive. Bennie is then committed for a minor crime and learns early that the color line is drawn rigidly. Negroes become associated with the vicious criminal among criminals as compared with the whites who, no less criminal in the eyes of the law, have the privilege of snubbing the Negro inmate. That is to say, caste and class on account of race continue in prison.

Orchid and Blueball, two more inmates who become disgusted, attempt to escape this segregated pattern but find no place of refuge so they return. Tony, who is somewhat saddened by it all, follows Jeff's paternal lead and succeeds; thus the story closes with the idea in the mind of the reader that each inmate feels that she is on an island far from the world, and hell is a comfort in comparison with the life that they know in the prison.

Swados' book is well-written, with Jeff as the most outstanding characterization. Social commentary in this book is an explicit statement of a need for reform measures in prisons for women. Life is grim here, and everyone knows that criminals must be punished if law and order are to be preserved. In the meantime there is very grave danger of correction institutions being headed by southern bigots who foster and maintain racial discrimination within the prison. Men who delight in sadistic behavior impose their compulsions upon unprotected inmates. Thus, the power delegated to the authorities is abused.

The picture of discrimination is painted with accuracy of details to give the full significance of the psychological reaction the Negroes have to this situation.[98] The arrival of the girls at the home is exactly as it is in the metropolitan area of New York. People live together here and work with any nationality

---

[98] George Froede, *New York Times Book Review*, Nov. 20, 1941, p. 20.

without restrictions. Granted that there is Harlem where there are more Negroes than whites, but whites are also in Harlem and all around the Negroes. Any type of life together that two racial groups prefer may be theirs if they choose. Friends are cultivated on the basis of personality and not skin coloring. In the confines of the institution, all free association with different races ceases immediately.[99] Criminals all, but color makes a difference in the treatment that the prisoners receive. It seems as if the idea is never to be eradicated that one group is to be treated differently from another because of melanin skin content. Justice is an impartial, abstract and cold concept. In the hands of none too careful administrators, justice becomes a warped idea, an issue in terms of the "mythical Anglo-Saxon heritage of superiority."[100] The psychology involved is to make a Negro utterly conscious of his race and, therefore, his crime becomes more than crime; it becomes Negro crime.

As a work of art, much needs to be done with organization of the material so that the author will curb her inclination to excesses. With an exercise of restraint, this story would drive home its forceful social commentary. As it stands, the story moves with such speed that the reader is not prepared for the suddenness of the luridness with which he is drenched immediately. Only in retrospect does the reader realize that this is a situation which needs correction. If the motivation of the characters were explained in a convincing way, the reader might be inclined to sympathize with the inmates as human beings who deserve consideration. The maturity of the girls

---

[99] Kaye Boyle, *New Republic,* Nov. 24, 1941, p. 707.

[100] A. L. Kroeber, *Anthropology,* pp. 175-181. ("Anglo-Saxon refers primarily to speech, incidentally to a set of customs, traditions, and points of view that are more or less associated with language. . . . It is doubtful whether as yet it is valid to speak of one race as physically higher or more advanced, more human, and less brutish than another.")

makes them appear to be women rather than girls in their teens. The seamy side of life hardens people at a tender age, but that does not justify the goriness and sordidness of the tales they relate.

Melodrama comes out in the novel to a great degree. Sex preoccupation of the girls makes of them women of the world, and it is overstressed. A realistic approach to the problem attempts to minimize an activity which will not have conventional expression. Furthermore, these are supposedly teen-age girls who are not of age.

Stranger and Alone is Dr. J. Redding's attempt to grapple with a serious matter in the South among Negro leaders in the field of education. His fable elects to expose conditions in a Negro college with special reference to the administrative activities. The institution is so organized and administered that the students become ineffectual individuals. They are trained to be failures in terms of American values. Redding delineates the all-but-white Negro leader who develops contempt for his less fair brothers in accord with his policy of collaboration with southern whites. In line with southern traditions, whites want to suppress the Negro on all levels. The novel develops two themes. First, that education in Negro colleges in the South is geared to keep the Negro in subjection. Secondly, militant leaders do not exist in the South. Those few Negroes who refuse to accept the present way of life stand isolated in their ineffectuality. They comment upon the cowardice of other Negroes and the effectiveness of the system called white supremacy in the South.

Fictional treatment of the mulatto has been an attractive subject for novelists. Willa Cather's *Sapphira and the Slave Girl* deals with the mulatto girl and the tensions which her presence causes whites. Lillian Smith's *Strange Fruit* is more in line with Redding's theme, for she indicates that Spellman

College for Negro girls is primarily a place for training Negro servants for whites, and the heroine and her sister, graduates of Spellman, are adjusted to menial jobs. Savoy's *Alien Land* deals with the Negro passing as *Southbound,* by Barbara Anderson, tells of a mulatto school teacher who leaves the North to find adjustment in the South similar to Redding's hero, Howden.

Shelton Howden, mulatto, registers at New Hope College in Louisiana as a conditional work student. With the help of his roommate, Thompson, he is able to pass his course. In his second year Miss Braswell's history class stimulates him. Dr. Posey, however, awakens him to the reality of the Negro's inferior position in American society in his sociology class. Dr. Posey, a Southern white, stresses the writings of Gobineau, Grant, Stoddard, and Chamberlain. These men disseminate the idea of racial inferiority of Negroes. Prof. Clark guides Howden effectively in building attitudes of self-esteem despite the college's policy of fostering racial inferiority.[101]

Valrie provides the romantic interest for Howden during his college career. After graduation Prof. Clark informs him that he is too old to begin medical school. So he takes a job on a train as a pullman porter. He receives an injury when he jumps from the train rather than be intimidated by a white supervisor. Prof. Clark brings him to his home where he recovers and is awarded a scholarship to New York University.

In New York Shelton lives at Harlem's YMCA, and after a year he receives his master's degree. Through the intercession of Prof. Bradford, Shelton Howden receives an appointment at Arcadia College. Shelton feels this way about New York and the East:

> When, at the end of the summer semester, Shelton Howden was granted his degree, and—thanks to the inter-

---

[101] Jacques Barzun, *Race: A Study in Modern Superstition,* p. 19.

cession of his major professor—was shortly thereafter
offered a job at Arcadia State College for Negroes, he
was glad to be through with the University and the
North.[102]

At Arcadia College in the South he prospers under the
patronage of President Wimbush. Given many administrative
details, Shelton executes them with dispatch. He becomes
involved with Ellen, the president's daughter, who is too
confused and neurotic to marry. Judge Stevens has arbitrarily
left the matter of appointing a supervisor of Negro schools to
Whimbush who gives Shelton the position. Shortly after his
appointment, Shelton marries Nan Marriot, a beautiful young
Negro woman. The book closes on a note of acquiescence on
Shelton's part, for he is committed to maintain the status quo.
He visits a Negro school which he finds below par, but the
Negro principal refuses to issue second-hand textbooks given
to the school by white authorities. Nor will this principal close
the school because of "cotton picking time." Shelton now has
a brittle hate for black people.

Negro leadership has always been a problem. Myrdal
points out that the Negro leaders fall into two categories,[103]
either collaborators like Wimbush and Howden or ineffectuals
like the country professor and the principal at the Negro
school. Militant leadership is not tolerated in the South, and
Shelton shows precisely why this is true. Not only does he
concur with whites, but he rather glories in his position. He
betrays his trust with a relish and abandonment. He is part of
the system and he knows it. Rather than give up his own
security, he continues blindly while others remain in subjec-

---

[102] J. Saunders Redding, *Stranger and Alone,* p. 108.

[103] Myrdal, *op cit.,* pp. 720-729. ("We base our typology of Negro
leadership upon the two extreme policies of behavior on behalf of the
Negro as a subordinated caste: accommodation and protest. . . . Accommodation is undoubtedly stronger than protest, particularly in the South
where the structure of caste is most pervasive and unyielding.")

tion. With Howden it is all for selfish interests, and may others perish.

As a work of art, the novel is well written, but it lacks certain technical excellencies. For instance, its organization permits the protest to bear the weight of the fable. The fact that Howden is successful in his determination to acquire a college education and to become a success turns into cynicism. Campus activities do not include one of the most important aspects of any college life, for there is no athletic program at New Hope College. The curriculum is weighted down with sociology, and the arts, along with music, have too little emphasis. Science, except for biology, seems to be outside the offering, as well as the knowledge of Howden. Thus, the whole college is out of focus with the first level of competence. It seems hardly fair to show that Negro colleges in the South have only an administrative side rather than a standard curriculum too.

Ellen is an unrealized character. Her neurotic escapades show only one facet of her personality. Surely, a president's daughter, by the mere fact of pretension, would have some intellectual accomplishment to her credit. Prestige of social position demands it. On the other hand, Howden's wife, Nan, is only half brought into focus. The reader is informed that she has crusading zeal in the conventional manner, but none of her actions prove it.

But as an exposé of the administration of the Negro college in the South from the inside, Dr. Redding does the job with consummate skill. He succeeds in achieving his purpose which was to write a realistic novel about the Negro leadership with sophistication. This is an "adult work"[104] with seasoned maturity in evidence. Glimpses of the social life on the college campus, with inadequate facilities, give a telling

---

[104] Harvey Breit, *The New York Times Book Review,* March 5, 1950, p. 12.

blow to the southern dual educational system on the highest level. The cowardice of the Negro in accepting an outdated second-rate status is convincingly done.

The achievement in characterization in this novel is Shelton Howden. Even though he is a "nondescript yellow,"[105] he is favored on account of it. He is a man who vacillates between moral rightness of the situation and his own personal security. One suspects that he does not have the exalted ideals that he is supposed to have proven by leaping from the train rather than destroy his individuality. As supervisor of Negro schools, he collaborates with white authorities without any feeling of remorse at all. In fact, he fosters a program of checking the advance of the Negroes as if he were the greatest Bourbon who ever lived. He can hate Negroes because they have darker skins. He can not even muster enough courage to love his wife with her olive colored skin even though he married her. He is not only a despicable character, but as experience shows, he is true to life. Mulattos, by and large, do have better positions, when they are educated, than their darker brothers in the South. Wimbush, with his name suggesting whimsicality, is drawn to scale so thoroughly that one is tempted to point him out in a southern Negro college. Wimbush lectures Howden and reveals his true character in this passage:

> Darkies who go around saying they don't give a roaring hoot what white people think, and who pretend they're independent of every and any white man ever born, just show their ignorance. They don't take a bit of skin off the white man's tail, though the damn fools seem to think they do. Why, son, if every darky in this country, including you and me, up and died this minute, it would no more affect tomorrow morning's ham and eggs and grits on white folk's table than a single unknown darky's dying

---

[105] Redding, *op. cit.*, p. 7.

would. White folks don't have to give a damn. But we do. We have to give more than a damn about them because no matter whether you love or hate 'em, the country's theirs by a kind of right of eminent domain, and, in a way people like you and me are theirs too.[106]

Novels like *Stranger and Alone, Native Son, If He Hollers Let Him Go, Lonely Crusade,* the *Last of the Conquerors,* and *The Street,* have the racial theme as a thread of commonality. They discuss the American Negro problem from various angles. These novels of purpose are effective because of their organization around an adamantine core of society. Reform of a social institution is implicit. In most cases the dispossessed Negro is the central point in the novel. This dispossessed Negro, selected from the minority group, is held up to the reader for scrutiny. Characters are involved in situations ordinarily viewed as commonplace, but ethnic differences heighten the sense of life. The stage is set for action—action based on the accretion of traditional social prejudices. By the by, the novels are fluid and dynamic. In the case of Richard Wright's *Native Son* and Ann Petry's *The Street,* the action has overwhelming momentum. Before one is completely aware of the spatial setting, the time of action inundates—drenches the reader. One responds to the violence. This set of dynamics of the novel relies upon dramatic conflict for effect. Three dimensional characters such as Bigger Thomas from *Native Son,* Lutie Johnson from *The Street* or Big Matt in *Blood on the Forge,* enter the stage of action calmly enough. But they are caught up in the maelstrom of compulsive action. Social forces in America serve as a magnet, drawing these figures to ultimate disaster. Spatial and time elements blend in the construction of these novels.

The novels in question have action in a dramatic frame which develops the naturalistic thesis out of social conditions

---

[106] *Ibid.,* p. 197.

as the drama unfolds. Mumford Jones definition in part finds illustrative reference and ready application in such works of art, particularly the aspect of literature which stresses the sociological and economic forces. Inadvertently, the imaginative whole addresses those who respond to social appeal.

Without essaying for perfection, the authors of this group of novels impress the critical and general reader with a high level quality of literary execution. Sociological in stress but psychological in effect, these novels, all of which are competently written, add up to distinctive artistic achievements for their respective authors. If they make no attempt at stylistic innovations, if they introduce no unchartered literary method or technique, they exhibit mastery of the genre in the American literary tradition.

The psychology of one of America's largest minority groups registers through the characters. These flesh and blood characters excite us. Inarticulate as Bigger Thomas is in *Native Son,* his emotionality has abysmal depths. Lutie Johnson, heroine in *The Street,* far more articulate than Bigger, and Lee Gordon in *Lonely Crusade,* register the consciousness of embittered souls. On the other hand, Shelton Howden in *Stranger and Alone* has the despicable role of accommodation. Modern tragedy is exemplified in the first instance; supreme irony and paradox in the second. The Biggers, Bobs, and Luties of the Negro group evoke the austere pity. They are little circumscribed human beings pitted against the unrelenting forces of society. These forces defeat, crush, and destroy these characters. They insist this set of circumstances need not exist in the land of opportunity. In the evocation of the tragic mood, this group of novels are sustained literary successes.

LIMITED PERSPECTIVES

Rude am I in my speech,
And little bless'd with the soft phrase of peace;

. . . . . .

And little of this great world can I speak,
More than pertains to feats of broil and battle,
And therefore little shall I grace my cause
In speaking for myself.
　　　　　　Scene 3　　Act I　　*Othello*　　Shakespeare

A group of novels falls in the category of sociological portraits of Negro family life.[1] Color and class consciousness play an important role in the author's treatment. Such works as Dorothy West's *Living Is Easy*, Lewis Caldwell's *The Policy King*, and George Henderson's *Jule* are typical. These novels postulate no thesis but show the Negro world in isolation with separateness of races a matter of course.

Levels of awareness among Negroes vary. Clearly one can enumerate hundreds of cases where Negroes are complacent. Problems of living are reduced to details within the group.

---

[1] V. F. Calverton, *The Newer Spirit*, p. 237.

Searching, seeking, or demanding opportunities for full participation in American affairs fail to form a part of life. What is, is good, seems to be the guiding principle in such a Negro family's life. Advancement to a higher plane of living or to responsible positions within the frame of American society escapes the consciousness of protracted characters in novels of this type. They have an uncanny method of ignoring the auspicious part that creative effort and ingenuity will gain for the persistent Negro. Contentment in a world which only vaguely echoes the standards of American living leads to stagnation. Progress becomes an impossibility and the status quo remains. Gains made by the ambitious Negro seem to make little if any impression upon the impervious Negro. The novels in this group indicate the effectiveness of subordination of the Negro by the majority group.

Several novels offer no thesis nor has the author any avowed axe to grind. These authors are content to relate a narrative which is descriptive of the American phenomenon, the Negro World. The novels simply emphasize the common knowledge that the "two races develop identical cultural patterns."[2] Their activities and their pursuits, therefore, are similar except for the incidental of color and the corresponding separateness that is the usual American way in race relationships. Such novels are Henderson's *Jule,* Powell's *Picketting Hell,* and sections of Alden Bland's *Behold A Cry.* The thread of commonality between the novels is their adjustment to the Negro world. The inevitable conflict of interrelationship between the two races is minimized. They differ in their manner of narration and show the flexibility of the novel form and the Negro author's skill in using his medium for various types of novels. They range, therefore, from the straight narratives of *Jule* and *Flour Is Dusty* to the semihistorical, socio-

[2] Ruth Benedict, *Race: Science and Politics,* pp. 17-27.

logical novel like *Behold A Cry* and the *Policy King* to the semi-biographical *Picketting Hell.*

As a group of novels, the works are technically good and prove stimulating to the reader. Particularly outstanding are the insights into the life within an adjusted world where the qualities of human beings are thrown into bold focus by stressing abstract qualities as, for instance, religion.

Alden Bland's *Behold a Cry* is the story of Ed Tyler's philandering against a background of "Chicago's race riots"[3] and union organization. The two themes seem to have less development than the personal escapades of the hero so that characterization becomes more important than the social documentation.

The plot is developed around the flight motif of the Georgia Negro to the industrial center. Ed Tyler, living in Chicago, builds his new life around employment and a love affair with Mamie. He forgets Georgia and his wife and family. World War I is in progress, and, seeking to escape service, he reveals his deception to Mamie and discusses the possibilities of bringing his family to Chicago to live with them. Mamie, chagrined and piqued by such a proposition, expresses her contempt for him. She agrees to this wild and unreasonable plan, and the life of deception begins with the arrival of Phom and the two boys, Dan and Jan.

Ironically enough, Ed does not pass the physical examination and is rejected for military service by the United States army. Ed takes the boys to the lake, and one of the several race riots breaks out. Some one accidentally hits a white boy with a thrown missile. Ed manages to get the boys home safely, and Phom in her own way informs the boys realistically what it means to be a Negro.

Ed discusses organized labor with Sam, a fellow worker.

---

[3] Alden Bland, *Behold a Cry,* p. 162.

He vacillates and refuses to cooperate with labor and thereby becomes a scab worker. During the first day of the strike, Ed suffers no injury on the job, but when he enters the streetcar he suddenly realizes that he is the only Negro present. Before he can get off the car, the members of the union attack and beat him soundly.

Phom insists that they move after Mamie's emotional outburst reveals her true relationship with Ed. In the new home with his friend Joe, Ed can not resist the advances made by Cleo, Joe's wife. Ed, having severed relationships with Mamie in a highly dramatic scene, decides to leave with Cleo. The two feel that their newly found love is more important than moral law and responsibility. Phom and the two boys are left to fend for themselves. By his desertion of his family, Ed destroys himself morally. But the reason of his destruction is a psychological reaction to his situation. The Negro type depicted bears the traits of the accommodating yet protesting Negro American. The conflict which American society produces in some Negroes equates compensatory indifference.[4] When such a Negro, say Ed for the case in point, attempts to examine critically his role in society and weighs subsequently the possibilities for immediate change, he discovers only futility.[5] For it is futile of one Negro to demand and get immediate and complete equality in America. Knowing this paradox and having made sex the elixir of life, he pursues this substitution exclusively. Duration of life is short, therefore, the excitement and satisfaction derived from the chase and conquest of women which is open to all virile and vigorous men provide Ed's reason for existence. Even so Ed is true to his narrow conception of life.

---

[4] J. Saunders Redding, *On Being a Negro in America*, p. 33.

[5] Harold Laski, *The American Democracy*, p. 468. ("There is no single vocation in which he does not suffer from being a Negro; there is no single environment in which he can hope, quite simply, to give expression to his own personality.")

The setting of the predominantly Southern novel, *Jule*, is rural Alabama. It is the sequel to *Ollie Miss*, the first novel by George Henderson, and in this work he attempts to continue the fortune of stalwart *Ollie Miss'* son, Jule. This simple farmer enjoys his life of abject poverty because he can "hunt coons."[6] Jule and Rollo, a white boy, are companions from childhood until the present stage of young manhood, when the companionship continues. Jule and Bertha Mae become lovers, but Bonyton Keyes, a white overseer, has sexual interests in her, and he and Jule fight over the issue. The result is that Jule beats him soundly and must flee from Alabama.

Arriving in New York, Jule takes any menial job that he can find and lives in the YMCA where he takes night classes. He recalls his mother, a worn out woman of the soil who had enough insight to insist that Jule aspire to a better life, and attempts to improve himself. Intervention of a white friend makes it possible for him to join the union. After several love affairs with Harlem elite, Jule returns to Alabama upon the death of his mother. He returns to New York bringing Bertha Mae along with him.

This plot outline indicates the scanty material used for this work. It is significant for the type of sectionalism among Negroes that it points up. Ignoring political freedom and the educational advantages, Southern Jules have the temerity to praise the life they leave behind in Alabama and other southern states. Shanty for a home, with corn bread pones and buttermilk diets, these staunch southern Negroes feel that such is superior to homes in New York and the different and more healthful diet. Harlem, crowded as it is, has to be better than a shanty depicted in *Blood on the Forge, Tobacco Road,* and the *Jule* variety.

Conditioning in this case proves successful because Jule

---

[6] George Henderson, *Jule*, p. 12.

is left completely oblivious of the life which makes Harlem a Negro metropolis. There is not enough apartment space, nor is there enough wealth to accommodate the large number of Negroes living there, but all of the political issues which affect America are part of the lives of the inhabitants of this community. In matters of national importance, the political life parallels the white world;[7] in fact, there are whites living in Harlem too.

Jule either deliberately seeks dives to frequent or finds only free-loving women because that is all of life that he sees. This is understandable to a certain extent because Jule's youthful experiences consist of only the most elemental and earthy variety. His world is made up of improper diet, work in the fields, and sex. Even though he is in New York, he finds outlet in the same pattern of life except the missing element of coon hunting. Such a character as Jule is an unwelcome intruder in New York, and Negroes consider him obnoxious because his impervious nature abuses advantages of Harlem life with his blundering and ignorant shortsightedness.

As a work of art only the first half of the novel is realistic and convincing. The second half is a preposterously biased picture which is not representative of Harlem life for Negroes generally. In direct contrast Ann Petry's *The Street* covers much the same seamy side of Harlem life, and she offers glimpses of "Sugar Hill" as *Jule* does. It is needless to add that it is more authentic and more artistically satisfying.

In comparison with his first novel, *Ollie Miss,* Henderson does not exhibit the technical advance one expects in a second work in his novel, *Jule.* This may be explained partially by the author's inability to disassociate himself from empty southern experience.[8] Many migrant Negroes to New York

---

[7] Laski, *op. cit.,* pp. 460-469.

[8] Laski, *op. cit.,* p. 467. (". . . he (Negro) is, in general, as ruthlessly exploited as the contempt and ingenuity of the South permit. He is

from the backwoods of the South are so maladjusted and shocked by the whirlpool of New York life as contrasted with the languid pace of southern existence that they are overwhelmed. They become psychologically blocked and never recover from the impact. Apparently, Jule suffers such a mental block making of himself a blind, sex-driven automaton.

Jule, like *The White Face* and *Flour Is Dusty,* exploits the flight motif. All three novels commence in the South and subsequently transfer action to the East. *The White Face* and *Flour Is Dusty* begin life by facing issues of life in New York and New Jersey respectively, while *Jule* careens through physical pleasures only. Most novelists agree that life has manifold responsibilities. Human beings know that the requirements are seriousness far more than indifference. In *The White Face* Chris attacks the Northern Negro who brags in the South and distorts his opportunities by overselling.

Picketting Hell by Adam Clayton Powell, Sr., is a well-written novel with biographical details. The principal character, Tom Tern, begins his career as one of the biggest liars in the South and progresses to the heights of a powerful and great minister in Massachusetts. He gives also the strong points and the appeal of religion to membership in the Baptist denomination.[9] A complete list of the characteristics of an effective preacher and executive is given in the portrait of Tom Tern. The author dares to expose the weakness and fallacies in the general church program. There are delightful moments of satire on the whole profession. His characterization of Tern is very much like the one drawn of Rev. Snow in Caldwell's *The Policy King.*

The events of the novel move at a rapid pace. Having

exploited as citizen, as consumer, as producer. Whatever institution can be so operated as to effect his being driven to a consciousness of inferiority and a sense of hopelessness, they are so operated. Even for the educated or wealthy Negro the South is a prison.")

[9] Adam Clayton Powell, Sr., *Picketting Hell,* p. 190.

been converted to the ministry, Tern takes his first church in New England. Here, he is involved in a love trial which is the legacy of his predecessor, Plymouth Rock. He keeps successfully his principles and marries Mary. Following marriage to Mary, he accepts a call to Falcon City. This charge affords him an opportunity to exhibit his strength and develop his character. He refuses to accept the program presented to him by the deacons of his church. He offers his own program and sees to it that it is put in operation. His wife loses her life in an automobile accident, but he marries a second time. Having become highly successful as a minister, he and his wife attend a European conference of churches. They represent the Christian Cavalcade for Christ. After an eloquent sermon in which he predicts the downfall of Hitler, the powerful Dr. Tern dies suddenly in the pulpit.

There is no social commentary in the sense of reform in this novel. But there is a great deal of insight into the life of the intelligent and successful minister. There is an engaging and delightfully satiric element in the novel which keeps it from becoming sentimental. The Negro church has played an outstanding role in the life of the Negro community[10] and continues to do so. The author is careful to point this out as he unfolds his success story.

In all of the Baptist churches, the women's auxiliary is an important organization in the church program. Tern, as minister, shows in his satirical description of a group that he works with that there is a great deal of ordinary sex attachment to the minister serving as a motive for the women. Again, he points up what is generally conceded to be hypocrisy among christians. There is the usual pose of godliness among hypocrites who hide a multitude of sins in the eyes of the earnest

---

[10] Bernard May, *Negro's God as Reflected in His Literature,* pp. 62-70.

Baptist christian. The international strength of the church is presented also. One reading his novel is impressed with the manner in which Powell handles the question of age. As a matter of record, Tern is happy to point out the outstanding accomplishments of the closing years of such great men as Verdi, Tennyson, and Goethe. This identification is the minister's way of showing his usefulness despite his advance in years. This is very pleasant reading and artistically well done as a novel.

Living Is Easy, by Dorothy West, *Taffy,* by Philip B. Kaye, *High Ground,* by Odella Wood, and *The Policy King,* are family chronicles of the fortunes of Negroes, and as such they give faithful renditions of middle-class prosperity among a few successful people. There is a greater similarity between *Living Is Easy* and *Taffy* than the other two. Both treat families who live integrated into white communities. As novels they suffer from the fault of the genre. There are too many insufficiently motivated incidents in both, and they place too much stress upon the commonplaces and surfaces of life rather than dealing with more profound aspects of human personality and man in his quest for understanding life. Action is at a minimum in *Living Is Easy* for the chronicle is told from the point of view of a "predatory woman"[11] rather than to mirror the dramatic business debacle of her husband. There are too many contrived situations in which Cleo, the heroine, is seen dominating the scene.

On the other hand, *Taffy* has too much melodramatic content. Practically every sensational scene found on the seamy side of Harlem life, the author describes. Many incidents occur at odd moments in the narrative so that one feels that the author lacks control of his medium.

But in the presentation of life among Negroes with under-

---

[11] Florence Codman, *Commonweal,* June 25, 1948, p. 264.

standing and authenticity, both novels come into the front for full honors.

Dorothy West, in her novel, *Living Is Easy,* writes of the experiences of Negroes in Boston, Massachusetts. This work is a family chronicle[12] and develops two themes. First, it deals with "the predatory woman" who has a color complex and secondly, it paints the picture of financial reverses of a Negro merchant in Boston.

The plot outline is rather extensive, but there is little action. The story opens with Cleo, a stalwart mulatto in North Carolina, where she plays with Josephine, a white neighbor. At fifteen the fortunes change for the two girls. One makes her debut into society while the other becomes her servant. Since Cleo is decidedly attractive, her mother is afraid that she will either be raped or bring disgrace to the family by bearing a child out of wedlock, so she sends her to Springfield, Massachusetts. Finding life uncongenial, Cleo goes to Boston and lands a job.

Riding her bicycle through the park, she knocks down Judson, a black man, who is walking through the park. He takes her name and address and promises to replace the wrecked bicycle. They marry and two children are born to them. Judy is dark like her father while Tim is lighter hued like his mother.

They move into a white neighborhood in a very comfortable home, since Judson has a thriving business on Market Street, opposite Fanueil Hall. Cleo invites all of her sisters from the South to live with her. She can not exactly compete with Boston society as such, but she is a leader among a certain group of Negroes. Family reverses make Judson sell his business. The saga closes with his departure for New York where he hopes to recoup his fortune.

---

12 Codman, *op. cit.,* p. 264.

"Luck is in the Lord and conduct in the people."[13] Cissie remarks, and the family chronicle bears her out. In this novel by Odella Wood, the title, *High Ground,* is suggestive of the goal of aspiring Negroes in American life. Such Negroes attempt constantly to improve their status. The two themes are World War I as it affects a Negro soldier, and moderate success as an American citizen.

The plot has highly motivated events since it deals with war. Our story begins in Akrona, Virginia, where Jim Clayton, one of a family of ten Negroes, lives on a plantation. This chestnut-skinned young man is vigorous and healthy and takes the rigid life on the farm in his stride. He is so intellectually isolated that a typewritten induction notice from the United States Army is a source of pride. Jim passes his physical examination and takes his second train ride in his life. Following basic training in the infantry at Camp Meade, Maryland, he is sent to France.

Life is excitingly new and different here. Jim is one among thousands who participate in the battle of Brest. Without food for four days, Jim goes to the front A.W.O.L. because he has become impatient and bored with inaction. Dead bodies are strewn all over the field, and Jim helps to clear the bodies of the soldiers from the field with the service unit. News of the armistice spread through the forest, whereupon Jim leads the company in singing the spiritual, "I'm going to lay down my sword and shield down by the riverside," in token of appreciation.

In Paris, France, the Negroes are greeted as heroes, but a farewell warning[14] is given by a white commanding officer that these conditions will not prevail in America.

At home again Jim marries Vargie, a former sweetheart,

---

[13] Odella Wood, *High Ground,* p. 90.
[14] *Ibid.,* p. 167.

rather than Clarissa. Marriage proves unsuccessful, so he leaves the South and begins life anew in Pennsylvania. He marries Marthana, and they become the parents of two children. Cissie, a sister, lives with them, and on a trip back to Virginia, Marthana is incensed over discriminatory practices. The book closes on a note of contentment in their home in Pennsylvania.

This novel is good for its authentic pictures of Negro life. Several scenes are particularly realistic. Jim's collapse aboard ship is presented with descriptive power.

There are several faults with this novel. First, there is the stylistic device of flashback whereby the story is retarded rather than advanced. It becomes confusing to follow both Marthana in her musings and keep the action and other characters into focus at the same time. At times there seems to be too much melodrama even after the violence of war. Strangely enough, there is less action in France than there is in America during peacetime conditions. Jim loses the stage after the return to America and his character becomes dull.

There is insufficient motivation for events which happen. For example, one does not know how Jim and Marthana succeed. They just blossom out, after having been relatively unsuccessful. But in the overall picture, this is a tale of family life with insights into the "enduring quality of Negroes."[15]

If there is hardly the quid pro quo flavor in *Living Is Easy,* there are complications in Philip B. Kaye's *Taffy.* Adolescence often victimizes youth so that development of stalwart and upright citizens becomes an impossibility. This very often grimy tale discusses such a youth.

Taffy is a thin bony youth of seventeen years of age who lives with his parents on 135th Street and Lenox Avenue, New York City. The family is about to move from the neighbor-

---

[15] Edmund Wilson, *Classics and Commercials,* pp. 467-472.

hood, having lived there for eight years. Taffy is filled with nostalgia when he reflects upon the congenial past with his friends. Recalling his previous life in the South, Taffy strikes a note of bitterness, for as a youngster he had been involved with whites in a fight. His parents inform him that it is rather futile to attempt fighting the world with your hands. Nonetheless, he has maintained his belligerent attitude.

Taffy and his friends burglarize an apartment on Edgecombe Avenue. They work methodically, taking valuables and any articles which strike their fancy, and Taffy is lucky; he finds sixty-five dollars in a wallet. They return to the poolroom and spend their time drinking and in idleness. The next morning the family moves into a large house in a white neighborhood on McDonough Street between Reid and Patchen Avenues in Brooklyn. Taffy returns from work the first day and finds that the living room is filled with white people who contend that the family would be happier in Harlem. Martha, Taffy's mother, is enraged and asserts her right of ownership, and the committee retires.

Taffy is sent to one of the best schools in Brooklyn, but he makes little progress because he has no genuine interest in school. His mother climbs steadily upwards as a political leader. She is appointed secretary of the Intercultural Committee which sponsors teas between whites and blacks in Brooklyn. She also becomes a leading woman in church affairs at Rock of Ages Baptist Church.[16]

Taffy becomes involved with Lillian, daughter of the minister of the family church, both at school and at church. The minister does not approve of the relationship.[17] Severing relations with Lillian, Taffy engages in an illicit love affair with Agnes, an unprincipled woman in Harlem. He can not

---

[16] Philip B. Kaye, *Taffy,* p. 169.
[17] *Ibid.,* p. 147.

resist the urge to go to Harlem. Quiet respectability as he knows it in his Brooklyn home bores him. In an attempted robbery Taffy's accomplice, Bill, kills the man. When Taffy is about to be apprehended for the crime, he resists arrest, and the policeman kills him. Mrs. Johnson, who is now a political candidate for office in Brooklyn, is overcome with grief. The tragedy of Taffy's untimely death reunites the family.

Taffy's tragic ending does not have the anguishing despair of Richard Wright's Bigger Thomas. He refuses to make the adjustment, yet he has all of the advantages. His is a case of parental neglect in part. Preoccupied with church and political leadership, Martha Johnson does not supervise Taffy's activities, and the unfortunate death results. Exposed to vice, Taffy can not resist gravitating to its centers, for it is more exciting than church to him. Divided leadership among Negroes has a certain telling emphasis in this novel also.

The Policy King is a family chronicle and discusses "Negro life in Chicago."[18] Lewis Caldwell projects his story around two major themes. The first consideration is that of race pride, and the second theme is the moral one—justice. In developing the second theme the author poses the question whether a high sense of justice, when it means the downfall of a member of one's family, is justified?

Rev. Marshall, a preacher and a failure, has the dominating idea of moral goodness as a means of making a contribution to the Negro race. He indoctrinates Helen, but Joe refuses to accept his notions of morality and piety. As a consequence, Joe leaves home at seventeen after a quarrel with Rev. Marshall, his father. He joins Ed Tyler, the policy king of Chicago's South Side. The rest of the family, Helen, Jerry, and his mother, are deeply concerned about his move into a world of crime.

---

[18] Arthur Burke, *The Crisis*, Dec. 1946, pp. 37-39.

Joe meets Mattye, Sam Laban's mistress, who recognizes in him capabilities likely to succeed. Under her expert guidance Joe learns rapidly, for he has business acumen. He is able, therefore, to purchase his own wheel which meant a direct share in the policy racket. Joe, as a result of the money he makes in the "number game," purchases an expensive homè and gives his mother enough money with which to live decently for the first time in her life.

Helen lives with a professional white woman, Mrs. Schultz, where she begins intense investigation of the policy racket in Chicago. Her idea is to have the racket outlawed. She knows that her own brother is connected with the racket.

As a consequence of the Citizens Committee League, Rev. Snow is able to bring the question before his congregation and the community. Helen is in favor of the movement. Joe is killed in gang warfare after Rev. Snow's church is destroyed by a time bomb which opposing factions place in the church. Helen becomes adamant when Jerry, the college student and brother, decides to follow in Joe's business. Although she earns a degree in sociology and has a family of her own, she will not give up the crusade to destroy the policy racket. She succeeds and Jerry is sentenced to prison.

Surface features of this novel might very well lead one to suppose that the Negroes in this novel are adjusted to their world of separateness. Unfortunately, the most segregated community in America has intervention from the white world without. There is hardly any situation of isolation where race does not become a factor. The topic of race and race pride is the subject of the Negroes' talks at Northwestern University where Jerry is a student. They begin with the following:

> We have a culture. It is much older than that of the American white man. Our civilization dates back centuries. Any true scientist will tell you about it, and no

intelligent white man will question the fact. The richest heritage that we have this very minute is race pride. But unless we are taught that the black man helped to make our country great pride of race can not be developed. We've got to shout the deeds of black Americans like Sojourner Truth, Crispus Attucks, Nat Turner, Frederick Douglass and others, I dare you to find these names in history books used in white schools.[19]

The second theme is rather pointed in its implications. Helen is typical of the crusaders as she is drawn who must be judged harshly in their overzealous activity in the name of justice.

Oscar Mischeaux's case is rather unique among Negro authors because he articulates his own grievances and builds up his own publicity.[20] His interest in establishing Negro films colors each of his novels. He can not rid himself of the idea of a scenario writer, and his books always bear the mark of sensationalism. His most recent books show the influence of pulp and detective periodicals. He attempts to be a serious writer, but he hardly has creative imagination and misses the reality of things by his theatrical posturing. His indictment of the Jews as usurpers of the Negro film industry apparently does not have sufficient evidence to support it. Immediately, one becomes a little skeptical about the issues and themes his books purport to develop. In effect he seems to say that Georgia white women crave Negro men, and there were black Germans interested in the cause of Nazism in the United States. Furthermore, he suggests that authorities in Tennessee accord a Negro detective the same courtesies extended white detectives from New York. The fact that Kent, a character in *Mrs. Wingate,* has to apprehend a Negro criminal winks at plausibility, but the known reactions of Tennessee whites to

---

[19] Lewis A. Caldwell, *The Policy King,* p. 73.
[20] J. W. Ivy, *Crisis,* June, 1944, p. 202.

Negroes are studies in reverse. Unless there has been new evidence to the contrary, such is not the case at all.

The one book by Oscar Mischeaux which may be considered his best is *The Wind from Nowhere*. Here, all of his theatrical sense comes to play. His plots and subplots with their stilted dialogue appear in full dress. It is the story of a Negro who goes to South Dakota and becomes a successful farmer. He marries a Negro girl from Chicago, but her father, a minister, interferes and the marriage is a failure. Finally, he marries an octoroon who does not know that she has Negro blood. This novel says most of what Mischeaux has to offer. In the subsesquent novels there is no advance over the first, technically or otherwise.

His novel, *The Masquerade,* may be dismissed categorically as a distinct failure. A novelist is always on dangerous grounds when he essays to write another novelist's successfully wrought novel. If the attempt is made, another medium such as drama may very well be successful, but rewriting a successful novel proves disastrous usually, and Mischeaux's *Masquerade* is a case in point. As a purported historical novel it shows bare and unrelated facts of history which become interpolation of historical fact upon a dramatic frame sufficiently moving to sustain interest without any additional material. The consequences are cumbersome and unwieldly research without any literary merit.

In Chesnutt's hands, *The House Behind the Cedars,*[21] a tale of Carolina Negroes passing as whites gains in dramatic intensity. It poses the problem with great plausibility and presents an exposé of social conditions. Mischeaux changes the story only to the extent that John North Cross reads Lincoln's Gettysburg Address and is inspired to become a lawyer. One has to infuse new life in a tale if he borrows it.

---

[21] Hugh Gloster, *Negro Voices in American Fiction,* pp. 84, 91.

Here is an author's limitation begging at a dying, if not dead, imaginative source.

The Case of Mrs. Wingate and *The Story of Dorothy Starfield*[22] complement each other. Oscar Mischeaux is a prolific writer. Of the two novels, *The Case of Mrs. Wingate* has more originality, yet it takes up the race question and places it in a fantastic frame of reference. Complicated plots and subplots mark the general state of confusion in this tale. Briefly outlined the fable runs in this manner.

Florence Adair, Georgia white girl, develops an incurable passion for Kermit, Negro barber. She comes into the barber shop in Georgia and flirts with him. Knowing the consequences of such relationships, Kermit avoids her. Determined to have him, Florence marries an old, tottering, wealthy white man who can not consummate the marriage. She employs Kermit immediately as her chauffeur. Florence succeeds in seducing Kermit, and they become lovers. Florence sends Kermit to Harvard where he obtains his Ph.D. After her husband dies, Florence marries Kermit and they begin their married life in New York City.

Mischeaux adds another story of Eutrina and Peter, lovers, who can not be married because of Eutrina's desire to be an actress. To this group of characters he adds a rather implausible spy ring in which a German Negro is sent to America to execute a master plan whereby the president's wife will be killed. The plot is discovered by a Negro detective.

Dorothy Starfield is a continuation of the same story with the detective angle recurring. The story of Florence and Kermit in New York as man and wife serves as an extensive filler.

Flour Is Dusty, by Curtis Lucas, presents biographical

---

[22] J. W. Ivy, *Crisis*, June 1945, p. 279.

data about the author. The novel follows the pattern of the Southern Negro in flight from oppression to the East. This work compares favorably with Carl Offord's *White Face* which uses the same type of opening. Curtis Lucas discusses in his novel two themes. First, he presents the conflict between father and son over the problem of education. Secondly, he describes a murder and solution in New Jersey. The usual line of action in straightforward narrative is presented in this first work. Few incidents occur. Among them are flight, crusading for the cause of Negro advancement, murder, and a conventional happy ending.

The plot is told through a series of flashbacks. Jim Farrell from Georgia recalls his past life in an Atlantic City hotel. When he was small, his father wanted him to stop school and "to help work each day on the farm."[23] A fight with some white boys decides the issue, for Jim is expelled from school. His father forbids him to read or to be caught with a book in his hand. This ultimatum causes a fight one day when Jim's father comes upon him unexpectedly while he is reading. After this fight Jim leaves home and enters school in North Carolina. He graduates and then comes to Atlantic City.

In Atlantic City, he works as a hod carrier, but his consuming ambition is to operate a business of his own. A romantic attachment develops between Jim and Crystal, niece of Mrs. Banning, owner of the hotel where he lives. Jim's political activity consists of membership in the Tolerance League. While at the movies, Mrs. Banning is murdered, and Jim is charged with the crime. Fortunately, Jim solves the murder, and he and Crystal pledge their love.

Although *Flour Is Dusty* presents a sensational tale with a great deal of biographical material, it also stresses the political action of the Tolerance League in Atlantic City.

---

[23] Curtis Lucas, *Flour Is Dusty*, p. 28.

Groups of militant Negroes make demands upon various public places of amusement and cafes to serve all of the public regardless of racial identification. In the case of Jim Farrell, he attends the meetings of the League where the crusading zeal for the cause of Negro integration takes this form:

> It exists in different guises all over the face of the earth. Here in Atlantic City, we call it segregation, and theaters, hotels, and restaurants are its living symbols. In the South it is Jim Crowism, and the Klansmen, with their flaming crosses and their flowing white robes, are its symbols. In Europe today they call it Nazism, and its symbol, the swastika has wreaked havoc with European social order. . . . Ladies and Gentlemen, these symbols, whether they are in Asia, Africa, Europe, or America, all represent the same thing—intolerance. Hitler must be destroyed. Mussolini must be beaten down. And just as surely, segregation and Jim Crowism in America must be wiped out.[24]

The novel as a work of art suffers from a contrived plot which leads easily into sensationalism. The deftness with which Jim apprehends Mrs. Banning's murderer seems far more professional than his experiences would permit. Flashbacks impede the action of the fable and his social commentary is in a much too obvious frame rather than to naturally arise out of situations.

Novels in the category of portraits of Negro family life have their raison d'être in American society. The principle of adjustment to social mores operates effectively with the characters in *The Policy King, Living Is Easy, Flour Is Dusty,* and to a great degree in *Taffy*. Family life with its corresponding ties comprises the main points of centrality in these novels. For instance, proud of belonging to a family group, the Marshalls in *The Policy King* establish a firm relationship between

---

[24] Lucas, *op. cit.,* p. 55.

individual members. Later, it develops that this family pride has in it a mixture of scorn, admiration, love, and hate. This compounded paradox accounts for Helen in *The Policy King* being able to maintain the integrity of a martyr when her own brother's life is in jeopardy. There are moments of tenderness and warmth between the members of the family.

Glimpses of the dominant role played by the Church in community affairs of Negroes come from *Taffy, The Policy King,* and *Living Is Easy.* It is through the church that the idea of reform is introduced in *The Policy King.* From the church Mrs. Johnson in *Taffy* is nominated for political office. Being under the influence of the church accounts for adjustment to the world where life and all activities center about race. Few interventions from the white world leave a tranquil note in the tenor of such existence.

Movement in this group of novels there is, to be sure, but it has a static quality—a leisurely pace. Years pass. A family history unfolds before the final scene spells out the tragic ending of *Taffy, The Policy King,* and *Living Is Easy.* In direct comparison with such a protest novel as *Native Son,* muted overtones characterize the foregoing novels.

Violence and melodrama stimulate the reader, but they fail to provoke pity of circumstance as in the case of *Lonely Crusade* or *Blood on the Forge.* On the contrary, the violence derives its impetus from calculation, jealousy, and envy. Moral compunctions over a matter of economics leave one emotionally undisturbed.

The novels in this category are uncompromising in their integrity, and truthful renditions of Negro life. They are realistically presented social documents which comment upon a competitive society.

EVERLASTING YEA: EVERLASTING NO

> I am black, but comely. Oh ye daughters of
> Jerusalem: therefore the king delighteth in me,
> and hath brought me into his chamber.
> > *Songs of Solomon*   Holy Bible

> And finds, with keen, discriminating sight,
> Black's not so black—nor white so *very* white—
> > *New Morality*   George Canning

Negro novelists of the forties have produced a group of works
which deal with an explosive racial theme. Novels in this
category discuss the sociological phenomenon of miscegenation.[1] Miscegenation has attracted Negro novelists repeatedly.
The all-but-white Negro faces the dilemma of selecting his
racial allegiance. Identification with the darker Negroes makes
an anachronistic note in the color pattern. Negroes have
readily acquired the American color phobia, and they are
squeamish over the issue. Assimilation with the majority group
leaves the mulatto the psychological torment of fear of dis-

---

[1] Otto Klineberg, *Social Psychology,* p. 167.

covery. Color in some cases permits assimilation which is an easily accessible escape from racial pressures. Not content with the ancillary role played by the Negro, these periphery cases make the desperate plunge into the white world. Having made this racial switch of allegiance, they find spiritual difficulties. Negro is an idea, a persistent idea, which never leaves the mulatto.

Throughout the twentieth century this theme has recurred. Beginning with Charles W. Chesnutt's *The House Behind the Cedars* (1900), continuing with Nella Larsen's *Passing* (1921), recurring with Walter White's *Flight* (1924), novelists demonstrate the vitality of this theme. *Alien Land* by Willard Savoy and *Counter Clockwise* by John Lee represent this theme during the decade under discussion. Each instance shows the cultural one-to-one correspondence between Americans of both groups. Conventions of American society, however, exact condemnation and denouncement of a discovered mulatto who passes for white. Scientific finding dismisses all fears of disaster from union with mulattos and whites, but emotional reaction to discovery continues the traditional pattern. Internal evidence in *Alien Land* and *Counter Clockwise* shows this to be true.

Counter Clockwise adds another novella to the list of Negro writings of this decade. The thematic structure here is obvious. The phenomenon of passing as white by the very light-skinned Negro is the issue. Social visibility does not deter the heroine in this story from reaping the manifold advantages of life without pressures of race in America. Lucas begins with a mixed couple who want a very beautiful child. Liom is the answer to her mother's expectancy and satisfies her criterion of infant beauty.

Liom, of age, rejects her Danish mother and Negro father completely. She lives with a white woman, Mrs. Sheridan, who strengthens her rationalization that "race does not matter it is only a product of thinking."[2] With this fortification she seeks and makes friends within the white group exclusively. A lively romance develops between her and Herbert Wilton, wealthy white socialite. This leads to an illicit love affair and Liom becomes pregnant by Wilton. She tells him of her condition and proposes marriage. Wilton knows that she has Negro blood, and it is perfectly permissable according to his code to be intimate with a near-white, Negro girl, but marriage is impossible. In positive terms he makes known his position on the issue and offers her money.

Accompanied by her friend, Helen Thompson, Liom arrives at Herbert's office. He offers her an envelope with money. Liom delivers a letter to him with the request that he read it after she has gone. Then without hesitation she leaps from the office window.

Helen, having heard his remorseless story, leaves Wilton and gives the money to Liom's mother. She, too, has made the mistake of falling in love with Stephen Keith, and commits suicide also.

Social commentary here is the attitude of American society on the question of mixed marriages. The mere fact that Liom has some Negro blood makes her objectionable to Wilton who insists that he must keep his race inviolate. Sleeping with a woman is one thing but begetting children and marrying a member of a different race is another matter. Liom knows this is the attitude and the conventional notion, yet she plunges into this impossible situation. Her attitude toward life, because of her color, is negative and serves as a premonition of disaster. For her only the pessimistic note must be sung, and she believes that:

> Everything was ugly, cold, unkind. . . . When you slept it haunted your dreams; it walked beside you to kill off

---

[2] John Lee, *Counter Clockwise*, p. 26.

hope, and it left you weak and sore in spirit. If you struggled it gripped harder.[3]

The customary attitude toward such a problem is contained in the curt and restrained notice reporting Liom's death. The fact that Liom was Herbert's mistress does not appear and indicates white hypocrisy in such matters and the strict observance of good form. A wealthy white man has the privilege of indulging himself with proper explanations to fit society's code as the following illustrates:

The girl was suffering from a persecution complex, and according to Herbert Wilton, her attorney, from whose window she jumped, she found it difficult to fit into the pattern of normal life. Mr. Wilton, who had taken a friendly interest in her welfare, had advised her to consult a doctor, and he stated that she seemed agreeable to his suggestion.[4]

"God won't do anything for Negroes but keep them fooled,"[5] sounds the bitter note in this book, and actions seem to prove the case. *God Is for White Folks* is the title of a novel dealing with the passing, all-but-white Negro. It is different from *Alien Land*, by Savoy, because it has its setting in Louisiana, and it makes no attempt at stylistic innovations.

The theme here is that the all-but-white Negro may pass anywhere in America. As to story there are many melodramatic incidents. The opening scene is a great fight between Beau, the main character, and Jeeter, who hates him because he is fair. Philip Beauchamps, owner of the plantation, is Beau's father. Since the Negroes will not respect Philip's son, Beau, he is permitted to leave the Garde plantation and go to Flamingo. Beau is an all-but-white Negro.

Beau, in the city, passes and takes a job in the oil mill of

[3] Lee, *op. cit.*, p. 19.
[4] *Ibid.*, p. 95.
[5] Will Thomas, *God Is for White Folks*, p. 4.

a friend of the family. He goes out on Saturday night and meets Elisse Lesseur. Gaynor, the banker's son, has an interest in her too. They have a shooting duel in the streets, and Beau is jailed. Jeeter informs the authorities that Beau is a Negro. The lynching party is called off when Gaynor recovers. Back home Beau is about to marry Elisse when his aunt attempts to murder her, and his father dies suddenly from a heart attack.

The conventionally happy ending completes the piece, for Beau inherits the plantation and is left with the alternative of marrying Elisse and remaining there or seeking a new life in another section of the country.

God Is for White Folks gives in its provocative title just what is expected in this novel. Will Thomas makes of his social commentary evident irony. At the same time he points to the farcical element in the whole race question. The reason for this is in his novel:

> White men had made the law and broken it, and the thing the law was supposed to prevent happened anyhow. Their own lusty sex urge, contemptuously ascribed to the animal blacks, had betrayed them, and it continued to do so. They bred mulatto children by sleeping with black women, and they bred quadroon offspring by those mulattos, and after that nobody could be sure who was white or who was not, until finally, the land was full of mixed breeds as white as their fathers.[6]

As a work of art, *God Is for White Folks* succeeds on two counts. First, it tells a likely story rather well. Secondly, it has some well-drawn characters, as in the case of Beau. The atmosphere of hatred and intrigue in the plantation counties is sustained.

It has several weaknesses. The fact that nothing happens to Beau is implausible. He is placed in some of the most

---

[6] Thomas, *op. cit.*, p. 227.

highly involved situations in the South and escapes uninjured.
The actual case would probably be the reverse. Whites hate
deception, and all of the mulattos know the law on this score.
Then, when a mulatto passes in the South and is discovered,
there is usually merciless extermination. Passing is recom-
mended for the North by some southerners but never in South.
The ending is unsatisfactory, while the cowboy shooting scene
is out of place.

Alien Land, by Willard Savoy, treats an aspect of the race
problem that is known as passing. This means that an offspring
of white and Negro parents whose skin coloring is white
identifies himself with the white race. Since the person involved has the same social visibility as another white person,
the transition from one group to another is easily accomplished.
But there is more to the process than mere externals. Savoy
develops the theme of the difficulties of this situation in
America. Passing is an attractive idea to the very fair Negro.
In fact, numerous individuals of this type feel that it is unfair
of the majority group to punish them by erecting barriers
that do not appear on the surface, as Kern in *Alien Land*
shows. Once the transition has been made, there seems to be
a spiritual torment which has its counterpart in no other
situation. The motives for passing are economic, social, and
political opportunities. In each case of the successfully passing
Negro, his materialistic gains increase tremendously. It is
a known fact that there are hundreds of opportunities in
America for white persons that are unknown to members of
the Negro group. Yearly, light-skinned Negroes move into the
all white world and profit thereby.[7]

The plot of this novel follows a straight line of action, but
the author uses an interesting device to relate his events. The
book is divided into interludes and chapters. This means that

---

[7] J. Saunders Redding, *On Being a Negro in America,* p. 116.

he employs the flashback method of narration and the stream of consciousness technique. Kern begins life in Washington, D. C., the curly haired, blue eyed son of Charles and Laura, two well-to-do octoroon Negroes. At a very early age Kern answers an ad in the newspaper to be a delivery boy for a white paper. He informs the white man that he is Negro and is promptly dismissed. As an adolescent he writes a story and wins a scholarship to the Evans school of writing in New England. He is expelled because his racial identity is made known. Then, Kern decides to pass. He accomplishes this act very easily and lands a job as a radio script writer. He becomes involved with a wealthy, white girl, Marianne. When the discovery is made that he is a Negro, she severs the relationship. Kern then takes a commission in the air corps and gets orders for foreign service. Following World War II, Marianne and Kern are married and produce a daughter. The novel closes with a reconciliation between father and son.

Social commentary in this novel is a topic which sociologists discuss under the heading of miscegenation.[8] To some observers this is a widening dilemma and *Alien Land* discusses it from every angle. *Counter Clockwise,* by Lucas, treats the same thing. Both books recall Chesnutt's *The House Behind the Cedars* during the first decade of the century. In the thirties Nella Larsen's novel, *Passing,* is suggestive of the contents. Similar in treatment in the broadness of scope and the lushness of life described is the very solid *Flight,* by Walter White. Many white authors have dealt with the same theme and a recent example is *Southbound,* by Anderson, in which the idea is stressed that this is a growing problem, and of necessity requires a reorientation in our thinking on the issue. The attitudes existing in Savoy's world betray cruelty and insensitivity to the feelings of human beings if they are Negroes.

---

[8] Gunnar Myrdal, *An American Dilemma,* p. 104.

The corollary of these qualities is white supremacy. Kern is conditioned in a white's world to behave just as they do, yet his better self cries out against it. He insists on balancing the sheet in favor of his role because it affords economic security and social privileges which are denied other Negroes. Yet the protagonist, Kern, longs for the Negro people. At the most inopportune time this urge comes out. For instance, he can not control his desire to drink liquor at a bar in Harlem with Negroes. Kern hates whites becauces he had to witness the brutal murder of his mother by a white man at a very early age. In the South whites tortured him and his aunt, killing her husband; he barely escaped death. He is torn between the two groups over his rightful allegiance, for he is more akin to whites in appearance than he is to Negroes. He is more in the conflicting position of one who insists on the advantages of the white group and the warmth and affection accompanied by poverty of the other. He belongs to neither actually but has to wander in that fringe region where his mind suffers aberrations. His persistence in being white and his honesty with his girl give Kern a mature mind and concerted action. His brooding, however, over the situation and the accompanying anxiety are the results of pressures from external forces in his world.

When Kern is asked to withdraw from the Evans school he resolves to pass. His decision, as he envisions it, will mean a great deal of difficulty. Yet, willing to take the risk, he fortifies himself for the new life with this slogan which sets forth with candor his new personality and transformation:

> New life an alien way.
> He was no longer Kern Roberts.
> He was Kern Adams.
> He was no longer a Negro.
> He was white.
> I have found security. I'm white.[9]

---

[9] Willard Savoy, *Alien Land,* p. 7.

Kern makes his resolution a reality, and then from the other side of the line he sees his fellowmen of the Negro race in a completely different light. Savoy, like Faulkner, is piqued by the endurance of the Negro despite his emptiness in terms of American standards of a full life.

> What force . . . that moves these people? What above all else is strong enough to make them feel life is worth living when covenants herd them into this jungle—when bare subsistence wages keep them in slavery? . . . Such a force must have a spiritual quality.[10]

Thus, Kern stands revealed to his reader completely assimilated and proudly scrutinizing the Negro with intellectual detachment.

As a work of art, C. V. Terry of the *New York Times* points out that Savoy writes with impassé. The book, however, suffers from an unwieldly stream of consciousness technique, and its organization into prelude, interlude, and chapters becomes confusing. But he registers his spiritual torment and his success as a white man.

God Is for White Folks, Counter Clockwise, and *Alien Land* confirm Hatcher's observation that Negroes "Again, like whites,—have shown their concern over mixture of their race with white blood."[11] Experience in American society shows this problem to be increasing in significance rather than diminishing. As works of art, the novels are technically good but not without faults. Kern in *Alien Land* decided and succeeded in ending the contra naturam of the situation. He passes into the white group and remains.

Counter Clockwise places Liom among the tragic figures. She can not make the adjustment to the Negro world. Rejection by the white suitor means inevitable death. Social commentary is far more significant in these novels than their

---

10 *Ibid.,* p. 24.
11 Harlan Hatcher, *Creating the Modern American Novel,* pp. 149-150.

purely artistic merit. *God Is for White Folks* has a very unrealistic gun duel between Beau and Gaynor.

The action in this group of novels has the mixed tempo of alternation. Fast and slow movements give an uneven quality to the work. In the matter of conscience over socially defined Negroes with white faces, they succeed in convincing the reader of their choice. Society has to make ultimately its decision as to reclassification of the fair Negro or better still become truly democratic in the acceptance of all people. The word is stated in the ethos of the society. Application lags. These social documents may very well be added to the list of remonstrances in the name of human relationships.

COMMON DENOMINATOR: MAN

. . . Here is man: and if you have man, black or
white is an insignificance. The intellect—that is mi-
raculous! Who has it, has the talisman: his skin and
bones, though they were of the color of night, are
transparent, and the everlasting stars shine through,
with attractive beams. . . . I esteem the occasion of
this jubilee to be the proud discovery that the black
race can contend with the white: that in the great
anthem which we call history, a piece of many parts
and vast compass, after playing a long time a very
low and subdued accompaniment, they perceive the
time arrived when they can strike in with effect and
take a master's part in the music.

Emancipation in West Indies
Ralph Waldo Emerson

This chapter, unlike the preceding one, discusses novels with
universal themes. Where the Negro novelist was concerned
with increasingly immediate problems, he now foregoes crusading and seeks to understand the imponderable aspects of

life. So, justice versus injustice, good versus evil, search for ultimate truth, everpresent problems of the human race, are his themes.

In a broadened perspective of this sort, understanding of life is far more significant than self-consciousness of race. Any ethnic group within American society provides characters for the Negro novelist. The novels are not suffused with disillusionment or denigration of a particular group because of race. On the contrary, they show the author's practical perspicacity in coming to grips with life. The Negro novelist attempts to render truth applicable to all humanity. This is a distinguishing feature of Negro novelists of the forties. Indeed, they exhibit a social imagination and a comprehensible awareness of the commonality of human experience.

As in all trends in literature there are, of course, exceptions, and all Negro writers do not conform to the pattern. Novels depicting life of whites appeared simultaneously with other novels by Negroes who treated racial themes exclusively. For example, *Behold a Cry* by Alden Bland, a picture of Negro life, was published in 1947, the same year Motley's *Knock on Any Door* appeared. *Alien Land,* by Willard Savoy, racial in stress on the all-but-white Negro, shared the publication year with Zora Neale Hurston's *Seraph on the Suwanee,* 1948. Both, interestingly enough, appeared with Sinclair Lewis' *Kingsblood Royal* which treats a similar theme. This novel by the Nobel Prize winner shows the reaction of whites to another who has a fraction of Negro blood, and it develops the theme in a controversial manner.

Rasmussen presents in *The First Night* a romantic tale of life in the Virgin Islands at the time of transfer of ownership from Denmark to the United States.[1] The themes are nationalism and miscegenation. The plot outline is conventional

---

[1] Charles and Mary Beard, *Rise of American Civilization,* pp. 777-778.

enough. The fable begins with the opening scene which is a flashback to events of earlier years. Two middle-aged lovers want to recapture that romantic spark which fired them in youth.

Lorenson, an archeologist, comes to the island for specimens of the products found there. He meets Dimitri, a very large Russian, who gives him fireflies and recites Shakespeare and Cromwell by turn. Dimitri has also an arrangement whereby he sleeps with every woman who marries before her husband. Many children have resulted from this practice. Clementia is about to be married to Dodo and is the next victim. Since Lorenson shares quarters with Dimitri, he has to listen in disgust to Dimitri. Clementia flees after her endurance has been worn out.

An earthquake shakes the island, and Lorenson in pursuit of Clementia finds the dead bodies of Father Dominic and Gracie, who have been lovers. Lorenson officiates at the funeral, and Kobobo, native chief, invites him to dinner. Clementia is there, and the darker girl, Zabatha, whom he met when he entered the island, is present also. The two girls are sisters. After a brief flirtation with Clementia, Lorenson falls in love with Zabatha. When the governments shift, Dimitri is tried and killed. Clementia finds a way of life with Rasmussen, while Zabatha and Lorenson sail to Denmark.

Stilted dialogue and the presentation of an unrealistic nostrum for race relationships mar this novel, but exotic amosphere compensates for the weakness.

Frank Yerby is a very successful and popular writer. He is rather distinctive because he has consistently provoked controversy as to his art. Adverse criticism which began after his first novel, *The Foxes of Harrow* (1946), in the *New York Times Book Review,* has failed to affect Yerby's popularity. His works for the most part are historical novels. In writing these works, Yerby has consistently drawn characters from all ethnic groups in the American scene. For instance, *The Foxes of Harrow,* his first novel, introduces the reader to French Creoles, Southern whites, Germans, and Negroes. Most critics agreed that these characterizations are well done.[2] In the historical novel few themes appear because such fiction gives merely characterizations against the background of history. Of course, there are issues which may very well have challenged the author for interpretation, but Yerby concentrates upon the pleasure principle of literature. He seeks to entertain by giving a recreation of a particular era in history.

The Foxes of Harrow recounts the conflict of the Civil War. It is a faithful account of events leading up to the actual war and the division of interests both in the nation and in individual families. Yerby shows systematically that Negroes participated in the Civil War on both sides. Those who went to war with Southern owners served as valets. On the other hand, those who served with the Union forces were soldiers. Yerby's major concern is not with the Negro aspects of the period. In fact, his central character is an Irishman. Yerby follows the pattern of the society in which he lives by giving subordinate roles to the Negroes while whites occupy the stage of action.

"The Vulpine Fox of Harrow," a caption of one reviewer, has a basis, for it seems that *The Foxes of Harrow* spreads out a broad canvas in which Stephen runs the gamut of human experiences. He endears himself to some readers with his gusto and temerity. *The Foxes of Harrow* invites comparison with Margaret Mitchell's *Gone with the Wind.* Both novels deal with the Civil War. Mitchell's book was exceedingly popular and so was Yerby's *The Foxes of Harrow.* The historical background of both novels is similar, and events follow the same pattern. There are differences in Negro characteri-

---

[2] Jennings Rice, *New York Herald Tribune Book Review,* Feb. 4, 1946, p. 4.

zations. Yerby makes his Inch a man of letters and his Negro slave a princess. The reverse is true in *Gone with the Wind.* There is more economy in *The Foxes of Harrow* than in the protracted work of Mitchell's *Gone with the Wind.*

With ripping speed the events of this historical chronicle piece unfold. Forty years are covered by this character-studded and melodramatically presented saga of life in old New Orleans from 1825 through 1865. The plot outline follows the pattern of the historical novel with many incidents and characters. The opening scene is a picturesque sand bar in a lake in New Orleans. Richly clad Stephen Fox has been deported from the ship, Prairie Belle, for cheating at gambling. Mike Farrel rescues him, and a friendship develops between them.

Once in New Orleans, his first acquaintance with the city is in the red light district. Here, he befriends Andre and in turn accepts his invitation to visit his home. Andre lives in luxury, and following breakfast, they go to the feast day celebration. Stephen falls in love with Odalie whom he meets there. Aurora, her sister, simultaneously falls in love with Stephen. He is very successful, and his dream house, Harrow, is the finest in New Orleans. Odalie consents to marriage and to them is born Etinne. Coincidentally, Achilles, a Negro on the plantation, and a princess, Le Sauvage, are married on the same day, and Inch is their son.

War between the states breaks out, and Stephen enlists. Since he has been a captain in the Mexican War, he maintains his rank. He fights on the side of the Confederacy, not out of loyalty but expediency. Etinne serves also, but in another state because he leaves with his bride, Cecile, after marriage. The Etinne-Inch relationship is the famous Dred Scott case in American history. With the war over, Inch occupies the stage, which infuriates Etinne. Reunited at Harrow, the novel closes as Etinne accepts Cecile, drowning his vow to murder her for infidelity with a kiss.

Some critics seem to think that Yerby did the Negro a disservice in writing *The Foxes of Harrow*. From the point of view of this author, such is not the case. Historical details are not only accurate, but the story does not intend to be a racial issue wherein the Civil War and the Negro's role is played as tragically heroic.

Yerby's second in the series of historical novels is *The Vixens* which deals with the period of reconstruction. This novel begins on an incongruous note aboard ship as Laird Fournais and his brother, Philip, make the journey home. Both represent the two factions in the strife, Laird of Massachusetts and Philip of the Confederacy. They encounter Colonel Duncan and his daughter. Later when it is known that Laird has served with the Union, he is an object of contempt. At home Denise, who has been schooled by her grandfather on the classics, Horace and Virgil and Ovid, awaits Laird anxiously because she loves him.

Laird marries Sabrina who had gone insane as a result of the impact of the massacre of Negroes in the street of New Orleans. On his plantation in the hills, Laird hires Jim Dempster to serve as overseer on his farm while he serves in the legislature. The conduct of his campaign for the legislature is typical of the honest men who are interested in the cause of justice during this period. But Hugh, an opportunist of the first rank, attempts to frustrate Laird's purpose in helping the Negroes, but loses. The dark record of the Knights of Camelia at this point enters the drama. Inch, the Negro servant in *The Foxes of Harrow*, reappears and utilizes his knowledge of the law in the Louisiana legislature.

There are too many ignorant Negroes, Laird observes, and they will lose their power. Meanwhile, Sabrina dies in a violent scene, and Laird kills Hugh so that Denise and Laird are reunited in the end.

The historical events of the reconstruction period do not deviate from the generally accepted interpretations of history. Indeed, Yerby is careful to point out that both sides were responsible for the plight of the South. In the tumultuous aftermath of the Civil War, many factions lost and advanced causes that are yet to be won. Jennings Rice of the *Herald Tribune Book Review* says "the historical background is well done."[3]

The last in the trilogy in terms of chronology is *Pride's Castle*. This novel covers the period from the seventies to the beginning of the twentieth century. In his prefatory statement to the novel, Yerby admits that this era in American economic development was exciting and a period of great opportunity for the magnates of Wall Street. This lush life is a memento today in the testimony of competition, gambling, and unbridled materialism. Yerby begins by taking a southerner, who is determined to have more than his share of the world's goods, and permits him to climb to the very pinnacle of success. Once there, he commits suicide when Esther deals him a crushing blow. She informs him with candor that Coppie is not his child but the offspring of her liason with Joseph Fairchild. More than in the previous two novels, Yerby develops definite thematic content. Out of his inordinate pride, man amasses wealth but loses his spirit. In the process capital tramples labor.

Pride is a hulking, big man who meets Sharon O'Neil on the streets of New York and promptly falls in love with her. She rescues him from a saloon brawl and takes him to her father's house. Tim, who is already married and the father of children back in California, accompanies them.

With fifty dollars that Sharon lends him, Pride, through a clever ruse, obtains a job with Stillworth whose daughter,

---

[3] Rice, *op. cit.*, p. 4.

Esther, offers to buy him for twelve million. Although he is pledged to Sharon, and Esther is engaged to Joseph Fairchild, Pride succumbs to his desire for money.

Esther and Pride are married in Pennsylvania after Pride and Tim disagree over the labor situation. Pride is determined to get the railroad through. He wins his million and builds a huge, massively conceived house which is ugly and in bad taste. He indulges in an affair with Sharon, and Esther and Joseph continue their relationship. Coppie, his daughter, is the one person that Pride really loves.

Sharon adopts Lilith after a brief marriage with wealthy Courtney Randolph. With the crash Esther tells Pride that he is not the father of Coppie. Disillusioned, Pride commits suicide. The novel closes with Sharon outsmarting the reporters, and Joseph rejects Esther. Coppie and Lilith are reconciled to the future.

Beatrice Sherman, in appraising this novel in *The New York Times Book Review,* found that the huge Pride succeeds in conveying the piratical vigor and ruthlessness of the fortune builders of the seventies and eighties.[4] Yerby makes a bow to social significance with the accounts of downtrodden labor. He pictures with a good deal of accuracy the misery of the panic years and even needling labor of the early communists. Beatrice Sherman concludes with a prediction of success comparable to *The Foxes of Harrow,* which time confirmed.

The Golden Hawk, by Frank Yerby, is his picaresque novel with an adventurous heroine, Rouge, and a seaman's seaman in Kit Gerado. Consequently, this is a readily understood novel and much less pretentious than *Floodtide;* indeed, the most objective. Immediately, Yerby presents the course of piratical action and maintains it. Gerado wins at once our approval, and Rouge excites our fancy. But Bianco and Don

---

[4] Beatrice Sherman, *New York Times Book Review,* May 15, 1949, p. 4.

Luis, Spanish characters, engage similarly the interest of the reader and occupy an important place in sea saga. The romantic interest which Gerado manifests in Rouge, only to lose her to Don Luis as a consequence of Spanish custom, suggests romantic delicacy. In the business of rescuing the gold bars, the fighting customs of the eighteenth century disclose wholesale violence and hysterical emotionality. The denouement may be irksome to readers because of its sadistic fight, fire, and sea battle. In the end Bianco retires to a monastery while Gerado and Rouge unite.

Yerby's historical piece, *Floodtide,* discusses the Cuban revolution and the American scene beginning in 1850. Even though the book covers roughly the same period as *The Foxes of Harrow,* the emphasis is upon the Cuban pro-Abolition sentiment which the Spanish people expressed during this period of history. Such incidental information as the number of slave owners and the legislation of the period supply pertinent historical fact. Certain people in the South were convinced that freedom of the Negro slaves, on principle, was inevitable. Ross is a good example in the novel.

The plot is more complicated than most of the Yerby novels. More incidents crowd its pages, and wider geography gives the book more breadth than is the usual case. Ross Parry, with his curling blond hair, stands on the steamboat, Crescent City. Among the spectators he sees dazzlingly attractive Morgan Brittany with her husband, Lance. Her face seems to be wicked like "Cressid of Iseult."[5] Ross, student from Oxford University and the University of Paris, is now ready to begin his business career as an architect. He lives below the hill rather than on the fashionable street.

At a party at the Brittany's, Ross meets Conchita Izquierdo and General Izquierdo. They discuss politics which involve the Clay Compromise of 1850. Ross leaves Natchez,

---

[5] Frank Yerby, *Floodtide,* p. 3.

Mississippi and joins the Cuban revolution. Spaniards lose their initial advantage. The group of men led by Ross are destroyed by the treachery of conniving Negroes in the group. Injured in the battle, Ross regains health under the expert nursing of Cathy. He in turn marries her, thinking Conchita is dead. Ross and Cathy honeymoon in Paris. Conchita is dancing in Paris at a theater, but the couples do not meet. Back in America, Ross is a successful architect and by 1859 frees his slaves. His brother, Tom, has been killed, and Jennie, his wife, gets her only consolation from the children, Annie and Peter. Morgan, who is more than a neurotic woman, explains her basic nature to Ross before she suffers a violent death in Finniterre, her home. Jennie receives a letter from Conchita, and hastens to inform Ross, for she knows that he is not happy with Cathy.

Floodtide shows everything that Yerby does as a writer. His artistic technique comes out in this book more fully because it is his most ambitious and the most loosely constructed. In the first place characterization with Yerby, in keeping with his historical themes, evokes a sense of the romantic with his swashbuckling heroes. In this saga Tom is more manly than Ross, who is too accomplished as a gentleman. Ross meets the demands of life, and he is amazingly successful. He seems to get more than his share of the good things of life. So do all of the Yerby men. They are all types, yet they have little more than cardboard character appeal.

Yerby is a conscientious worker, and his historical material shows accurate research. His deftness with Spanish customs is an achievement. Even though Yerby is a writer for a reading public which does not want the weighty or ponderous books, he includes in all of his books a mixture of seriousness. This admixture of lightness and seriousness spills over, and a definite point of view greets the reader. Yerby insists, rightly so, on presenting the Negro as an unusual person of stature and dignity in some cases despite the shackles of slavery. He is keen in giving the white psychology behind the rejection of black people. His characterization of Brutus is a little more than mere formulae.

Ross and Cathy are married, but she is opposed to his attitude on the question of slavery. In fact, she detests his point of view, but she loves him. He gives this counterargument after she has asserted how unjust everyone is but a southerner:

> "We gentlemanly Southerners killed a few ourselves," Ross said dryly. "It was back in '55 that five thousand Southerners invaded Kansas and took over the polls. And, if I remember correctly, it was May 25, of '56 that John Brown and his men killed those five slavery men at Pottawatomie Creek—four days after we chivalrous Southerners had burned the free soil capital of Lawrence to the ground—the same day that another Southern gentleman beat a small frail Massachusetts Congressman almost to death with a Gutta Percha cane."[6]

As to characterization in this novel, Yerby gives another blond man with a very handsome face. Ross is slightly more advanced on the chart because he has not only an excellent education but a European background as well. This makes it possible for him to have an opposing point of view to his fellow southerners. He agrees with the Cuban general in his pro-abolition sentiments. He has a sympathy for the Cuban revolution because he studied in Spain and knows the language. Association with Europeans gives him a breadth of understanding which his less informed brother, Tom, could never have. Ross is weak in battle but strong in intellectual accomplishments.

Morgan Brittany, who occupies the stage, is explained as a neurotic. She has compulsions which give her more than

---

[6] Yerby, *op. cit.*, p. 314.

ordinary passion and hardness. Her beauty is used only for gaining material possessions. After her sordid history of poverty and rape, she delights in making men suffer in their lust for her. She is empty.

Even though Yerby's books are designed for sheer entertainment, several serious passages appear. He displays more than commonplace understanding of white psychology behind the rejection of black people in his characterization of Brutus in *Floodtide*. Much nearer to a dimensional character than mere formulae, such a projection is far removed from cardboard technique. The following passage is illustrative:

> There was a sound of motion in one of the cabins, and a woman came out, leading a little boy. She was as black as night, and just as beautiful. It took Ross some minutes to realize this fact. For a man of Anglo-Saxon heritage and traditions to be able to see beauty in a black skin involves long and torturous mental readjustments. That Ross was able to do so quickly was indicative of the sensitivity of his perceptions. Rachel was nearly as tall as himself, and she bore herself like a queen. . . . The boy was a fine, sturdy youngster—an exact replica of Brutus in miniature.[7]

Yerby gives an acceptable point of view in terms of Spanish attitudes towards the institution of slavery during the discussion of the Clay Compromise of 1850:

> "The Negroes are an inferior race," Ross began patiently, but Conchita flashed her eyes at him.
> "What nonsense!" she said. "Plácido was a mulatto, and he was a great poet, and a great man, and Pimienta was as black-as-black as her hair. I knew them both as a child. They were friends of my father. It so happens that I have not the blood of the blacks, but only Spanish

---

[7] *Ibid.*, pp. 188-189.

and *Indio,* a little. But many of my best friends are mulattas, and my tutor, a graduate of the University and the most brilliant man I've ever known, was a black. My father freed his slaves because of them—that's what started all the trouble. I'm afraid, Señor, that you Norte Americanos are not very civilized."[8]

A. Q. Jarrette's *Beneath the Sky* is a novel which deals with whites on a plantation in Greenville, South Carolina. The theme is infidelity. This fable is an account of unholy passion and its consequences.

The plot outlines a set of incidents which end in disaster for the main character, Jim Robinson. This middle-aged man begins his day with his family which consists of Sue, his wife, and Frank, his son, at breakfast. At the same time Jake Logan and his family composed of Lucille, his wife, and Margaret and Jane, his daughters, begin their day. Jim Robinson owns the plantation and the bank. He is an enterprising Yankee from Maine. Jake Logan is his southern white overseer and hates him because he is a Yankee.

Daisy Johnson and her sons, Willie and David, are servants. These Negroes work in the field under Jake Logan who dislikes the Negro boy, Willie, especially because he feels that he will rape his daughter, Margaret.

Margaret begins to work in the bank through the intercession of Jim Robinson, who falls in love with her, and they indulge in an illicit love affair. Frank, Jim's son, is in love with Margaret also. Jim is so infatuated that he asks his wife for a divorce. Since she refuses, he poisons her.

Meanwhile, Willie is seen swimming in the pool with Jane, one of Logan's daughters, and he is lynched. Jim Robinson's attempt at intervention is ineffective.

Demanding an investigation, Sue's sister discovers, upon

---

[8] *Ibid.,* p. 57.

questioning by a detective, that Jim confesses to the murder of Sue. Margaret and Frank are able to marry, since Lucille kills Jake when he attempts to prevent Margaret from marrying Frank.

A performance that exhibits a high level of competence in fictional writing is Ann Petry's *Country Place*. The author's second novel differs from her first best selling, *The Street*. *Country Place* is her assertion of freedom as a creative artist with the whole of humanity in the American scene as her province. Petry's departure from racial themes and the specialized Negro problem adds to her maturity. As such the book does not develop a thesis with the ultimate indictment of the social order implicit, but it does present several themes. In the tradition of Sinclair Lewis' *Main Street,* which informs the world that behind the façade of humdrum, ordinary life of a small town seethe charged emotions which erupt unsuspectingly upon the town, *Country Place* describes a similar set of circumstances. The dilemma reaches ultimately the greater world, for, in fact as in principle, human nature is essentially the same in the small town as in the metropolitan city. Sophistication of the city replaces the provincialism of the small town in matters of morality such as church attendance and certain human relationships. Winesburg, Ohio, in the Middle West provides the setting for *Main Street* while *Country Place* is set in Lennox, Connecticut, on the eastern side of the nation.

The theme of justice versus injustice permits Petry to weave her story of disillusionment of the returning veteran from World War II. In keeping with the high esteem which is accorded virtues in the New England scene, this pointed narrative unfolds through characterization precisely how such a view affects individuals. Without any preaching which such a theme might easily tempt an author, Petry points her moral implicitly. For instance, the conclusion of the story corrects the mounting evils that have been in the ascendancy. Injustice might easily have triumphed if the author's sense of poetic justice and honesty had not prevented it. The old aphorism "right triumphs in the end" is applicable to the conclusion in *Country Place*. Resolving the conflict in such a way that the unjust are punished and the just rewarded satisfies our concept of morality. The influence of the Victorian standards of high moral conduct and strict decorum breaks through such a presentation. Despite our sophistication and frankness, solid virtues remain an integral part of our morality as *Country Place* shows.

Natural beauty and distinctive charm mark the New England village as Ann Petry describes it. To her, more than in any other section of the country, there abounds more of peace and quietness with a time for reflection on the ordinary processes of life at a leisurely pace in New England. The author knows the custom of the people of the region first-hand, and this knowledge appears with compelling force as she reveals her insights into the life of the characters about her. Ordinarily, one can easily rhapsodize about the beauty of the region and the provincialism of the people. New Englanders demonstrate their loyalty to their section, but there intrude upon the idyllic charm of the reader malice, gossip, and adultery. In the course of the novel, fights and violent death impress themselves upon the reader. All is not right in this Connecticut village.

The plot outline of *Country Place* is slender, but in Petry's hand there emerges a keen sense of timing and incidents of mounting intensity. The story begins with the narrator who is the druggist relating the tale of Gramby house. Johnnie Roane, veteran of World War II, returns to his home town, Lennox, Connecticut. Naturally, he is excited over the prospects of reunion with his beautiful wife, Glory. The Weasel, who is the taxi driver for the small community, gossips incessantly. Immediately, he plants the seeds of doubt in Johnnie's mind:

> The Weasel smiled. "You never can tell about women. Not being one I couldn't say. I guess after they been married awhile they get kind of restless. It ain't what they expected. Kind of monotonous, especially since the movies show 'em how it could be. Mebbe Ed shows 'em how it could be different. Gives 'em a little excitement."[9]

At the moment Johnnie does not permit this malicious gossip to register, but Glory is really interested in Ed Barrell, the Lothario of Lennox. Her reception of him is cold on his first night home, for she refuses to be affectionate.

Lillian, her mother, has married Mearns Gramby with the idea of becoming wealthy. Mrs. Gramby, his mother, who is a wealthy woman, dislikes Lillian intensely, for she considers her beneath her station both in character and in wealth. Lillian has had a checkered past, and Mrs. Gramby knows it. She, therefore, controls the family wealth in such a way that Mearns has to obey her whims.

Glory finally makes an engagement with Ed Barrell to accompany him to his cabin. Meanwhile Mrs. Roane and Mrs. Gramby discover them making love in a lane in Ed's car as they ride past with the Weasel, who knew of the rendezvous.

Glory, who has been affectionate with Johnnie the previous night, meets Ed in the woods at his cabin. Johnnie, who calls for her at the store, encounters the Weasel, who informs him of Glory's departure with Ed. Now, Johnnie knows about Ed's cabin, and in a violent storm he finds Glory in a very compromising situation in Ed's cabin, and a fight follows. Having beaten Ed, Johnnie receives a very crushing blow from

---

[9] Ann Petry, *Country Place,* p. 17.

Glory who, after failing to placate him with feminine wiles, reveals her true feelings in the matter:

> "Yes, I slept with Ed. And I'll do it again." Her face at that moment was like her mother's face the day she found them on the porch, sitting in the glider, their arms wrapped tightly about each other. The voice was the same, too, ugly, emerging from lips that curled back in a snarl.
>
> "He's a man," she said. "And you're not. I wouldn't go on living with you if I was to be paid for it."[10]

Johnnie decides to leave at once for New York.

> Tomorrow, he would go to New York, taking the first train out; New York was what he wanted. . . . The ache of the dying lingers over and beyond the living.[11]

Meanwhile the Weasel takes a letter from Ed's wallet and gives it to Mrs. Gramby, who intends promptly to disinherit Lillian. Driven to the courthouse accompanied by Ed Barrell, Mrs. Gramby posts her will, and through a quick turn they miss the step and plunge down to the street meeting a tragic and untimely end. When the will is read, Lillian is utterly amazed to find that she will receive nothing. Mearns also comes to life and feels that their marriage should be dissolved. With this set of incidents, Petry closes on a tragic note, for neither Johnnie, Ed, Glory, nor Lillian has achieved happiness.

One of the distinctive features of *Country Place* is the competently written nature descriptions. The storm, amounting almost to a hurricane, illustrates some of the better writing in modern fiction. On reading the passage one almost gets the feel of being in the rough downpour of rain with its accompanying lightning, thunder, and winds. The writing at

---

10 *Ibid.*, p. 198.
11 *Ibid.*, p. 199.

this point paints word pictures which enable the reader to visualize the scene with amazing clarity. Although the passage described strikes the reader with emotional impact, little details, such as the yellow coat blazing against the wet and dripping greenery, make the whole scene realistic for its contrasts. Aside from the force of the rain which makes travel difficult, the slushing and falling along the way, coupled with the blackness of night, add to the authenticity of the scene.

The storm stands out, but not in isolation from human passion. The author uses this device to heighten the human drama which takes place in the cabin. Johnnie's pent-up emotions of four years are about to be released. In effect the impression conveyed to the reader at this point ties up neatly with the relationships between human beings and nature. Almost symbolically an angry nature whipping puny man because of its superior force serves as a prelude to a man wreaking revenge upon another man because he disrupts his marital life.

Nature in a tempestuous mood in combination with human passion equals conflict, for Johnnie feels that the adultery of his wife with Ed Barrell will be verified. His reaction, following a night of bliss with Glory, is a trenchant etching of human personality under mental strain as a consequence of shock. The passage reads:

> Once across the bridge he found he was enjoying the storm. I hope to Christ it wipes out the town of Lennox, leaving not a single building standing on its foundation, no blade of grass, no tree or shrub to mark the spot. I hope it destroys every home down to the last shingle, every chimney, every plant; so that no one will ever know that people lived there. I want every one to lose tonight. I want them to watch the death of the things they loved;

> I want them to stand at windows and huddle in door-
> ways and peer from the shelter of barns and corncribs and
> see what they love blown down, violated. I want all of
> them to be in at the death of their dreams; held there,
> immovable and defenseless, as they witness the last gasp.[12]

Of course, that is exactly what happened to him. He not
only finds his wife in an adulterous position with Ed Barrell,
but she, failing to trick him with feminine allure, dismisses
him scornfully by attacking his virility.

Ed Barrell and Mrs. Gramby lose their lives on the courthouse steps, and in reflection Ed admits that he has never
found that satisfaction in the body which every woman promised him in the invitation but only Glory approached in the
embrace.

> He closed his eyes, took a deep, shuddering breath, and
> the pain in his chest made him gasp. Yes, it was like
> making love to Glory. Down and down and down like
> this, falling, falling, drop in space; hit and stop, roll over
> and go down again; and then the drop, sheer, straight
> down, no pause. Perhaps he was going to find it now, the
> thing he had sought for so long. There seemed to be a
> hush all around him. It was like entering a vacuum, an
> enclosed unoccupied space, alone there, something wait-
> ing for him there.[13]

Characterizations in the novel attest Ann Petry's skill as
a novelist. The Weasel recalls faintly a Dickens' creation in
his personal appearance and his marvelous sense of timing.
He, as taxi driver, knows all of the secrets of the people in the
community and the town. He turns his insatiable urge to pry
and gossip into sleuthing and ferrets out all of the personal
scandal that he did not already know about the central char-

---

[12] *Ibid.*, p. 186.
[13] *Ibid.*, p. 256.

acters. Really, the Weasel approximates a type of perfection which is annoyingly irritating. One does not hate him, but he is exasperating in his role as the motivating force for action in the story. He is a wise choice on the part of the author. He pries into the affairs like this:

> I ought to be able to smell out who wrote him that letter, The Weasel thought. I wasn't born in Lennox, but I know as much about the town as anyone else.

Gossiping:

> You know, Glory's Mother—Lil. Cheap people.

Escapes death:

> The Weasel, smaller, slighter, more agile than others, went down three steps, reached for his balance, found it, stood still.[14]

Lili and Glory are women on the make. The fact that they are mother and daughter simply adds to the effectiveness of their negative personality traits. As a mother Lili is representative of the undesirable qualities to be found in mothers. Her selfishness and her gold digging interests color her life. On the other hand, Mrs. Gramby stands out in bold contrast as a solid, rich, old lady who enjoys holding the family fortune under tight control. She maintains a stately home in good form. She is a replica of a good old, Boston society woman in retirement but maintaining a way of life becoming to a lady of wealth and means.

> Then she thought, this comes with age, this standing bemused, thinking of something that happened long ago, while the urgent task that had been uppermost in your mind slips away, forgotten.[15]

Johnnie is the least realized of the main characters. His

---

[14] *Ibid.,* pp. 109-112, 256.
[15] *Ibid.,* p. 249.

sensitiveness registers, but somehow he does not stand in full stature of the fighting veteran. He takes life too emotionally and permits his better self to be crushed by love. After four years in the trenches and all of the battle weariness that he experienced, there should emerge a more mature personality. His war experiences should have served as a stabilizing influence. In the end his decision to go to New York and begin a new life gives him the power of determination. The author stresses the point that there are two well-defined camps, namely, the just and the unjust. Strangely enough, the just or the good rarely interest the reader so much as the fallible person. This accounts for our seeing in Johnnie only two dimensions. Our sympathies go to him because he does not deserve this punishment, and he operates at a disadvantage.

Incidentally, the characters in *Country Place* belong to three ethnic groups. The central characters are white while a Negro and a Portuguese may be said to represent the minority groups. Intermarriage between these two characters is of no moment, for they are in the role of servants, and this minimizes the importance of the amalgamation angle in some American, class conscious circles.

In the transition from one aspect of life, to concentrate on a treatment of another aspect, Ann Petry displays the same level of competence which characterized her first novel, *The Street*. In society, always, there is material for the author to interpret and to illustrate all its features.

The book suffers from a certain sense of artificiality. The use of the druggist as narrator of the most intimate details in the lives of the characters proves distracting and unconvincing. The shift from narrator to characters is somewhat cumbersome. At such times one does not know exactly where the story is. Bradford Smith of *The Saturday Review of Literature* found that the book lacks sufficient explanation of the social forces which produced the people in the book who are bad. He expresses his idea this way:

> The reader is made to understand the social forces which produced Studs Lonigan but there is no comparable explanation by Ann Petry.[16]

There is a strong melodramatic element in the book which mars the work because it is overdone.

Ann Petry ties up the threads of her narrative in *Country Place* and registers the principle of modern tragedy. Out of the mounting incidents which have occurred, all persons miss the true significance of life. Each is defeated in the objectives that he set for personal happiness. Mrs. Gramby dies, while Lillian and her daughter are left without men or money. Ed, who could hardly behave differently, is rid of the nuisance of excessive sex. Perhaps, unrealized Johnnie will be mature in his new life. Frustrations of this sort become modern tragedy, for inability to achieve adjustment to life, because of forces outside of one's self, is tragic. One very admirable feature about this novel is the view of an aged, wealthy woman. Continuing life in style, she has knowledge of lurking death as always with the aged who hold on to life.

William Gardner Smith's contribution to the trend among Negro authors to delineate characters of all ethnic groups is *Anger At Innocence*. It is a work in which the author points up the themes of environment against a spiritual force. The two attributes, good and evil, are juxtaposed in such a way that they become absolutes in terms of characterization.

In this second novel the competence displayed in his more controversial work, the *Last of the Conquerors*, which has been discussed earlier, is in evidence. The plot is simple and in keeping with Smith's ability at understatement. Book One

---

[16] Bradford Smith, *The Saturday Review of Literature*, Oct. 18, 1947, p. 17.

opens with Theodore Hall, the hero, having coffee in a diner
in South Philadelphia. He is forty-years old and frustrated
because his marriage is a childless one. As he leaves the diner
in the rain, a girl attempts to pick his pocket. He seizes her
wrist and lectures her. Before he releases her, he exacts from
her a promise that she will not do this again.

At home Theodore is disgruntled with his wife. By chance,
Rodina, the girl, meets him again. They continue to meet,
and finally he takes her home to her mother where he listens
to this character sketch:

> "Rodina was born evil," Mrs. Baleza said with passion.
> "When she was eight years old, *eight years old*, she was
> caught on a couch with a man twenty-five. She stole and
> she lied and was too lazy to work. She didn't go to church.
> She did just what she pleased. She was evil, Mr. Hall.
> She always will be evil, and her evil will spread to any
> man who fools with her. Mark my word."[17]

Ted is incensed with Mrs. Baleza's estimate of Rodina.
His reaction to her warning is to promptly begin living with
Rodina, for he walks out on his wife, Sylvia, demanding a
divorce.

Huck, a frustrated lawyer, now a truck driver, is one of
several men with whom Rodina has been intimate. Ted and
Rodina share an apartment in the same neighborhood where
Rodina is known for her criminal activities. Huck lives in the
same building. He dislikes Rodina's new mate and avoids her
as much as possible. Having successfully found a job, Ted and
Rodina live as soul mates rather than man and wife, for Ted
will not cohabit with her. Ted continues to correspond with
his wife. Meanwhile, Mrs. Baleza dies and Rodina becomes
listless and falls into mental lethargy. Finally, she picks a cop's
pocket and runs to Huck for protection. His price is that she
sleep with him.

---

[17] William Smith, *Anger at Innocence*, p. 42.

Fearful that Ted will leave her and guilty over her affair with Huck, she demands that Ted shoot her. The scene is like this:

> "Shoot! Shoot!" she cried. He looked up at her in surprise. Shoot? He was conscious of the gun in his hand, and surprise turned to something near amusement. Shoot? The *Liebestod?* "Coward!" she screamed, "Coward! Woman! *Shoot!*" . . . Screaming soundlessly, she pointed the gun at him and pulled the trigger twice.[18]

Sylvia and her friend Howard are united, while Rodina is left to face a murder charge. At the police headquarters the men wondered how an innocent looking chap could have become involved with a young girl so depraved.

Around this flimsy plot Smith attempts to give importance to the two forces, good and evil. In this choice of subject matter, he has an opportunity to probe the spiritual depths. In keeping with his purpose, Smith has selected one of those very poor sections of Philadelphia. He does not balk for one moment at the seamy side of life; he gives it with candor and realistic pictures. "Southern Philadelphia is a checkerboard of bricks and lots and narrow streets."[19] Here, vice brews and the people, no less human beings than in other sections, make the struggle for life. Rodina is a part of this limited world of work and dull home life. Excitement is derived from crime. Furthermore, there has been deeply implanted in her that she is evil. This stems from the teachings of a father who was a minister. She attempts and succeeds in making everything that is said about her come true. She is a girl who has a spark of decency in her, but it is stifled by her belief that she is doomed and bad. She is surrounded by bad people. If they are men they want her body because she is attractive. Women

---

[18] *Ibid.*, p. 297.
[19] *Ibid.*, p. 54.

simply ignore or hate her. Yet there is a curious quirk in her make-up which makes her yearn for good people.

Theodore has never done in his life the things he has wanted to do. He feels that the one thing that he needs to make him know that he is alive is a child. Denied this, he feels that writing poetry is sustaining. He is good for the sake of goodness.

When he meets Rodina, he feels that he will be able to reform her. She needs actually to be reformed. For the first time in her life, she has an incentive for goodness. Unfortunately, Theodore does not measure up to the task. Just when he should have asserted himself, Theodore sinks into the habit of his old life and permits himself to be torn between Sylvia, his wife, and his conviction. The two poles can not be reconciled, for Rodina, sensing that she can not be good, attempts to make Theodore bad. Added to this mental stupor, Huck and Juarez interfere always; one intrudes masculinity and the other gossip.

The novel exhibits competent writing, but Smith has a false premise. As a matter of fact, good and bad applied to human beings are never absolutes. The most vile person has some good traits; conversely, the most pious person has some evil tendencies. The ascendancy of the one over the other accounts for the label ascribed to either type of individual. In making Rodina predominantly evil and Theodore predominantly good, Smith rules out a great deal of the human quality in the two characters. Then, the author weakens his drama with improbabilities. In the event that a forty-year-old man, who is frustrated sexually, has enough courage to take a mistress, he would undoubtedly sleep with her. A passionate young girl would hardly permit a man to continue relationships with his wife. Such conduct is unlikely. The one attribute that would make Rodina alive, the author takes from her—

the role of a woman. She is a tart and frump without motivation. The novel, therefore, is only partially successful. Yet it gives the tragic view.

From *Their Eyes Were Watching God* to *Seraph on the Suwanee* charts the literary course of Zora Neale Hurston as novelist. This author of long standing and high attainments makes the transitional course with characteristic skill. Hurston, a graduate of Columbia University, has several anthropological studies to her credit. Nonetheless, she manifests interest in varied activities and manages to accomplish a great deal in all. Her transition from preoccupation with racial themes to the psychological novel with Florida poor whites as characters does not surprise her readers at all. In *Their Eyes Were Watching God,* she made a significant contribution to the field of American literature, using Negro themes. Her character, Teacake, introduced to literature a particular type which remains unique. Even then Hurston displayed an interest in the morbid. Even though the cause of Teacake's madness could be attributed to snake bite, the force with which this madness comes to the reader makes Teacake a memorable character in Hurston's earlier novel, *Their Eyes Were Watching God.*

Seraph on the Suwanee places Hurston at once among the many American writers who have paid homage to Sigmund Freud. One has only to recall the Freud vogue of the twenties and thirties in American literature. Freud at this time was accepted as the modus vivendi of uninhibited sex. Hurston deals with a different phase of Freudian psychology although sex appears. Her point of departure subscribes to the more recent Freudian treatments in literature which popularizes the neurotic character. In the particular case in point, Hurston gives a study of the hysterical woman.

Seraph on the Suwanee depicts the psychological dilemma

of blonde and shapely Arvay Henson who finally overcomes her neurotic condition. Maria and Brock Henson want their daughter, Arvay, to marry, but they do not realize that she is neurotic. They explain her spasm as being "tetched." Arvay's main interest is Rev. Carl Middleton, organist at the Baptist church, and husband of her sister, Larraine. For six years now, she has lived in vicarious adultery with Larraine's husband. Most of the young men attempt to win her affection, but Arvay rejects them all.

Into this picture steps Jim Meserve, a man whose ancestors once owned property. He pays court promptly to Arvay whose efforts to repulse him fail. After a short time, Jim wins Arvay's consent to marriage. Jim, who is a favorite at the mill where he is foreman, consults Joe Kelp, a Negro worker, on the subject of marriage. Arvay and Jim marry after he has seduced her.

The first child is born an idiot, and they leave for another section of Florida. Jim prospers as an orange plantation owner. Angeline and Kenny complete the family unit. Arvay, even though she is the mother of three children, and Jim is faithful, is still self-conscious and fears that she will lose Jim's affection. Aside from her own personal neurosis, the children fashion for themselves completely different lives. Kenny plans a musical career in New York, and Angeline marries a Yankee.

After the death of Arvay's mother, she returns to Jim with a new sense of freedom and resolves her conflict in passionate embrace.

Arvay introduces the reader to a neurotic woman known to clinical psychologists as the hysterical female. This type has certain repressions which originate in the libido.[20] Here the emphasis is upon sex. The case study of Arvay follows the

---

[20] Karen Horney, *Neurosis and Human Growth*, p. 173.

conventional pattern of the type. For instance, when Arvay appears on the scene she has a chronic case of repressed love for the minister, Carl, who later marries her sister. The feeling of guilt engendered by her secret love comes out in the form of spasms or fits. Most men shy away from her once they know about the malady from experience. Now the psychology behind such behavior remains grounded in the individual's private world where she indulges in romantic love without the attending reality of physical love. Even when married, such women, although they bear children, derive little sensation from passionate love and remain essentially frigid. Arvay's tendency toward fainting equates epileptic seizure, which belongs primarily to the Freudian hypothesis of sexual repression. Arvay, once faced with a physically appealing man, is awakened sexually. She transmits to her first-born intellectual deficiency.

The strained relationships between Jim and Arvay are explained partially by personality differences and the attending conflict between highly defined types.[21] Jim robs Arvay of her security by the very nature of his integrated personality. Arvay is alienated from her mother because life with Jim removes parental control and childhood associations. Still she remains a hysterical woman in the psychological sense. The figuration associated with the hysterical type comes to its logical termination after twenty years of married life when there is complete surrender on Arvay's part. Hysterical women in midlife, with the approach of the end of fertility, realize suddenly that true sexuality has passed them by. By furtive or overt effort they become aggressive for sexual sensations; yielding, and responsive. Arvay does this, and in a passage that shines with erotic brilliance, Hurston reconciles the lovers and frees Arvay from her neurosis at last. Hurston knows her neurotic

---

[21] *Ibid.*, p. 178.

types well, and with "Freud in one hand and a pen in the other,"[22] as one critic observes, she dissects professionally her types. In the field of fiction, Hurston has come up again with a contribution to the types created by Negro authors. She, more or less, is of the avant-garde in Freudian literature among Negro authors. In the main stream this sort of thing happens quite frequently. The artistic talent of Hurston continues to be evidenced in her successful description of Florida whites, whom she observed scrupulously.

Characterization of Arvay and Jim are competent portraits by an author who develops animated characters that live throughout the novel.

Hurston introduces a number of comments on American society in this novel. The scene at the railroad station is typical. The little white and Negro children, playing with affection and enjoyment together, rather than with friction or race consciousness, is a subtle comment on the paradox entailed in the adult world. Inhibitions here prevent the daily freedom of human relationships on a man-to-man basis. Another instance of this type of comment is the shrimping trip. When the men go out on the Atlantic ocean, Arvay meets Negro captains of ships with whom business men are congenial. In addition there are mixed crews, and people accept racial equality in the situation as a matter of course. These nuances are fraught with potent suggestions which the writer handles well.

Hurston is so successful with the idiom of the Florida whites that one critic had to express amazement. The manner in which the scenes are built up in this work marks Hurston as a meticulous writer. She develops episodes and corresponding actions—all related—and finally she resolves the conflict in

[22] Frank Slaughter, *New York Times Book Review,* Oct. 10, 1948, p. 3.

a satisfactory ending. Hurston has no concern for the tragic view of life in her characterizations. On the contrary, she is filled with the comic view of life. The characters reveal a heartiness of life; even with Arvay, people around her constantly affirm life.

Psychology applied to literature often finds objections from the camps of the psychologists who feel that the artist can not scientifically get over the facts. This is a reasonable position, but Hurston succeeds in getting most of the facts in her novel.

Hurston does for Florida in the South what Petry does for New England in the North. If Petry describes with brilliance and remarkable finish the storms of New England and the beauty of the country side with the flora and fauna of New England in cheerful dress for the occasion, Hurston relaxes in the sun-baked sultriness of Florida with its oranges and palm trees. She gives even a precise description of shrimping on the Atlantic ocean. Hurston knows the locale of Florida as well as Petry knows her beloved New England in general and Connecticut in particular. In this connection sectionalism comes out in the work, and the inhabitant of a particular region, writing about life, illustrates the differences to a great degree. Petry selects a typical New England personality while Hurston depicts a typical lower middle-class white known as the cracker. Both writers achieve notable success. Perhaps the more difficult task was Hurston's because she not only gives special cases or types of Florida whites, but she adds to the fable Freudian overtones and a complete diagnosis of neurotic personality. The idiom which the Florida cracker uses becomes a problem in itself since it does not conform to the accepted pattern of cultivated, general, American speech. Hurston mounts successfully all of these difficulties with a characteristic finesse which has made her an outstanding American Negro author. Worth Hedden of the New York *Her-*

ald-Tribune expressed her amazement in this manner: "It seems incredible that one not born to the breed even though a neighbor and an anthropologist could be its biographer."[23]

Hurston captures the flavor of ordinary speech in her dialogue in this novel. Arvay and Jim are about to be married and as they ride along in the carriage after a seduction episode this is their conversation:

"Don't be looking so sick over it, and putting on a long face, Arvay. Missionary work is for old maids and preachers. Youse a married woman now. You ain't got no time for that."

"Married?" Jim was cruel to be making game of her at a time like this.

"Why, sure you're married, Arvay. Under that mulberry tree."

"All I know is that I been raped."

"You sure was, and the job was done up brown."

"I could have hollered for Pa."

"And it would not have done you a damn bit of good. Just a trashy waste of good time and breath. Sure you was raped, and that ain't all. You're going to keep on getting raped everyday for the rest of your life. You couldn't be hollering for your Pa everyday for the rest of your life, could you?"

"Everyday?" Arvay looked across and up at Jim in startled bewilderment. "You sure got plenty nerve."

"So I've been told. But that's the way the cloth's been cut, and that's the way it's made. No more missionarying around for you. You done caught your heathen, baby. You got one all by yourself. And I'm here to tell you that you done brought him through religion and absolutely converted his soul. He been hanging around the mourner's bench for quite some time, but you done brought him through religion, and saved him

1948, p. 24.
[23] Worth Hedden, New York *Herald Tribune Book Review*, Oct. 31,

from a burning shell. You are a wonderful woman, Arvay."

The elements opened above Arvay and she arose inside of herself. This must mean that she had been forgiven on high. Her secret sin was forgiven and her soul set free. Else why would Jim be talking like she thought he was? She had paid under that mulberry tree.[24]

An imaginatively wrought world, yet realistically sustained, describes best the remarkable first novel, *Knock on Any Door,* by Willard Motley. Charles Lee of *The New York Times Book Review* labeled Motley "A Disciple of Dreiser,"[25] and that title serves adequately as a description of his achievement. Motley's *Knock on Any Door* is similar in many ways to Dreiser's *An American Tragedy.* This is especially true of the materials selected and the style in which the two books are written. Both novels deal with sensitive boys who desired to be different, but the warping influence of environment changed the course of their development. Instead of becoming upright, honest, and useful citizens, they became criminals. Society in both cases imposes on them the extreme penalty for its own preservation of law and order. The moral pointed in both instances is a paradox. Society must assume the responsibility for the crimes perpetrated by each boy; yet the same society must take the lives of the boys in order to protect itself.

Both writers use the technique of accumulation of details, and they insist on interpolations. At times the writing fascinates the reader by its clarity. Motley has some economy in his novel. Neither Willard Motley nor Theodore Dreiser is subtle, but Dreiser has more subtlety than Motley. Both authors impress the reader with their humaneness and the sense of compassion. Both men seem to admire the central

---

[24] Zora Neale Hurston, *Seraph on the Suwanee,* pp. 50-51.

[25] Charles Lee, *New York Times Book Review,* May 24, 1947, p. 3.

character and display unquestioned honesty and integrity in reporting their cruel yet realistic fables. Both are naturalists and obey their compulsion to render the situation as truthfully and faithfully as their observational powers will permit. Dreiser's naturalism has more of the seemingly cosmic sweep than Motley's, but the latter has massiveness. Like James Farrell, Motley employs the shock technique, and in the deftness with which he handles his theme he recalls both Theodore Dreiser and James Farrell. The proponents of naturalism will immediately recognize the type of thesis that Motley develops because it is not new. One of the readily recognizable qualities of naturalistic writings registers as social criticism. Even though Motley does no preaching, the commentary on a calloused society strikes with impact. Simply stated, Motley advances the thesis that society, by providing unwholesome environment, corrupts the youth and is, therefore, responsible for the crimes they commit.

In its own terms, *Knock on Any Door* posits the sociological case study of Nick Romano. In developing his thesis that environment conditions a sensitive boy negatively, Motley selects incidents where social custom is broken, the law flouted, and a man murdered in order to prove his case. The inherent elements in such an environment that could change a very sensitive boy, whose ambition was to become a priest, into a hardened criminal are slums, poverty, and ignorance. In another sense police brutality, parental neglect, and failure of the church must be brought into the picture, for they are guilty and responsible for Nick's tragic end, too.

Nick's development into a criminal who proudly faces the electric chair forms the first half of the methodical reporting of Motley in his *Knock on Any Door*. The picture in contrast from the sensitive altar boy, who was almost too handsome, to the conscienceless murderer presents one of the more effective and emotionally charged portrayals in modern American writing. The plot is rather slender with an interpolation of the story of the Schultz family.

Nick Romano, one of a family of five, lives with his parents and Aunt Rosa in Denver, Colorado. His father enjoys reasonable prosperity as a small businessman. Reverses, however, cause him to give up his business, sell his car, and move to another neighborhood. Nick, fortunately, has been confirmed by this time. On his way from church, he sees a little dead mouse. He is so struck with compassion by the sight that he cries and takes the mouse home with him in order to bury it. His mother is impressed by such a display of tenderness. She relates the story to everyone and boasts proudly that Nick will become a priest. Nick serves as an altar boy as this passage indicates:

> Nick lit the tall candles on the altar, touching them with the long taper and seeing them come alive; he genuflected before the tabernacle where Christ was, returned to the sacristy.[26]

With the family misfortunes the first set of degenerating influences begin to operate against Nick. Friendly with the neighborhood petty thieves, he consents to hide a basket of stolen fruit in his home. When it is discovered, Nick is sent to the reform school. Instead of correcting Nick, the reform school warps him. Here, the brutal treatment of the authorities makes Nick hate life. While Nick is an inmate at the school, he takes the side of the Negro boy against the order of the school bully, Rocky, who introduces discrimination in the reform school. Nick becomes the hero of the school because he defeats successfully Rocky in a fight. Nick's hatred of the school increases when Tony, a really conscientious and, perhaps, good boy, is indirectly murdered by the guards. At this point Grant, a sociologist, visits the school and meets Nick.

---

[26] Willard Motley, *Knock on Any Door*, p. 7.

But his attitude makes it quite clear to Grant that more than mere persuasion will be necessary in order to win incorrigible Nick back to the folds of society. Reform school facilitates the process of Nick's deterioration.

Once out of the reform school, Nick returns to Skid Row where a motley crowd of depraved people admire him. At first he simply confines his activities to the young, corner juvenile delinquents. Later though, he becomes friendly with panhandlers, professional prostitutes, gamblers, and jackrollers. He learns the sleight of hand of the criminal rapidly. Now that he knows about sex from experience, he adds homosexuals to his acquaintances. His father is concerned about him, but he beats him unmercifully, whereupon Nick leaves home and lives with Owen, a friend from Skid Row.

Nick is so hardened now that he blossoms out into a criminal and turns professional with gusto. He and Vito have just robbed a man, and this is the way they appear:

> They dumped the guy and ran down the alley. They came out at the other end and ducked into another alley. Panting hard, they finally stopped so they could see what they got. ". . . I even got his change," he (Vito) boasted. He grinned professionally.[27]

Continuing this type of lawlessness, Nick is apprehended by the law, and the police tactics of sadism bring the tendency to be a criminal to a climax. Nick's attitude is now antisocial:

> Nick came out two months later, mad at the world. Still thinking about Riley's rabbit punches, he went over to Maxwell street and into a store.[28]

Nick now enters willingly a duel with death, for he can no longer be considered a borderline case with the street. The street has won.

---

[27] Motley, *op. cit.*, p. 135.
[28] *Ibid.*, p. 198.

Two decent girls have entered his life now, Rosemary and Emma. Of course, there had been many prostitutes. The second half of *Knock on Any Door* relates the story of Nick's marriage and his subsequent crimes which lead him inevitably to the electric chair. Emma, the girl Nick marries, has had more than her share of life's hardships at a youthful age. Nick is, for the first time in his life, serious and is enamored of her. He learns briefly the joy of real love and ennobling passion. They spend a pleasant afternoon and evening in the park. Nick listens to Emma as she recites her favorite poetry which defines and explains her spiritual life and personality:

> Lying close to him Emma told him the story of the Lily Maid. And some of the poem she remembered. Blushing self-consciously, she recited what she remembered. "Elaine the fair, Elaine the loveable, Elaine—the Lily Maid of Astolat, high in her chamber up . . . up in a tower to the east. . . ." Her words drew a long and solemn note from the woods; he listened, everything in him slipping down to a low hush. Now guessed a . . . now guessed a hidden meaning in his arms . . . now made a pretty history to herself of . . . every dint a sword had beated in it and . . . every scratch a . . . lance had made upon it. . . . "That's all I remember, Nicky, . . . oh," her lips smiled, "the part I liked, it goes—'In her right hand the lily, in her other the letter, all her bright hair streaming down, and she . . . she did not seem dead but fast asleep.'" Leaning on her elbows, Emma smiled gravely at Nick. Nick's eyes came back from Camelot.[29]

They marry and Julian, Nick's brother, marries Rosemary, the other girl whom Nick has known. Marriage proves unsuccessful because Nick is impotent. Even more alarming in a sense is his inability to maintain a job. He is too temperamental to fit into the practical world. When he announces to

---

[29] *Ibid.,* p. 255.

his wife that he has lost the job he is made to feel ashamed by Emma's reaction which is:

> "Oh, Nicky, that's too bad! But you'll find another job." And she kissed him. He was more ashamed when she kissed him than he had ever been in his life.[30]

Since Nick can not make a living in private industry, he again takes to crime with his friends on Skid Row. Nick is again jailed and sentenced to one year in prison. But Emma is faithful and waits on him patiently. When she learns of his confinement, she comes to the jail and this scene is graphic:

> Emma walked into the barrel cell where at last they let her see him. "It isn't your fault! It isn't your fault, Nicky!" She moved quickly toward him, almost running. "It's what reform school did to you, the way you grew up." She threw herself hard against him, her fingernails scratching down the material of his coat at his shoulders, digging into his back. "I love you, Nicky, I love you!" With his face buried against her hair and neck, Nick choked and didn't answer. With his arms around her he patted her back, gently.[31]

At this point Nick has lost his battle against the street. The persuasion that Grant tries proves ineffectual and Julian's suggestion that he reform seems an effrontery to him. All along he has had the love of his invalid mother, his Aunt Rosa, and Emma. When he is finally released from jail, he does make an attempt to be less reckless in his crime. He and Vito rob the L station after Emma has committed suicide. Of all the policemen in Chicago, Riley, Nick's enemy, pursues them. They manage to get away but it is only a temporary escape for Riley follows him in the alley in the rain. Nick has his gun poised and kills Riley. He is finally jailed again. After a

---

[30] *Ibid.*, p. 277.
[31] *Ibid.*, p. 289.

sensational trial Nick defiantly walks to his death in the
electric chair. Nick's attitude is:

> Maybe they could kill him but they couldn't break him!
> He threw back his shoulders, widely, and looked straight
> ahead, a grim tightness of defiance across his lips. With
> him moved the guards and his shadow. He walked with
> a little of Rocky's loose, easy grace. With some of Tony's
> hardness. With something of Vito's *I-don't-give-a-god-*
> *damn* in the toss of his head, Butch's razzberry in the
> twist of his lips.[32]

Motley is not a moralizer as such, but the social commentary in his novel, *Knock on Any Door,* strikes with unmistakable force. He follows the principles of the school of
naturalism very closely. This set of circumstances without
God and without successful educative forces makes of Nick a
pawn in the hands of malevolent society. Nick makes the decision through the exercise of his own volition after he has been
warped by society's agencies which are theoretically designed
to mold character and to develop upright citizens. In this act
Nick is determined in his course of development by the street.
This means that in the end he does a fair amount of damage
to himself and to others. This gives to the naturalistic writer
a case which not only has sociological content and implications
for society but proves Motley's thesis that unwholesome environment corrupts youths and makes criminals of them.
Motley's approach to the problem of living is very stark and
realistic, and many of the dispossessed lose in the struggle for
a decent and happy life. Indeed, Nick Romano is an example.

Society's institutions, when they are unsuccessful, produce
cockiness in a person like Nick. This cockiness is characterized
by his statement, "Live fast, die young, make a good-looking
corpse."[33] Such a statement indicates the extent of society's

---

[32] *Ibid.,* p. 497.
[33] *Ibid.,* p. 186.

warping influence. Nick means that he is conscious of the reform school, and of his unpleasant home life, and the brutality of the police and his own fate. In another mood this is Nick enamored of free sex and easy money. He rejects conscience because he is in a state of mental confusion. He knows only the sordid side of life and can not ascertain his proper course. Society betrayed him by not offering him conditions which would permit him to develop into the priest which was the embodiment of good and his childish ambition. Nature is on the side of this criminal, for Nick is handsome and charming. This characterization shows the author's concern for the problem. It is out of compassion for those who inhabit the underworld, and who are doomed to untimely destruction, that he wants this condition improved, the corrupting influences eradicated. With his tremendous energy, Motley turns upon society and registers his disgust for such an environment.

The characterization of Nick is the achievement in this book. He has a magnetism which works for him at all times in a rather satisfactory way. Somehow the author transmutes this same magnetism to the reader, and despite all of his obviously antisocial attitudes, Nick attracts and exacts sympathy. Loyalty to Nick comes out at the trial where his friends fabricate a lie in order to save him. The clannishness of the habitués of Skid Row is of a distinctive kind. The lady who administers to Nick's need after he has murdered Riley knows that he is the hunted "pretty boy killer."[34] But out of enmity between her type of life and the course of the law she harbors him.

Motley permits the defending attorney at the trial to quote from Darrow, famous attorney. This is a condemnation of society, for the crimes of the children are the crimes of society. This is a plea for the alleviation of human misery caused by

---

[34] *Ibid.*, p. 352.

bad social conditions. Nick, on trial for his life, charged with
the murder of Riley whom he killed and maligned after he
was dead, gives Morton an opportunity of relating history. It
is literary history of the nineteenth century when French literature had its Emile Zola participating in the Dreyfus affair
and writing *J'Accuse!* The scene in Motley's hand reads this
way with the attorney speaking:

> "We—Society—are hard and weak and stupid and selfish.
> We are full of brutality and hate. We reproach en-
> vironment and call it crime. We reproach crime—
> or what we choose to label crime—without taking per-
> sonal responsibility. We reproach the victims of our own
> making and whether they are innocent or not once we
> bring them before the court, the law, Society—once we
> *try* them, we *try* them without intelligence, without sym-
> pathy, without understanding! . . . And—we—cut—down
> —any—we—choose!" . . .
> "I bring no platitudes. I bring no suavity. I accuse—
> you and me—this precious thing we call Society—of being
> the guilty parties who have brought Nick Romano, inno-
> cent, here in this courtroom before us!"[35]

In a sense, the attorney for the defense almost wins his
case, for it is not actually Nick in the final analysis who is
guilty. Conditions out of which his sordid history of crime
is written share the responsibility. Remove the conditions, and
you remove the criminal. This is proof of the naturalistic
thesis which is handled with skill and a deftly sure touch by
Motley. These conditions which indict society are both explicit
and real. Sociology here has more of the graphic reality than
the textbook on the subject can permit in terms of realistic
description.

The world created by Motley strikes with the power of
reality in the best naturalistic tradition. For instance, observa-

---

[35] *Ibid.*, pp. 442-443.

tional ability to note the minute details of the underworld, that is to say, the truly seamy side of life, appears in his description of one of several dives. Life on Skid Row, which he incisively describes, is his contribution to protest literature. It has a certain shock value and is, very suggestive of the danger awaiting the person who dares to travel its route. After Nick and Vito successfully rob the L station, and they have to flee with Riley of all the policemen in Chicago in pursuit, Nick enters by a secret entrance to the Sunshine Inn. This dive is typical of the type on Skid Row. It has a cheap neon sign, peepholes, and several secret entrances. The bar is ordinary with combination grill and drinks. Cheap tables spread over the place, and the gaudy juke box which lights up a corner completes the atmosphere of an underworld hang-out. A clientele of the Skid Row variety, as cheap as the sign and as gaudily dressed as the many-colored juke box, frequent this place. These men and women attempt to drown out their sorrows in cheap liquor and easy sexual pleasure. The proprietress of the place knows life as only a prostitute or an inmate of Skid Row could.

With disarming calm she administers to Nick when he enters the place after he has murdered Riley. There are no questions asked except the obvious statement that he is wounded. Such an attitude speaks eloquently the language of the underworld in its attempt to evade the law. She even brings Nick breakfast.

Knock on Any Door contains an array of characterizations that move and convince us of reality. Of course, the masterpiece in the book is Nick. He moves in front of us as a lad with a halo of curls and lighted candles. This is a veritable paradise from which he is expelled by adversity, but through no fault of his own. Later, he is pushed into the evil depth of degradation by gradual forces. He can neither resist nor control these forces. Nick, who is sensitive, handsome, and animated, longs for self-realizations but is frustrated because of his inability to cope with life. His behavior reveals his character, and his development comes slowly, gradually, and even painfully. For example, after he has arrived from Denver in Chicago, he becomes aware of conventional sex between boys and girls, and he is shocked. Later, he indulges with relish.

His frustration mounts when his domestic life is not a success. With a none too satisfactory job he tries, but even there the forces will not help him in the struggle to live decently. He has to go back to the street which at this point is disgusting. His greatest psychological upheaval comes when Emma commits suicide. If ever Nick really sees himself, it is at this moment. If Nick actually has a chance at respectability and happiness, it is this all too brief interlude with Emma. His tormented soul and tortured mind are momentarily calm. This tender spot identifies Nick with the human family. Without this tenderness one would have to judge him unsympathetically and dismiss him as a calloused loutish brute.

Grant, Owen, and Morton all have vitality and a sense of reality. Minor characters such as Rosemary, Sunshine, and Mrs. Schultz have that quality of fictional reality which is easily transferred to the experience of the reader and become in the process not only arresting but disturbingly realistic.

Single episodes may be picked at random and they shine with brilliance even out of context. For instance the trial scene with Nick's life at stake delivers tremendous force. The battle between the two lawyers, Gleason versus Morton, gives the point of the entire case history of Nick Romano. One recalls Studs Lonigan by Farrell at this point. These are illustrative passages which show the drama.

Morton cues:

We first meet him on a dirty, rainy, foggy night. All of his life has been a dirty, murky, rainy, foggy night. . . .

I don't know what evil star was in its ascendancy when Nick Romano was born but I know that its baleful glare has beaten down upon him for twenty-one years of his young life. There was never any happiness in this boy's life nor was there even any tinge of happiness unless it was when he was serving God at the altar. . . .

Kerman storms his realistic answer:

. . . "—he—Pretty Boy, Baby Face Romano—is a mur-der-er! . . .
"The fate of this one murderer is of small importance. The protection of our city and our decent, upright citizens is paramount in this trial and in every murder trial! Nick Romano is a menace to Society! He must be done away with as you would have a mad dog disposed of!—without sympathy! . . .
"Mercy is a wonderful attribute of human nature—a godlike gift—to us all. But"—Kerman shook his head no slowly—"if it ever lodged in this murderer's heart it was suffocated by the vileness that has characterized all his life. . . . He *has had* his chance! Society tried *innumerable* times to reform him. He is beyond reform, beyond hope."[36]

As an example of modern tragedy Nick Romano of *Knock on Any Door* illustrates the principle with pristine simplicity. Modern tragedy springs from a sympathy with the ordinary man who fails to achieve happiness or success in life. It is man in the clutch of adverse circumstances with its corresponding helplessness. Nick is the product of an environment which does not provide for him either the opportunity or the agency whereby he may realize his potential as a person. Nick faces the problem of having his values distorted by the same agencies that society maintains for the protection and development of the individual. Nick subconsciously reveals his knowledge of his impending tragic destruction by his actions. His motto: "Live fast, die young, and have a good looking corpse," is an

---

[36] *Ibid.,* pp. 449-460.

objectified expression of frustrations. Nick plunges deliberately into the mires of crime with full knowledge of the outcome of his acts. His compulsion drives him deeper and deeper until he is lost completely.

Knowledge of his frustrations and intensity of feeling give Nick a passionate desire for life, yet he makes of it self-destruction. He can not find a solution to the problem of living. To place an individual in a situation where he has to reject his very soul in order that he may kill himself constitutes Nick's tragedy. The list of failures that he has to live with is staggering indeed. They include lack of education, lack of skill for work, unsuccessful marriage, and crime. Nick is a man caught in the strangulation of life.

Even though Motley's *Knock on Any Door* is significant as a novel, and proves to be a remarkable first work, it has several flaws. The first defect and the most important, it seems, is the overall architectonic of the novel. It attempts to include too much. More economy for a fable of this type is required. Too many details and too many characters appear so that the reader may very well have difficulty in keeping in mind the threads and fortunes of all characters along with the narrative. The interpolation is too long. Actually, the Schultz family becomes a novella, thereby throwing the frame of the novel out of proportion. At times the plot is obviously contrived, and Motley nearly makes it impossible to find the required amount of plausibility in his case. For instance, he permits Julian to find an adjusted life without influencing Nick at any stages in their development, yet they live in close relationship and intimacy as members of the same family. The point of the issue may very well be forced; furthermore, the indictment of society may very well backfire because of the successful operation of the same forces for good in the lives of useful citizens.

Yet the flaws melt away in comparison with the positive

virtues of the novel as an artistic accomplishment. Motley is in the new trend of Negro authors. He has his thickly populated world made up of all ethnic groups appearing in the American scene in this region.

This is very realistic, for the actual section of Chicago which is described in this novel has a variety of racial groups in close proximity; Italians, Swedes, Polish, White, Negroes and Mexicans. All have their place as individuals in the work. It seems that the adversities of life and the underworld activities integrate all people with little difficulty. The psychology behind this condition is perhaps the knowledge that all are attempting to escape the law. Evasion gives them a common objective, for they know that the law is no respector of persons. Kinship in adversity is the principle that is known to people of this type. Motley accomplishes his objective in this work, which deals with a different racial group from his own. His central character is true to life while his Negro character does not betray the author's identity nor his, perhaps, natural bias. On the contrary, he is restrained and does not for one moment betray his special interest in Negroes beyond their role in the novel.

Motley has a working, artistic principle which assumes the artist is a person who belongs to the world and his art is for mankind. In this connection he is in line with the truly great writers in European and American traditions. The universal man is far more significant than any particularized group, that is to say, human beings make up the human race and as such are alike in many ways.

Motley is in the new trend with the younger generation of American authors such as Gore Vidal and Truman Capote, to mention a few, who have written successful works in which they utilize new material for the novel. Homosexuality has been introduced in novels by these writers. Exploration of the possibilities of new material offers an opportunity to add additional dramatic content and a new type of hero where frankness is the emphasis. Motley in his *Knock on Any Door* treats the same problem. Nick and Owen indulge in a relationship which does not end until Nick is electrocuted. The interior of Owen's apartment with its feminine paraphernalia is described. The build-up to the actual relationship between the two men with liquor as the agent which destroys inhibitions so that Nick is conscious only of a hairy hand has a tone of authenticity. The naturalistic tendency in fictional writing is to mount details in order to shock the reader into a complete awareness of the hideousness, the sordidness—even repugnance to the environment. Motley observes and reports the brutal hard facts regardless of their effect upon certain sensibilities. In this regard he does more than this; he focuses attention on the warped personalities in their relationship to society. In a word he displays the crusading spirit. He realizes a solution through the characterizations of the lawyer and Nick, for he implies that environment such as the one which corrupts Nick is still with us for:

> The sad faces of the houses line the street, like old men and women sitting along the veranda of an old folks' charity home. . . . Nick? Knock on any door down this street.[37]

Novels written by Negroes about members of the human race evidence aesthetic properties. Noteworthy is the imaginative quality of the design along with poetic rendition of the sense of the beautiful in language and in human personality. Rooted in society, these created characters discuss social values. The intransigent forces of good and evil impress the reader of this fiction. The sense of nobility in man is far more significant than his destructive nature. The duality of man in society comes out in aspects of *Country Place, Anger at Innocence,*

---

[37] *Ibid.*, p. 504.

and *Knock on Any Door*. Straightforward, historical narrative characterize *Floodtide, The Foxes of Harrow,* and *The Vixens*. Political thinking is not so much a part of the internal structure of these novels as it is an incidental part of the activities of several characters.

In the sense that James Jones's *From Here to Eternity* may be called a social document, these books are also. That is to say, they create a world in which social values must be constantly scrutinized. In American society material possessions are tremendously important. In *Country Place* social climbers seek to attain wealth by marriage. In the case of *Seraph on the Suwanee,* the main character attempts to and succeeds in being an opportunist. All of the novels show happiness a value of society in relative proportions. Spiritual and emotional stability come only out of struggle. *Knock on Any Door* is strictly speaking more sociological in its emphasis. These works show authors who in their comprehension of life describe the process of ambivalence, that is to say, fear and desire, attraction and repulsion as the key to man in modus vivendi.

REPUTATIONS

He who tells me that there are defects in a new work,
tells me nothing which I should not have taken for
granted without his information. But he, who points
out and elucidates the beauties of an original work,
does indeed give me interesting information, such as
experience would not have authorized me in anticipating.

Biographia Literaria
Samuel Taylor Coleridge

The preceding chapter dealt with the tendency of Negro
novelists to write narratives pertaining to all ethnic groups in
America; that is to say, they broadened their perspective
rather than to concentrate exclusively on racial themes and
Negro life. This chapter discusses Negro authors' reputations
as serious writers. Critical reception of novels by Negro authors
established their reputation in current and reputable periodicals such as *Partisan Review, Antioch Review,* the New York
Herald Tribune Book Review, and the *New York Times
Book Review.* Of course, many other sources were examined
and findings are quoted and discussed.

The decade 1940-1950 proved remarkably fruitful for Negro novelists. Indeed, it might seem a real fulfillment of Dr. W. E. B. Du Bois' prophecy of a "flowering of Negro genius."[1] The productions of the twenty-seven Negro authors who have been treated in this book reflect varied aspects of the American scene. As a matter of fact, the novels constitute a substantial contribution to the main stream of American literature. They are novels of considerable literary merit, in most cases, and have attained sufficient stature to be acclaimed by reputable critics as serious works of art. Such reception negates the erroneous notion that Negro novels serve only as an incidental and negligible appendage to American belles-lettres, and that they are all concerned with one theme, the injustice of racial discrimination.

Critical reception accorded Negro novels of this period surpasses in quality that of any other decade in our national history. During the first twelve years of the twentieth century, craftsmen such as Charles W. Chesnutt, *The House Behind the Cedars,* 1900, *The Marrow of Tradition,* 1901, *The Colonel's Dream,* 1905; W. E. B. Du Bois, *The Quest of the Silver Fleece,* 1911; and James Weldon Johnson, *Autobiography of an Ex-Coloured Man,* 1912, erased all doubts of the capacity of the Negro for creative writing. So successful were the works of fiction that William Dean Howells, the dominant critic of the era, made it quite clear that separate standards for judgment of Negro novels were unnecessary.[2] Thus, critics dealing with Negro novels expected them to display as much technical skill, comprehension of human nature, and concern for morality as any other works of fiction do. These earlier writers, however, reached only a limited audience. As a consequence, they are familiar only to the specialist in Negro literature and to a very few intellectuals.

---

[1] W. E. B. Du Bois, *The Souls of Black Folk,* p. 293.
[2] William Dean Howells, in "Preface," *Colonel's Dream,* N. Y., 1905.

In direct contrast with the past neglect, several Negro authors of the decade 1940-1950 have achieved national prominence. In fact some are household names as, for instance, Richard Wright, Ann Petry, Willard Motley, or Frank Yerby. For the first time the public stampeded book stores for a copy of a novel by a Negro author.

In 1940 Harper published Richard Wright's *Native Son*. To be sure, works by Negro authors had been published by the firm before but for the first time a novel by a Negro author was phenomenally successful. Critics received the book favorably and established Wright's reputation as a serious writer of fiction. Of the many critics who dealt with *Native Son,* David Daiches, author of *Literature and Society,* gives one of the most penetrating estimates of the book. In his significant treatment of the book, Daiches selects six novels and appraises them collectively. There is a common literary thread among them, and Daiches considers *Citizens,* by Meyer Levin, *Native Son,* by Richard Wright, *Trouble in July,* by Erskine Caldwell, *River on Earth,* by James Still, *Triumph of Willie,* by Caroline Slade, and *Crazy Hunters,* by Kaye Boyle. These novels, according to Daiches, attempt to come to grips with aspects of contemporary American life. They are alike in their desire to show, to illustrate, sometimes to interpret, rather than to prophecy. In this they manifest a new trend in fiction. The solution of the world's problems in the form of ready-made systems and neat conclusions has proven inadequate and fails to withstand careful and critical scrutiny. Many novelists, therefore, endeavor to arrive at reinterpretation and reappraisal of society before rashly advocating any particular nostrum. David Daiches writes:

> The sullen helplessness of an oppressed race living in the midst of its oppressors, yet cut off from them is well portrayed, and the conclusion—that under these circumstances a man will find the only freedom he has ever

known in accepting full responsibility for a crime which was unpremeditated and unintentional, and that we can only understand this by understanding the psychology produced by his environment—is convincingly pushed home. There is real honesty in the book, a patent desire to understand thoroughly, and to make the reader understand, what the story of Bigger Thomas *means*.[3]

Native Son is an important and persuasive work, and Daiches continues in his inclusive critique of the novel. His reflection on the negative qualities of *Native Son* appear in this passage:

It is a pity, therefore, that the actual crime of Bigger Thomas should have been made so violent and unusual. To hack off the head of an accidentally smothered girl with a hatchet so as to be able to stick her body more conveniently into the furnace is not the kind of an action to which the Bigger Thomases of America are likely to be driven, and consequently (Richard) Wright's novel, as interpretation, suffers. . . . The whole point about a novel of this kind, which is trying to probe behind action to an explanation of the nature and origin of the typical situation the action presents, lies in its general applicability, and the action, therefore, should be conceived as illustrative fable. The fable would have been more powerful had it been made up of events of less melodramatic quality, showing the murder of personality by environment and the death-in-life that follows by suggesting the cumulative effect of petty crimes and petty frustrations. (Richard) Wright is trying to prove a normal thesis by an abnormal case, and though the case he chooses is one proof of his thesis it is not the most convincing.[4]

Another critic found the book lends itself easily for comparison with an outstanding contemporary of Richard Wright, John Steinbeck. Malcolm Cowley, author of *Exile's Return,* writes:

---

[3] David Daiches, *Partisan Review,* May-June, 1940, pp. 244-245.
[4] Daiches, *op. cit.*

> *Native Son* is the most impressive American novel I have
> read since *The Grapes of Wrath*. In some ways the two
> books resemble each other: both deal with the dispos-
> sessed, and both grew out of the radical movement of the
> 1930's. There is, however, a distinction to be drawn be-
> tween the motives of the two authors.[5]

Steinbeck, as the article suggests, comes from a more or
less economically secure background in American society. For
his *Grapes of Wrath,* he had to identify himself with his characters through pity. The difficulty for Steinbeck to overcome
was sentimentality. In Richard Wright's case, on the other
hand, who comes from a substandard American group on the
economic scale, he had experienced hardships characteristic
of the existence led by Bigger. His hurdle was to refrain from
hating every white character. The article points out further
that Wright keeps continuously before the reader his role as
spokesman for all of the underprivileged, exploited, and persecuted Negroes in America. And, because he speaks for the
nation, without permitting himself for one moment to cease
being a Negro, Cowley suggests that the book has more force
than any other novel by a Negro author. He adds that the
end of the novel is artistically satisfying. His position stems
from that fact that frustrated Bigger Thomas performed the
first free act in his life when he accidentally killed Mary
Dalton. Life imprisonment as a sentence for his crime would
have robbed Bigger of his one opportunity to claim the nobility
of dignity.

Clifton Fadiman, critic for the *New Yorker* and author,
observes:

> Richard Wright's *Native Son* is the most powerful Amer-
> ican novel to appear since *The Grapes of Wrath*. It has
> numerous defects as a work of art, but it is only in retro-
> spect that they emerge, so overwhelming is its central
> drive, so gripping its mounting intensity. No one, I think,

[5] Malcolm Cowley, *The New Republic,* March 18, 1940, pp. 382-383.

except the most unconvertible Bourbons, the completely callous, or the mentally deficient, can read it without an enlarged and painful sense of what it means to be a Negro in the United States . . . seventy-seven years after the Emancipation Proclamation. *Native Son* does for the Negro what Theodore Dreiser in an *American Tragedy* did a decade and a half ago for the bewildered, inarticulate American white. The two books are similar in theme, in technique, in their almost paralyzing effect on the reader, and in the large, brooding humanity, quite remote from special pleading, that informs them both.[6]

In continuing the discussion of the novel, Fadiman reacts to the profundity of the underlying philosophy. He feels that the book presents more than a facile thesis of economic determinism and penetrates deeper into the layers of consciousness where only Dostoyevsky and a few others have gone. Wright clarifies his position in bold language and no uncertain terms in attempting to rescue *Native Son* from the category of the mere proletarian tract. Furthermore, this stand eliminates soft pleading and saccharine approaches to the acceptance of the Negro under the heading of generosity. At the same time the novel escapes the pitfall of bellicosity. Fadiman is convinced that *Native Son* is a remarkable novel regardless of the amount of melanin in Richard Wright's skin.

Imperfections in the novel for Fadiman are the following:

> Wright is too explicit. He says many things over and over again. His characterization of upper-class whites are paper-thin and confess unfamiliarity. I think he overdoes his melodrama from time to time. He is not a finished writer.[7]

Henry Seidel Canby, author, critic and editor of the *Book-of-the-Month Club News,* writes candidly in announcing the selection of *Native Son*:

---

[6] Clifton Fadiman, *The New Yorker,* March 2, 1940, p. 60.

[7] Fadiman, *op. cit.,* p. 61.

Certainly, *Native Son* is the finest novel yet written by a Negro. Like *The Grapes of Wrath* it is a fully realized story of the unfortunates, uncompromisingly realistic, quite as human as it is Negro.[8]

Peter Monro Jack, *New York Times Book Review* critic, follows Canby's pattern and is equally lavish in his acclaim of *Native Son*. He writes in agreement with Fadiman of the *New Yorker*. He does not hesitate to compare the novel with a great American author of the present century, Theodore Dreiser. For Jack the point is essential to say:

A ready way to show the importance of this novel is to call it the Negro "American Tragedy" and to compare it roughly with Dreiser's masterpiece. Both deal seriously and powerfully with the problem of social maladjustment, with environment and individual behavior, and subsequently with crime and punishment. Both are tragedies and Dreiser's white boy and Wright's black boy are equally killed in the electric chair not for being criminals —since the crime in each case was unpremeditated—but for being social misfits.[9]

Jack recognizes only one minor imperfection in the novel and he writes of it in this way:

Wright does spoil his story at the end by insisting on Bigger's fate as representative of the whole Negro race and making Bigger himself say so. But this is a minor fault in a good cause.[10]

Jack continues in the article to account for the antisocial behavior of the two youths. He attributes their acts to their drab surroundings which forced them into crime. The two young men are victims of society. Jack beams enthusiastically

---

[8] Henry Seidel Canby, *Book of Month Club News,* March, 1940, p. 6.
[9] Peter Monro Jack, *New York Times Book Review,* March 3, 1940, p. 20.
[10] *Ibid.*

as he appraises Wright's success, thereby establishing Wright's reputation in these concluding words:

> Certainly *Native Son* declares Richard Wright's import-
> ance, not merely as the best Negro writer, but as an
> American author distinctive as any of those now writ-
> ing.[11]

Milton Rugoff, well-known critic, observes in The New York *Herald Tribune Book Review*:

> It is difficult to write temperately of a book which
> abounds in such excitement, in so much that is harrow-
> ing and in so profound an understanding of human
> frailty.[12]

Admitting his difficulty in exercising restraint, Rugoff explains the work further. He confesses readily that *Native Son* is a work with certain extraordinary qualities. Moreover, it deals with the tragedy of the American Negro in an unconventional manner. As a matter of fact, Wright substitutes a criminal for the ordinary, second-rate, Negro citizen. With this technique accomplished, Bigger Thomas becomes doubly offensive to the general white reader. He further evokes excitement by permitting Bigger to commit such criminal atrocities that the reader cringes in amazement and horror at such audacity. Therefore, the work is not intended for queasy stomachs. Rugoff finds that the book

> . . . does not beg; it indicts. It hits even those like the
> Daltons who give millions to Negroes; for even they
> sanction discrimination. It bends no knees, it asks no pity;
> it seeks to scourge.[13]

The principle is that high tragedy can not be wrought from horror and hate alone. Wright, however, achieves the

---

[11] *Ibid.*

[12] Milton Rugoff, New York *Herald Tribune Book Review,* March 3, 1940, p. 5.

[13] Rugoff, *op. cit.,* p. 5.

sense of tragedy with an overwhelming impact upon the reader. Accordingly, part of Wright's triumph is that he has complete knowledge of the fathoms beneath Bigger's terrifying personality. With feverish intensity, Wright supplies the key to such a frustrated Negro. Beneath the insolent and metallic exterior of Bigger lies the quivering flesh where rots the seed of the man who might have been.

Faults of the book for Rugoff are drawn to the attention of the reader in the following:

> The faults of the book should be recognized; it is more than once guilty of melodrama, adding artificial excitement to a sufficiency of the natural kind; it heaps up complications beyond the reader's powers of assimilation; occasionally the plot skates on thin ice; and several times Bigger's confusion seems to baffle even his creator—but in the end these all seem easy to overlook. . . .[14]

In *The Saturday Review of Literature*, Jonathan Daniels, critic, writes in the same vein as Rugoff of the *Tribune*, and he reflects:

> For terror in narrative, utter and compelling, there are few pages in modern American literature which will compare with this story of the few little days which carried Bigger Thomas, Negro from Mississippi in Chicago, from bullying cowardice through murder to the position of black fiend against the hating world hunted across the roof tops in the snow. It is authentic, powerful writing, about a young Negro driven by his cramped destiny to crime, but only flung up by accident and anger as quarry for roaring fury.[15]

Daniels feels that Wright has written with an objectivity that is irresistible in this almost aching narrative. He discovers

---

[14] *Ibid.*

[15] Jonathan Daniels, *The Saturday Review of Literature*, March 2, 1940, p. 5.

only one objectionable feature to the book which is the preaching in the courtroom scene.

Dr. Sterling Brown, Negro author and critic, passes critical comment on *Native Son* in this way:

> Richard Wright is the first . . . to give a psychological probing of the consciousness of the outcast, the disinherited, the generation lost in the slum jungles of American civilization.[16]

He further discusses the power of the novel as having potential cunning to steal into the inmost recesses of the human heart. In pointing out the differences between the techniques of Dreiser and Wright, Sterling Brown feels that Dreiser piles detail upon detail as a naturalist in order to gain verisimilitude, but Wright, seeking truth to a reality beyond naturalism, makes use of the devices of the symbolic novel as do Steinbeck, Caldwell, and Dos Passos.

Marguerite Wyke joins Dr. Brown in her estimate of the book. She writes:

> The Harper's prize novel is the year's most compelling and trenchant.[17]

Marguerite Wyke further observes that Wright, a young American Negro writer, deals with the problem honestly and fearlessly, and his method, therefore, is in contrast to the manner in which white writers have handled the Negro question. Like Malcolm Cowley, prominent American critic, Wyke found similarities between Wright's *Native Son* and Steinbeck's *The Grapes of Wrath*. This parallel is most readily seen in the themes treated. Steinbeck pictures the migratory worker while Wright shows us another dislocated segment in the economic picture. He presents Negroes condemned to live in the ghetto areas of large industrial centers. She considers

---

[16] Sterling Brown, *Opportunity*, June, 1940, p. 185.
[17] Marguerite Wyke, *Canadian Forum*, May, 1940, p. 60.

Wright a realist who goes below the surface to the root causes, and the tragic climax of the book shows clearly that violence and racial strife have become accepted modes of American life. But they are the inevitable consequences of our social system. Wyke feels that:

> This book should arouse in Americans an awareness of the dangerous status of these inarticulate masses.[18]

Margaret Marshall, critic of *The Nation,* writes a far less restrained critical review, but her statement appears to be equally honest:

> The Negro in America is confronted by two attitudes. He is treated either as an inferior and an outcast or as the member of an oppressed race who is therefore owed special consideration by "enlightened" whites. These opposite attitudes are in fact the two sides of the same coin of race prejudice, since both deny to the man who happens to be colored his standing as a human being—to be accepted or rejected as such in his relations with other human beings. This is the real tragedy of the black man in America, and this is the basic theme of *Native Son* by Richard Wright. As narrative the story of Bigger Thomas carries its own dreadful fascination. Bigger's world is made real and terrifying; the theme is developed with such passion and honesty . . . that the critical faculties tend to be held in abeyance while one reads his book.[19]

David Cohn writing in the *Atlantic Monthly* found little in *Native Son* to recommend it. His article has been discussed in an earlier section of this book. But Don Stanford, critic, of the same opinion as Cohn discusses the book in *The Southern Review*. His article cites several novels of violence, such as *Native Son* by Richard Wright, *The Hamlet* by William Faulkner, *Windless Cabins* by Mark Van Doren, *Citizens* by

---

[18] Wyke, *op. cit.,* p. 60.
[19] Margaret Marshall, *The Nation,* March 16, 1940, p. 367.

Meyer Levin, *Tommy Gallagher's Crusade* by James Farrell, and *Rogue Maule* by G. Household. All of these novels, according to Stanford,

> contain numerous murders, cases of rape, street fights, scenes of torture, and brutal shootings.[20]

In defense of his revulsion to such literature, the writer recalls T. S. Eliot's condemnation of brutality in modern literature in his essay discussing D. H. Lawrence and Thomas Hardy. The writer deplores the fact, yet he admits that brutality seems essential in order to stir the blunted sensibilities of a large segment of our reading public. Don Stanford candidly states:

> *Native Son,* in many ways a fine psychological study of race hatred, is marred by two unnecessarily brutal murders. . . . We have here all the earmarks of the naturalistic technique—sordid atmosphere of violence and terror, a crude, repetitious prose, and a central character who is not a free agent but who is completely at the mercy of his environment and of his ungoverned passions.[21]

Appearing in the mid-forties, Chester Himes' novel, *If He Hollers Let Him Go,* received favorable critical reception. Herbert Kupferberg, critic, the New York *Herald Tribune Book Review,* in a favorable vein observes:

> Nevertheless, Chester Himes gets across his main point, which is that in a different sort of world the Bob Joneses would be able to lead wholesome and happy lives.[22]

In Kupferberg's discussion of the novel, he begins by giving his opinion of Himes' approach to the subject. Obviously, the chip on the shoulder attitude, which the author

---

[20] Don Stanford, *The Southern Review,* Winter, 1940, p. 618.

[21] *Ibid.,* p. 619.

[22] Herbert Kupferberg, New York *Herald Tribune Book Review,* Nov. 4, 1945, p. 10.

undoubtedly realizes, is no help in solving the race problem. There are too many people ready to knock it off, yet Himes permits the hero of his first novel to use his shoulder when he should use his head. He leads the reader to suspect that he admires this truculent hero. Himes draws a clear picture of the world of Bob Jones for the reader, and the glimpses the reader gets of this world are disheartening to say the least.

Henry Tracy, critic, writes in *Common Ground* that:

> *If He Hollers Let Him Go* . . . is a ruthless analysis of an emotionally unstable Negro whose finer qualities are so quickly blacked out by ungovernable compulsions that no high motive outlasts the contact that evoked it.[23]

In the same article Tracy poses the question:

> How warping an influence can bitterness and hatred toward white folks be for a Negro? Chester B. Himes in his novel, *If He Hollers Let Him Go* . . . answers through Bob Jones, a shipyard worker who lives a nightmare existence ruled by unreason, in a blinding confusion of loyalties, hates, and lusts. . . . "White folks sitting on my brain" is Bob's explanation of his madness. He resents "the look on white people's faces"; the "living everyday scared, walled in, locked up" by the barrier of race; the word "nigger," used by the vilest white slut with impunity.[24]

Roy Wilkins, writing in *Crisis* anticipates the critic in *American Mercury* in his comments on Himes' style. Wilkins feels that Himes writes well, often brilliantly, studding his prose with action words and blunt colorful phrases in *If He Hollers Let Him Go*. Himes, for Wilkins, is a talented, young, Negro author who gives the story of Bob Jones, shipyard worker, on the Pacific coast during the war years. Wilkins informs us:

---

[23] Henry Tracy, *Common Ground,* Summer, 1946, p. 110.
[24] *Ibid.*

It is a tale of confusion over the race problem and of
blind revolt, a revolt that thrashes out against every
incident, every idea, every unuttered whisper that would
separate, humiliate, and shackle American Negroes on
the basis of color.[25]

The *American Mercury* in reviewing the book writes:

Himes style, though too faithful to that of James M.
Cain, is nonetheless effective in defining sharply the inner
turmoil of an intelligent Negro . . . violent mental conflict
drives him to the verge of rape and murder, but circumstance and a little reason in the end forestall irreparable
damage to his life. He is left bitter, almost broken.[26]

Placing Himes in the main stream of American literature
for an origin and a parallel, *American Mercury* reviewer cites
James M. Cain. Himes' style is too faithful to that of James
Cain for the reviewer, and, therefore, the book suffers because
it is undisciplined.

Stoyan Christowe, author and critic, in *The Atlantic
Monthly* does not panegyrize in writing about Himes' second
novel, *Lonely Crusade*. Favorable on the whole, and impressed
with Himes' artistry, Christowe recounts the historical background for such a novel. A generation ago such problems
became literature about immigrants. Writers gave descriptions of the immigrant and his struggle against the obstacles
of prejudices. Today there is a recurrence of the same theme,
newly dressed as the race problem. Relative to Himes' novel,
he writes:

Chester Himes' new novel is a study of the American
Negro, a brave and courageous probing into the Negro
psyche. His diagnosis reveals a racial malady for which
there is no immediate remedy.[27]

[25] Roy Wilkins, *Crisis,* Dec., 1945, p. 361.
[26] *American Mercury,* Feb., 1946, p. 249.
[27] Stoyan Christowe, *Atlantic Monthly,* Oct. 1947, p. 138.

Later Christowe admits that Himes' ability for effective writing is unmistakable in his merciless vivisection of the Negro personality. The book says in effect the whole Negro race in America, as a result of centuries of brutal oppression, is sick at soul.

Nash K. Burger, critic of the *New York Times Book Review*, begins his critical estimate of the book with the explanation of fear. In fact, he thinks that *Lonely Crusade* as a work of art equates *Fear in Our Midst*, and he points out:

> *Lonely Crusade* is a novel of fear, of the fear ever present in the mind of a Negro living in a white man's America. It is a fear that . . . case of Lee Gordon . . . Himes' protagonist, so preys on his mind and emotions that his actions become unaccountable, even to himself. But as . . . Himes tells it, Lee Gordon's lonely crusade to put down his feeling of fear and isolation becomes only an exaggeration of every man's struggle to find himself and his place in the world.[28]

Himes in this second work has again shown his ability as a serious writer, and he has used similar material to that employed in his first novel. But *Lonely Crusade* is broader in perspective.

Burger adds that *Lonely Crusade* is complex for:

> Lee Gordon operates in a tough, jungle world, and . . . Himes presents it like it is. It is a world that, in the end, was too tough for Lee himself and, as caught in . . . Himes' pages, may be too tough for some readers as well. Lee's tortured odyssey through drunken orgies, police beatings, murder, and riot; Lee's strange inability to achieve satisfaction in his relations with his patient, loyal wife or the white Communist girl with whom he has an affair—these things are presented as bluntly as they happened, and they keep the narrative broiling.[29]

---

[28] Nash K. Burger, *New York Times Book Review*, Sept. 14, 1947, p. 20.

[29] Burger, *op. cit.*, p. 20.

The anti-Semitism which crops out in the novel is pointed up in this review. Burger concludes his estimate with the idea of the effectiveness of Himes' narrative gift.

Feeling that the work is very artistic, Arthur Burke, critic, in the *Crisis* is more laudatory than Burger. His enthusiastic reception of the work appears in the following excerpt:

> Himes has the knack of developing character rather than explaining it. Himes is a cross between Dickens' characters and George Eliot's psychological analysis together with the newer Freudian psychology with its emphasis on pathology of race.[30]

In addition Burke detects certain elements of the coarseness characteristic of *Tobacco Road* and *Forever Amber*.

Arna Bontemps, author of *Drums at Dusk,* adds to the positive side of Chester Himes' achievement. In relating the book to a vital issue among Negroes, he interprets the significance of the economic problem when he writes:

> The problem with which Chester Himes deals in his second novel follows logically the crusade for fair employment practices and other efforts to integrate Negroes into American life. He is concerned less with spearheads than with the struggles of individuals who find themselves occupying newly won ground and trying to make the personal adjustments the task requires. This is no light matter, and Himes examines it with the passion of hurt pride.[31]

Since Himes is a realist, he finds the situation and its outlook for Negroes like Lee Gordon hopeless. The book is hardly a tract as Christowe suggests, for Lee Gordon's confusion, his search for reality in a hostile world, has many parallel cases in literature apart from the issue of racial

---

[30] Arthur Burke, *Crisis,* Nov., 1947, p. 365.

[31] Arna Bontemps, New York *Herald Tribune Book Review,* Sept. 7, 1947, p. 8.

tension. Bontemps ends his critical analysis favorably this way:

> Chester Himes's talent, apparent to many in *If He Hollers Let Him Go,* has produced an even more provocative book this time.

The critics found numerous defects in *Lonely Crusade,* and Bontemps writes incisively about the thematic structure of the work. He disagrees with the approach advanced by Himes toward a practical working philosophy. Himes implies in *Lonely Crusade* that the Negro has no honor and never will have in America. With this knowledge a principle with him, materialism, narrowly interpreted to mean dollars, is and should be the sole purpose of existence for the American Negro. Bontemps disapproves of such a position in this refutation:

> Certainly this is not exactly the mood in which to work for any kind of progress, and those who look to *Lonely Crusade* for a chart are likely to turn away sour.[32]

Eric L. McKitrick, critic for *The Saturday Review of Literature,* criticizes *Lonely Crusade* favorably. He gives a very personal point of view relative to the novelist's prerogatives as a writer, particularly when he is dealing with painful material. He explains his position in this sincere manner:

> I feel that as an artist he, like all others, is entitled to paint with the broad brush, to objectify any way he wishes the complex, often highly contradictory, sometimes violent, almost always suppressed inner torments of the sensitive Negro who tries only to keep his head decently above water. There is no one better qualified than he to explore to their bitter depths all these painful processes.[33]

---

[32] *Ibid.*

[33] Eric L. McKitrick, *Saturday Review of Literature,* Oct. 25, 1947, p. 25.

On the negative side McKitrick finds that Himes gives us a psychologically unstable protagonist which to stay with requires too much of the reader. The hero pries the racial problem through many eyes. For instance there are the Marxists, Southern whites, patronizing appeasers, and phony intellectuals.

By discussing the race problem from every angle, Himes only confuses the issue. In the business of living, a person usually has his own immediate concerns to occupy his mind. The protagonist has a job, but he also has an attitude which is not conducive to promoting understanding of himself nor of life. His inability to accept life on its own terms comes from his confusion. He has real and imagined fears that are not explained by his actions, for he betrays inadequacy in private and public life. Bitterness and materialism may combine, but they will hardly produce happiness.

Diana Trilling, critic writing in *The Nation*, gives a cursory account of Carl Offord's novel, *The White Face*, which reads:

> A first novel by Carl Ruthhaven Offord, a young Negro newspaperman, is worth study as a sociological report on one of the less well-known aspects of the Negro problem —the activities of fascist agents in Harlem. On the principle of divide and rule, and taking advantage of the bad feeling that already exists between the Harlem Negroes and their Jewish landlords, shopkeepers, and domestic employers, fascist agitators are evidently finding Harlem a fertile territory for anti-Semitic propaganda ... Offord's book may not be a good novel, but it is a chilling account of something that is much more than a footnote to the problems confronting us on the home front.[34]

Far more receptive and sympathetic in its attitude and tone is Henry Moon's précis of Harlem in fiction. In his criticism of Carl Offord's *The White Face* he writes:

---

[34] Diana Trilling, *The Nation*, June 5, 1943, p. 815.

For nearly a quarter of a century, Harlem has been widely publicized as the world's most populous Negro community. At times it has been glamorized as a vast night club with gay and bizarre entertainment provided by the dancing feet and singing hearts of its carefree citizens. Often it has been smeared . . . promised land . . . seldom . . . depicted . . . American community differing because of restricted opportunities afforded its people for economic security, social welfare, and cultural advancement. In this first novel by a young Negro author, the attempt is made to portray the warping influences of these limitations upon the lives of Chris and Nella Wood, refugees from a Georgia peonage farm. Making their way to Harlem. . . .[35]

Moon is rather colorful in ascribing to the books its value by pointing up its faults. His comments run like this:

Color there is a plenty in Harlem. And joy and pathos, beauty and ugliness, triumph and defeat, indifference and revolt, hope and frustration. Yet out of this melange, there has come no novel of enduring quality, no story which has probed deep into the social and economic conditions and given a representative picture of the community—nothing to compare in vividness, scope and understanding with James T. Farrell's portrayal of Irish-American life in his "Stud's Lonigan" trilogy . . . Offord has not succeeded, naturally, where more experienced and talented writers have failed.[36]

In direct contrast with the point of view advanced by Diana Trilling and Henry Moon, Lisle Bell of the New York *Herald Tribune* becomes excited about the social implications of the novel. He begins his review by framing this question:

Has New York the right to call itself a civilized and human city? This is no question from a quiz program, to be punctuated by a musical gong if you fail to answer

---

[35] Henry Moon, *New Republic*, May 31, 1943, p. 741.
[36] Henry Moon, *op. cit.*, p. 741.

in so many seconds, but it is one that unhappily asks itself
when you read *The White Face*. And your inward reply
will not be the prompt and confident affirmative it might
have been before you opened the book, a first novel which
is a stark catalogue of crime and hatred, persecution and
poverty. Even if one concedes that Carl Offord's bitterness had led to touches of exaggeration, this story of life
in Harlem, showing how injustice and ignorance have
been exploited by the forces of Fascism, is close enough
to the grim truth to leave one depressed and shaken.[37]

The articles express concern over the possibility of the
existence of such forces at the present. Insidious as they are,
by making capital of antagonism of race and color, they do
not illustrate the whole truth. Offord hits hard and his characters speak a language of the gutter without reticence, but
the novel was hardly written to whitewash facts.

J. Welfred Holmes of the *Opportunity* writes:

There is always the implication, seldom expressed but
ever present, that the black peasant would be better off
if he had stayed where he was. One wonders if this might
not be true of the main characters in *The White Face*
and *The Darker Brother*. Both novels deal with the
southern rural Negro transplanted to New York. Both
novels give a picture of the disruptive forces that assail
the Negro newcomer to the Big City. Both tell of people
with little money and less moral and spiritual stamina
fighting desperately to stay above the maelstrom of New
York life.[38]

For comparison, events in *Darker Brother* point out that
Negroes are human beings and as such are no different from
others, while *The White Face* points up Fascism in Harlem
with cardboard characters. They move in a vague and confused background which shows the complexity of the Negro

---

[37] Lisle Bell, New York *Herald Tribune Book Review,* May 16, 1943,
p. 12.
[38] J. Welfred Holmes, *Opportunity,* June, 1944, p. 35.

problem. Conflicting ideologies not only undermine Chris' remaining personality-security but also distract him. Ignorant as he is, only half truths and meanings come within his mental grasp. Trained to accept any statement a white man makes as the unadulterated truth of Jesus Christ, he can not understand both sides of questions nor the duplicities involved in politics. His response to the agitators denotes the extent to which unlettered people may be influenced detrimentally. The American Negro needs an education which will develop in him movability in an industrialized American society. He needs it more than majority groups because he will inevitably face greater difficulties in the problems of living in the same society. Chris has emotionality now rather than rationality. Confronted with issues and values totally unfamiliar to his original southern setting, he resorts to old modes of responding to a newer and fuller life which are inadequate for his present life. His tragedy lies in the convention of American society which stamps the mark of oppression upon Negroes like Chris.

William Attaway's second novel, *Blood on the Forge,* received favorable critical acclaim. Drake De Kay, critic of the *New York Times Book Review,* begins by warning the reader of the rawness of the content of this competently written novel. His review reads:

> This novel portraying life in the raw is not for those who shun the unlovely aspects of human nature, who have a distaste for bloodshed and the cruder manifestations of sex. Indeed one of its chief claims to literary distinction consists in its author's refusal to sentimentalize his earthy men and women. The artistic integrity Attaway evinced in his first book *Let Me Breathe Thunder* is equally evident in the faithful depiction of the primitive approach to life of a social group on whose laborious efforts the whole scheme of modern industrial life is based.[39]

[39] Drake De Kay, *New York Times Book Review,* August 24, 1941, pp. 18-20.

With notable objectivity, De Kay feels this novel written by a Negro author is a starkly realistic story involving social criticism as searching as any to be found in contemporary literature. Although the protagonists are of Attaway's own race, he does not single out the Negro as the sole victim of unjust conditions. He shows native white Americans, Slavs, Italians, and others working under the same injustices of the system. The double theme is realistic and well done. Attaway describes convincingly the Negro in competition with the white man on the labor market, and the rural Negro of the soil in his attempt at adjustment to urban industrial life.

The faults of the novel did not impress De Kay who reacted favorably throughout his review of the work. In the same manner, Milton Rugoff of the New York *Herald Tribune Review* appraised the novel, for he writes:

> It is inevitable that *Blood on the Forge* should recall the work of Richard Wright—not simply because the author is Negro, but because he writes of the frustration and suffering of his people and does so with crude power and naked intensity. *Blood on the Forge* is a short novel packed with the same sense of animal terrors of the hunted and the dream of the long oppressed that marked *Uncle Tom's Children*. William Attaway is willing to portray Negro life at its lowest in order to make stunningly clear to what a pass life in a white land has brought his people.[40]

Big Matt and his family's shanty is painted this way as Rugoff continues:

> Their farm is a Negro *Tobacco Road*—which means that it belongs even lower on the social scale than the demesne of the Lesters, descending in fact into a region where the only relief is an iron stoicism or crazy yearnings.[41]

[40] Milton Rugoff, New York *Herald Tribune Books*, Aug. 24, 1941, p. 8.
[41] *Ibid.*

Rugoff extends his description of the characters once the transition has been made from the hell of peonage to the new situation in the steel mills which is problematic too. He says:

> If the picture of Negroes-against-the-soil seemed raw and shocking, that in post war Pennsylvania steel towns is like something out of a revivalist's damnation-sermon conception of hell—a vision of writhing souls seen through smoke and flame, heightened by glimpses of the debauchery of Sodom and Gomorrah and the smouldering dump heaps of Gehenna.[42]

James C. Hopson, critic, writing in *Crisis* presents biographical material about Attaway and his reception by critics as a novelist. His observations are:

> With the publication of his first novel, *Let Me Breathe Thunder*, . . . Attaway, then only twenty-five, broke with the traditional pattern of Negro authors by projecting a narrative about whites instead of Negroes. The promise indicated in this first novel won for the author a Rosenwald Fellowship that has made possible the speedy appearance of his new volume, *Blood on the Forge*.[43]

Hopson continues that the novel is essentially the story of steel. Symbolically this giant steel matches strength with mere humans and each time the men withdraw defeated spiritually and physically. Attaway displays his insight into the economic surroundings. These men who are already exploited fear that the intrusion of the Negro will mean a lowering of the wage scale. Therefore, realizing that both whites and blacks are hemmed in by the system, finally the whites identify themselves with the Negroes in the cause of labor.

The story is told in a vigorous, lusty style of writing which produces a tone of credibility. In the last half of the novel,

---

[42] *Ibid.*
[43] James O. Hopson, *Opportunitiy*, Nov. 1941, p. 346.

Big Matt rises to proportions of a tragic figure, Hopson discloses.

James W. Ivy, critic, reviewing in *Crisis* writes of Attaway's reputation in this manner:

> This second novel of William Attaway is certain to make more secure his position as one of the coming masters of American prose fiction. . . . The dialogue is simple, lifelike, straightforward, and cuts to the bare essentials.[44]

Attaway restrains himself within the pattern of his narrative. He gives subtle modifications of the brutal emotionality involved in the plight of his characters. He knows that in the area of economics the Negro suffers most, for it is only with the possession of fundamentals that one is able to exist. Unfortunately, his characters fail to attain the fundamentals.

Ann Petry's novel, *The Street,* appeared appropriately in February, in the sense that in numerous sections of the country Abraham Lincoln's birthday celebration was in progress. The novel commanded immediate attention among book lovers. It drew from critics commendable reviews.

Diana Trilling, critic of the *Nation* and the *New York Times,* selects two works: Fannie Cook's *Mrs. Palmer's Honey,* George Washington Carver Award, and Anne Petry's *The Street,* Houghton Mifflin Literary Fellowship novel. In comparing the two novels, she feels that *Mrs. Palmer's Honey* is more cerebral of the two. Her opening comments on the problem is a tribute, in a manner of speaking, to those who write about the Negro problem with a certain missionary zeal. Her contention is that if the literary people had their way there would not be racial bias in America. She expresses this strong point of view:

> The American novelist's pen is firm, if not sharp, in defense of minorities. . . .[45]

---

[44] James W. Ivy, *Crisis,* Dec. 1941, p. 395.
[45] Diana Trilling, *The Nation,* March 9, 1946, pp. 290-291.

Diana Trilling berates elements in the novel relative to patronage, condescension, oversimplification, and self-deception and her article continues:

> ... "Mrs. Palmer's Honey" fails to take into account the fact that is so frankly and unself-consciously admitted by "The Street"—namely, that class feelings are as firmly ingrained in the colored population of this country as in the whites; that there is nothing inherently virtuous from a political point of view or any other point of view, about being a member of a mistreated minority.[46]

In reference to the artistic weakness of the book and in her assessment of value judgment on the novel, Diana Trilling informs us:

> While Mrs. Cook's idealism on the score of class solidarity does credit to her, it asks, in the light of Mrs. Petry's straightforwardly middle-class document, to be corrected by a confrontation with our class realities. "Mrs. Palmer's Honey" also—and again in the light of "The Street"—calls attention to a profound but common error in so much of our contemporary political thinking, the error of assuming that it is only in the degree that people are virtuous that they deserve just treatment. Basic to a great deal of our writing on minority problems, especially in fiction, there seems to be the idea that we must prove that members of minority groups . . . are good, even better than the rest of us, before we have the right to demand that they be treated like everybody else. Must a white protestant resident of Westchester be certified for character before he enjoys his full rights as a citizen?[47]

David Dempsey, critic writing in the *Antioch Review,* relates in a detailed article about the novel a decidedly different point of view than the one given by Diana Trilling. Using the very suggestive title, "Uncle Tom's Ghost and the Literary Abolitionists" David Dempsey declares:

---

[46] *Ibid.*
[47] *Ibid.*

(Ann) Petry underscores her meanings with action rather than editorials, and avoids the sentimentalization of character which one finds in such a "protest" writer as (John) Steinbeck.[48]

He compared Ann Petry's Lutie Johnson with Lt. Brett, hero of *Deep Are the Roots*. In his opinion the two characters are espècially representative of an emergent class of Negro professional men, teachers, artisans, and government workers about whom our literature has been strangely silent. *The Street* again shows how segregation ultimately defeats the best in people just as surely as it brings out the worst in them. Very provocatively Dempsey notes that a tree grows in Harlem, but it is less likely to survive. Along with the attractive elements in the book Dempsey found that Ann Petry's tragedy lacks the sense of the inevitable that we find in Richard Wright's *Native Son*. Furthermore:

> [Her] tragedy is enacted more on the level of the adventitious and contingent, and one does not feel that her heroine's commission of murder stems from any thematic necessity of the novel.[49]

Dr. Alain Locke, author of *The New Negro*, writes:

> The artistic success of the year is, of course, Ann Petry's *The Street* . . . local color carries only its share of the story; the main burden is borne by probably the deftest characterizations skill of any Negro novelist to date; for . . . Petry's characters etched out vignette fashion at first and then etched over in later episodes, eventually they stand out fully and intimately known, from the logic of their personalities as well as from environmental forces that bear down upon them. The story flows with a sense of conviction and inevitability, even down to the tragic end. They symbolize the environment which made them, and in realism, that is the height of art.[50]

---

[48] David Dempsey, *Antioch Review*, Sept., 1946, pp. 442-447.
[49] *Ibid.*
[50] Alain Locke, *Phylon*, March-June, 1947, p. 18.

Alfred Butterfield, *New York Times Book Review* critic, writes:

> Ann Petry has chosen to tell a story about one aspect of Negro life in America, and she has created as vivid, as spiritually and emotionally effective a novel as that rich and important theme has yet produced. *The Street* is a work of close documentation and intimate perception. It deals with its Negro characters without condescension, without special pleading, without distortion of any kind.[51]

Butterfield contends that the writer produced a gripping tale peopled with lifelike, United States citizens, and it exudes the qualities of classic pity and terror in good imaginative writing. He finds also that the novel clearly describes the filth and litter that swirl on the sidewalks of sections of New York. It introduces us to people who inhabit overcrowded houses who live trouble as one lives with a member of the family. In such a setting Lutie wages gallantly a battle against overwhelming forces of the street.

Continuing the favorable reception of the work, Arna Bontemps, Negro novelist and critic, commences his review by referring to Ann Petry as a fresh new talent who deserved the Houghton Mifflin Fellowship prize. He asserts:

> As a novelist (Ann) Petry is an unblushing realist. Her recreation of the street has left out none of its essential character. It is a part of her achievement, however, that the carnal life of the slum never seems to be hauled in for its own sake. Even the earthy language, like something overheard on a truck or in a doorway, fails to draw attention to itself; in every case it seems to blend into the situation.[52]

Bontemps has the reader know that Ann Petry follows a rich heritage of predecessors who have been intrigued by

---

[51] Alfred Butterfield, *New York Times Book Review*, Feb. 10, 1946, p. 6.

[52] Arna Bontemps, New York *Herald Tribune Weekly Book Review*, Feb. 10, 1946, p. 4.

Harlem as material for novels. Such a roster includes Carl
Van Vechten, with his excursions to this section of New York
in the twenties out of which grew his *Nigger Heaven,* and is
associated with the Harlem vogue. Others are: Randolph
Fisher, James Weldon Johnson, Wallace Thurman, novelists;
while Leroy Ottley of the staff of *Life* magazine, has written
articles and books about Harlem. None, however, achieve
more than Ann Petry in her realistic recreation of atmosphere,
characterization, and the environment itself with its very
stultifying effect.

Henry Tracy, critic for *Common Ground,* writes the following account of *The Street*:

> What are the pressures on security and decency within
> the overcrowded black ghettos . . . ? Ann Petry demon-
> strates the answer in her novel, *The Street,* written out
> of a living and working experience of six years in New
> York's Harlem . . . For until the meaning of those in-
> human pressures and warping experiences is burned into
> the conscience of all America, such things as . . . Petry
> describes will continue to happen to the Lutie Johnsons
> of our cities. *The Street* is an outstanding novel from any
> angle.[53]

Lucy Lee Clemons in *Phylon,* joins Petry in her attitude
about Negro women. She, therefore, was particularly affected
by the skill of the characterizations in the novel. Her point is
expressed in this way:

> The actions of Ann Petry's heroine are not provoked by
> desire for white men, for either pleasure or profit. Lutie
> spurns Junto with revulsion. It was her uncompromising
> attitude which led to tragedy for Lutie and Bub. . . .
> But it gives her stature among Negro heroines of modern
> American fiction.[54]

Ann Petry attacks the stereotyped concept of Negro women

[53] Henry Tracy, *Common Ground,* Summer 1946, p. 109.
[54] Lucy Lee Clemons, *Phylon,* Jan., 1946, pp. 98-99.

who are reputedly immoral, unprincipled, and easy prey of
any white man. There is in Petry's *The Street* a basic understanding of fundamental qualities of humanity. In her realistic
presentation she exhibits no squeamishness concerning the
sordid side of Negro life.

The *Catholic World* critic wrote favorably of the book.
It reads:

> Here is a fast moving, well-written story. It comes from
> the Executive Secretary of Negro Women, Incorporated,
> an organization which keeps an eye on legislation and in
> various ways tries to redress some of the scandalous in-
> justices from which our colored fellow citizens are suf-
> fering.[55]

In fine, the articles admonish the white reader who ought
to bow in shame at this reminder of that criminal indifference
to the Negro's inalienable rights still prevails.

Theodore Pratt, writing in the *New York Times Book
Review,* was not very impressed with the novel, *Behold a Cry,*
and his critical assessment begins:

> There is bitterness from the Negro view-point, and there
> is wisdom, too, when at the end one of the characters
> says "Maybe it just happened." The woman who says
> this is referring to the tragedy of her race as well as to
> her own misfortune.

In sections Pratt finds *Behold a Cry* to be pretty good
reporting especially when it gets away from Ed's woman-
chasing and treats of his sons asking questions as they become
aware of the color of their skin. The brief description of
Chicago race riots is vivid and evokes in the reader a sense
of horror.

The flaws in the book according to Pratt are:

> Alden Bland, the Negro author of this short novel, has
> none of the power of a Richard Wright. His style is

---

[55] *Catholic World,* May, 1946, p. 187.

jerky, sometimes making it as difficult to follow his story as it is to discern what he is getting at.[56]

Furthermore, Pratt contends that there is confusion as to whether the author wished to tell of infidelity and unholy passion in his first novel or to tell of his people's problems.

Arthur E. Burke, critic in the *Crisis,* received the work with enthusiasm and writes:

> *Behold a Cry,* spanning a brief period, is one of the most cogently and succinctly written interpretations of life among Negroes published in several years.[57]

Burke continues by telling us that the book is interesting for its rapid movement and its interplay of social, economic, and racial factors. At times the diction is delicately poetic to Burke.

Jule by George Wylie Henderson failed to impress Hubert Creekmore, critic in the *New York Times Book Review,* and he appraised it this way:

> To the large volume of literature by and about Negroes, George Wylie Henderson has added a few rather unfamiliar features. Most striking is the fact that his Negro hero, Jule, seems impervious to any anxieties or pressures of his race. The others—a caustic picture of Harlem's well-to-do, Jule's two close friendships with white men and a Negro farmer who keeps tenants—are not quite so novel.[58]

The faults of the book far outweighed its merits and its failure may be attributed to the following:

> For telling his story . . . Henderson has used a kind of writing that may be best called a primer style. Almost

---

[56] Theodore Pratt, *New York Times Book Review,* March 23, 1947, p. 18.

[57] Arthur E. Burke, *Crisis,* Jan. 1948, p. 27.

[58] Hubert Creekmore, *New York Times Book Review,* Oct. 13, 1946, p. 22.

every sentence is simple, declarative, and short. The dialogue is similar and has much the same rhythm and cadence no matter who speaks, white or Negro. It may have been his intention to project some of the Naïveté of Jule in his prose, but the results are often monotony, exasperation and unnecessary explanation. . . . From such a passage—and there are scores—a reader gets no insight and no pleasure. It's passable in a melodrama where the focus is on acting. But in the story of the Negro's struggle upward in this American world, Henderson owes it to his characters to give them, by his writing, minds and souls and qualities that will come out of the prose to the reader, touching him with the warmth and reality of people he knew.[59]

Fannie Cook, author of *Mrs. Palmer's Honey,* reviewing in the New York *Herald Tribune* attacks the book also and expresses herself in the following:

Jule is a novel about colored people by a colored man, George Wylie Henderson. In the first third of the book the story of Jule as a small boy in rural Alabama is told convincingly and well . . . Henderson's deliberate repetitiousness of style is admirably suited to the simplicities of events and honest relationships between persons.[60]

Unfortunately the vividness does not continue as the story progresses and the author's indifference is one of intolerable naiveté.

Two authors whose critical reception was meager are Curtis Lucas, author of *Flour Is Dusty* and *Third Ward Newark,* and Lewis Caldwell, author of *The Policy King.*

Common Ground, commenting on Curtis Lucas' *Third Ward Newark,* observes:

. . . Swift moving race-relations novel by Curtis Lucas. A vivid series of incidents, revealing the blighted social

---

[59] *Ibid.*

[60] Fannie Cook, New York *Herald Tribune Book Review,* Oct. 20, 1946, p. 10.

background of a Negro ghetto in a northern city give an intense and moving character to the book.[61]

Arthur Burke, *Crisis,* reviews Lewis Caldwell's *The Policy King* in the following manner:

> *The Policy King* . . . is in several respects an unusual novel. First of all, more than any other novel about Negro life, it deals frankly with a racket which, though widespread, has received less attention in literature than one might expect. Secondly, the ramifications of this racket into the social, economic, and educational problems of Negroes primarily and others incidentally are handled with a sureness of knowledge which gives the book a tone of realism and verisimilitude.[62]

He feels that the artistic defects consist in melodrama and a poorly wrought, literary style of writing.

Oscar Mischeaux, prolific author of the *The Wind from Nowhere* and *The Case of Mrs. Wingate,* has received no favorable critical appraisal in periodicals during the forties. For example, J. W. Ivy, writing in the *Crisis,* appraises the novel this way:

> *The Wind from Nowhere* tells the story of Martin Eden, an ambitious and successful Negro pioneer settled in rosebud county of South Dakota. . . . It is really a cinematic melodrama and not a novel of Negro life at all. . . . This book is simply the old dime thriller with Negro characters substituted. As a story the book is structurally faulty and drippingly sentimental . . . and even the love story and the villainy are stagey.[63]

The Case of Mrs. Wingate simply drew a descriptive notice indicating that Mischeaux had written a fourth novel which is not a war piece and has a Negro spy as the heroine.

---

[61] *Common Ground,* Spring, 1947, p. 111.
[62] Arthur Burke, *Crisis,* Dec., 1946, p. 378.
[63] J. W. Ivy, *Crisis,* June, 1944, p. 202.

Felice Swados in her *House of Fury* described life in a woman's house of detention. The work received the following review:

> . . . (Felice) Swados' earnestness and the fact that she has written the book as if from within the walls and completely without venom or motive should be signaled, but that is all. Apart from this, awkwardness, even diffidence, mar the characterizations, and although many of the scenes are as violent and depraved . . . Faulkner has dealt with, they stir the reader about as much as would the description of a taffy-pull at a young ladies' seminary . . . Swados' recording of them—and of all the other scenes—is bloodless, ineffectual and dull.[64]

The *New York Times Book Review* with George Froede, critic, writing was more favorably impressed and he writes:

> The author seems very sure of her material, and the primal, amoral intensity of life in a corrective school is sympathetically told. For sheer cyclonic pace the book is unusual.[65]

The *New Yorker* gives almost a favorable comment:

> The girls themselves are interesting, varied, and appealing, but they seem much older than the thirteen or fourteen years the author makes them.[66]

Taffy by Philip B. Kaye impressed Richard Sullivan of the *New York Times Book Review*. His favorable comments are:

> This is a novel about Negro people in America in the same way that *Main Street* and *The Grapes of Wrath* are novels about white people in America. The author fixes upon a given segment of our national population

---

[64] Kaye Boyle, *New Republic,* Nov. 24, 1941, p. 707.

[65] George Froede, *New York Times Book Review,* Nov. 2, 1941, p. 20.

[66] *The New Yorker,* Nov. 1, 1941, p. 90.

and treats certain characters within it exclusively intensely
and with some sociological concern. Yet the racial question as such comes only incidentally into this strong narrative. The essential matter supersedes race; it is simply
and rather terrifyingly human, and the novel is a fierce,
jarring, and important piece of work.[67]

Dr. J. Saunders Redding reviewing in the New York
Herald Tribune Book Review failed to find any qualities which
distinguish this book as a work of art and his negative remarks read:

> There is no thematic line, and no narrative structure.
> Because it lacks the one, the book has not the tone of
> voice either of purpose or of point of view. Because it
> lacks the other, it is without method and control. The
> why is never answered, and the how is broken into a
> dozen fragments that must be pieced together with pa-
> tience.[68]

Dorothy West in *Living Is Easy* received critical acclaim
with the publication of her first novel. Florence Codman
writing in *Commonweal* rather enthusiastically observes:

> In Cleo Judson, (Dorothy) West has created a woman
> smitten by the virus of Agrippinas of all races, the preda-
> tory female on the loose, a wholly plausible, tantalizing
> creature. There are some loose places in the framework
> of the book, but the style has a professional, ready grace,
> and there is nothing "stock" about the characters. In-
> deed, in her first novel, (Dorothy) West displays all the
> talents of a highly competent writer.[69]

Arna Bontemps, novelist, writing in *Herald Tribune Book
Review*, gives a crystal clear estimate:

> Dorothy West's novel is of course a chronicle of twisted
> lives, but an honestly written one in which sociological

---

[67] Richard Sullivan, *New York Times Book Review*, Nov. 5, 1950,
p. 32.

[68] J. Redding, New York *Herald Tribune*, Nov. 19, 1950, p. 4.

[69] Florence Codman, *Commonweal*, June 25, 1948, p. 264.

implications are only a small part of the author's full intention.[70]

Stranger and Alone, by Dr. J. Saunders Redding, is considered by critics to be a really significant book. Certainly, the tone of *The Yale Review* with Paul Pickrel, critic, writing is favorable indeed when he says:

> This book adds more to our understanding of Negro life than many more sensational books; it is, in a sense, more shocking than the shockers, because it shows the critically weak points in those very institutions which most of us look to as the solution—in part, at least—of the problem of the Negro.[71]

Ann Petry, novelist, reviewing the book favorably in *The Saturday Review of Literature* points out:

> Negroes react in a thousand ways to the loose and unwritten code which governs relations between Negroes and whites in the United States. In order to survive they resist the code. This resistance ranges from a do-nothing withdrawal, a kind of passive resistance, to the active resistance which becomes open defiance. . . . But there is . . . another, much less publicized response to prejudice. It is based on complete acceptance of the code, approval of it. The people who show this reaction believe that Negroes are inferior and work to preserve the code. This response is the basic theme of J. Saunders Redding's first novel, *Stranger and Alone,* a book which evokes pity and terror in the reader as effectively as any of the fiction which dramatized the death agony of the protesting outraged victims who hurled defiance at the code. . . . This is a first-rate novel and a moving one. J. Saunders Redding has added a new and wonderful set of characters to the annals of the fiction that deals with race relations.[72]

Ralph Ellison, writer, reviewing the book favorably,

---

[70] Arna Bontemps, New York *Herald Tribune Weekly Book Review,* June 13, 1948, p. 16.

[71] Paul Pickrel, *Yale Review,* March, 1950, p. 576.

[72] Ann Petry, *Saturday Review of Literature,* Feb. 25, 1950, p. 18.

weighed both the positive and negative aspects of the book in order to ascertain its true literary value. The overall impression is favorable which reads:

> The first thing to be said is that *Stranger and Alone* is sociologically important; the next is that unlike many novels presenting Negro Americans, it is but superficially a racial novel. . . . it is actually about treason and that complex of mixed motives, snarled emotions and allegiance found in the collaborator. The distinction is important, for although the immediate impact of treachery depicted is received by Negroes, the ultimate victim is our society. *Stranger and Alone* concentrates on revealing the blasting effect upon both personality and society which so-called and loudly defended education can have . . . Shelton Howden learns that the white South has set aside its highest rewards for Negroes who are traitors to democracy. Shelton Howden on his first day at New Hope College for Negroes . . . resembles that of the hero of nineteenth century novel described by Lionel Trilling as "the young man from provinces."[73]

Negatively Ellison writes in muted tones about the novel in this passage:

> If in his first novel Redding has selected a protagonist too limited in personal appeal, and if his writing lacks the high quality that marked his autobiographical *No Day of Triumph,* he has done, nevertheless, a vastly important job of reporting the little known role of those Negro "leaders" who by collaborating with the despoilers of the South do insidious damage to us all.[74]

Malcolm Cowley, editor and critic in the *New Republic,* displayed his critical judgment and literary taste in his acclaim of William Gardner Smith's the *Last of the Conquerors.* For him the novel fills the gap in the group of war novels, and he explains:

---

[73] Ralph Ellison, *New York Times Book Review,* Feb. 19, 1950, p. 4.
[74] *Ibid.*

It is the first novel of army life to be written by a Negro.
. . . It is a straight-line narrative in the early Hemingway
manner, written neither better nor worse than most of
the novels by returning veterans. Smith deserves credit
for reaching their level of competence at such an early
age. . . .[75]

Cowley alludes to the misconception that foreigners might
receive from such a book. Concerning this point, he is particularly enlightening:

. . . the two races in this country have developed identical
cultures which are kept apart only by force and fear.
Except when questions of race are involved, the Negroes
act, speak and think exactly like the whites—and even
write like them, so that one could read whole chapters of
this novel without suspecting that they were written by a
Negro about Negroes.[76]

Charles Enrich Wheeler, critic, writing in the *Crisis,* receives *Last of the Conquerors* this way:

This excellent first novel is the story of American GI's in
occupied Germany. It is a disturbing story of Negroes
caught up by the divergent influences of two worlds: the
prejudices of their white comrades and the friendliness
of the Germans.[77]

The estimate of *America* of the book is in agreement with
Cowley on a number of points when it comments:

A tale that has its shocking elements but which is unique
in letting one see, through a Negro's eyes, a view of
postwar Germany which seems at times a better country
for a Negro to live in than the United States.[78]

Reviewing in the *Atlantic Monthly,* Charles J. Rolo ex-

[75] Malcolm Cowley, *New Republic,* Sept. 27, 1948, p. 33.
[76] *Ibid.*
[77] Charles Wheeler, *Crisis,* Nov. 1948, p. 337.
[78] *America,* Nov. 13, 1948, p. xiv.

presses in much the same language the point of view of other critics when he observes:

> It's the story of a Negro soldier in the Army of Occupation, who discovers in Germany what it feels like to be treated as a human being. In Berlin there is no color line. The women find him attractive, *the more so because of the fact that he is colored.*[79]

Rolo adds that this first novel by a twenty-year old Negro is certain to attract attention because of its highly charged theme. A social document of this type achieves a powerful impact, and the novel is strong and solid in structure. On the other hand, Rolo finds the novel weak in style from a literary point of view.

Joanna Spencer, critic, in the New York *Herald Tribune,* writes with depths of feeling in her article which dealt with the *Last of the Conquerors.* She rather engagingly writes under the caption "Across the Color Line" in this manner:

> The love story is moving and real. Dawkins is a young, pleasant, well-mannered Negro who is bright but not aggressive, courageous but not heroic. Smith writes with a single-mindedness that perhaps oversimplifies but his extreme restraint gives his cruel story a gentleness which is both skillful and effective. This is a very good first novel.[80]

William Harrison weighing the merits of *Counter Clockwise* in *Crisis* writes:

> This novel has two claims to uniqueness. It is the first novel issued by the only Negro publishing company in New York. It is the first novel written by a Negro author who contrasts the social phenomenon of "passing," or the attempt of a light-colored Negro to escape membership

---

[79] Charles J. Rolo, *Atlantic Monthly,* Oct., 1948, p. 110.
[80] Joanna Spencer, New York *Herald Tribune,* August 22, 1948, p. 3.

in an underprivileged racial minority, with that of the endeavor of a working class white to rise to a higher social class and jettison all the domestic and other ties which normally bind the individual.[81]

The heroine attempts also to avoid the working class and severs all the domestic ties which normally bind the individual. The conclusion of the story may appear shocking to some readers, but under the circumstance it is hardly possible that events could have taken any other turn. Obviously, this conflict seems forced and somewhat removed from reality. For there are hundreds of fair Negroes who make the adjustment.

Edward Lawson, critic in *Opportunity*, advances much the same point of view, and he informs us:

> [*Counter Clockwise*] is a story of the color line, and the misfortune that seems inevitably to dog the footsteps of those who attempt to cross it. Written by a young Negro author and published by a Negro firm, it is a creditable achievement that holds promise of better things to come from such a combination.[82]

Flaws that appeared to Lawson center about the presentation and general manner of execution. The author gives an episodic and jumpy narrative, and it is only in spots that the writing rises to a high level of communication.

For a first novel, *God Is for White Folks* by Will Thomas drew some good critical comments. N. L. Rothman, critic, in the *Saturday Review of Literature* evaluates the book in this manner:

> The character of Beau's aunt, and the whole episode of her vengeful madness, are, I think, extravagant, something out of the popular romantic mode to give this book a turgescence it does not need. Let it rest upon its true

---

[81] William Harrison, *Crisis,* Sept., 1940, p. 299.
[82] Edward Lawson, *Opportunity,* March, 1940, p. 93.

talk. There is enough of vitality and challege here to stand without embellishment.[83]

Rose Feld, critic in the New York *Herald Tribune Book Review,* writes:

> Concerned as it is with social implications, the book, nevertheless, emerges as an old-fashioned romantic tale highlighted with moments of racial conflict and melodrama. One wishes that (Will) Thomas had forsworn an ending which, though conventionally happy, lacks credibility.[84]

The *New Yorker* in its review found little of importance in this work and dismisses it in this fashion:

> An earnest first novel whose subject . . . the author might better have left alone until he had developed a little more as a writer. Right now, unfortunately, (Will) Thomas sounds too much like a man who fears that his readers may at any moment get bored and wander away, an anxiety that may account for the murders, assaults, lynchings, and other forms of violent action with which he has festooned this story of race prejudice in the Deep South.[85]

Hal Borland, critic in the *New York Times Book Review,* prefers a work by John Hewlett, *Wild Grapes,* or Victor Johnson's *Horncasters* for a true portrayal of a reported lynching in literature. His estimate of Will Thomas' *God Is for White Folks* is "undistinguished on all counts."[86]

C. V. Terry, *New York Times critic,* appraising the novel, *Alien Land,* writes:

> An angry work, this first novel deals with a special aspect of an ominous and ever-widening dilemma. Here (as in

---

[83] Nathan L. Rothman, *Saturday Review of Literature,* Oct. 4, 1947, p. 20.

[84] Rose Feld, *New York Herald Tribune Weekly Book Review,* Oct. 19, 1947, p. 24.

[85] *New Yorker,* September 27, 1947, p. 112.

[86] Hal Borland, *New York Times Book Review,* Sept. 27, 1947, p. 6.

the recently published *Southbound*) we have the spiritual torment of the all-but-white-negro who can "pass" with ease, and the deepest torment he faces when he moves into the all-white world. . . . Savoy, a young public-relations specialist in Washington, writes with understanding of this impasse. His reporting is as honest as his over-all purpose: the hate that flames on both sides of his grimly drawn color-line is both real and terrifying. . . . Savoy pulls no punches on either side of his battle line: his portrait of Kern's self-righteous father is no less merciless than his two-gun sheriff; the scarecrows he sketches in Negro ghettos from Georgia to Harlem are as bitterly real as his white night-riders.[87]

Arthur E. Burke, critic in the *Crisis,* informs us in his acclaim of Willard Savoy's *Alien Land*:

The problem of living as a Negro in the United States has been told in fiction . . . so many times that one might imagine its ramifications had been exhausted. Yet Willard Savoy in *Alien Land* tells a new-old story with such variations and power that one realizes how vital the tale still is and how much it needs to be repeated. . . . Almost every shade and variety of insult, humiliation, and even of physical violence, from the subtle slights of the North to the outright emasculation of the race in the South is here painted always in vivid and sometimes hideous colors.[88]

This is the story of the half-white Negro reminiscent of Chesnutt's *The House behind the Cedars* and Walter White's *Fire in Flint* and *Flight*. Savoy writes with broad, firm strokes, telescoping the action as he moves from section to section of the country. Washington, D. C., New York, Vermont, and the Deep South appear and are minutely described in terms of race relationships.

In 1946 several novels by Negroes were published, and

---

[87] C. V. Terry, *New York Times Book Review,* April 3, 1949, p. 20.
[88] Arthur E. Burke, *Crisis,* Oct., 1949, p. 219.

among them was *The Foxes of Harrow* by Frank Yerby. He
is a prominent figure in the new trend among Negro writers.
A rather prolific writer, he holds a unique place because of
his attitude toward the novel. His characterizations come from
any ethnic group, and he delineates them well which is in
part proof of the thesis of this book. His books have not been
favorably received for even an initial volume by a Negro
author very often receives unfavorable reviews which is in
keeping with American attitudes on such matters as race.
Yerby is partially responsible for this attitude. By his own
admission he is not a serious writer but is content to be a
popular one. Nonetheless, he is a talented author with a keen
imagination and unquestioned narrative gift. Richard Match
of the *New York Times Book Review* received the first volume
this way:

> Here is a good, old-fashioned, obese historical novel of
> the Old South that seems, more than once, to be haunted
> by the affluent ghost of Scarlet O'Hara. It is the story of
> Irish Stephen Fox—"tall, red-haired, with a face that
> looked like Lucifer's so soon after the fall that the angel-
> look was still on it"—who came to New Orleans in 1825
> and parlayed a pearl stickpin and a devilish way with
> cards into the greatest sugar fortune in Louisiana.[89]

Match continues with a brief biographical sketch of this
Negro literary figure:

> Frank Yerby, who won an O. Henry Memorial Award
> for a short story last year, is a former student at Fisk
> University. In this, his first novel, one might have hoped
> for the ideological intensity of, say, Howard Fast's *Free-
> dom Road* and, indeed, there are some sympathetic evi-
> dences of the Negro's deep resentment against slavery. . . .
> Yerby has chosen, however, to concentrate on a conven-
> tional historical narrative of passionate amours and gen-
> tlemanly swordplay.[90]

---

[89] Richard Match, *New York Times Book Review*, Feb. 10, 1946, p. 8.
[90] *Ibid.*

Harriet Kane, author of *Plantation Parade,* reviewing in the New York *Herald Tribune Book Review,* wrote less objectively about the book. Her critical comments discussed the technical aspects of publication after she admits that the book has merits. She begins:

> Yerby . . . carefully conned his New Orleans guide books and other standard sources. He has set up a properly robust hero and driven him hard through French quarter streets, Louisiana plantation driveways, boudoirs and other appropriate places.[91]

Frank Yerby's *The Vixens* appeared in 1947 and Jennings Rice' review in the New York *Herald Tribune Book Review* received it favorably as this passage indicates:

> But the suspense is sustained, the historical background well done, and readers who like their heroes noble but rakish, their heroines rash but faithful, their villians properly villianous will find it a difficult book to put down once they have begun it.[92]

He then mentions the fact that there are also several moving portraits of Negro leaders, murder, massive rapine, the dark record of the Knights of Camelia, and bloody clashes between the races. One very remarkable aspect about this book is its honesty. He continues:

> . . . when he comes to grips with Southern history he displays balance and understanding. His Southern whites, the great mass of them, are not shining knights fighting gallantly for a lost cause, as certain earlier writers would have them. But neither are they proto-fascists cynically bent on grinding down the black proletariat. They are, like their Northern opponents, people fighting bravely in defense of standards which they believed, however erroneously, to be right.[93]

---

[91] Harriet Kane, New York *Herald Tribune Book Review,* Feb. 24, 1946, p. 8.
[92] Jennings Rice, New York *Herald Tribune Book Review,* May 4, 1947, p. 10.
[93] *Ibid.*

He adds that Yerby is careful to point out that the scoundrels and opportunistic carpetbaggers and southerners are guilty.

Frank Slaughter in his *New York Times Book Review* article on Zora Neale Hurston's novel, *Seraph on the Suwanee,* begins by defining for his readers the term:

> "Seraph: One of an order of celestial beings conceived as fiery and purifying ministers of Jehovah," says Webster. Arvay Henson, the heroine of this long novel of the Florida sand barrons and turpentine forests, probably never heard of a seraph, but she set out to be one nevertheless. Arvay never heard of Freud either, but she's a textbook picture of a hysterical neurotic, right to the end of the novel. The author knows her people, the Florida cracker of the swamps and turpentine camps intimately, and she knows the locale. One gets the impression that she took a textbook on Freudian psychology and adapted it to her needs, perhaps with her tongue in her cheek while so doing. The result is a curious mixture of excellent background drawing against which move a group of half-human puppets.[94]

Common Ground, where Eddie Shimano gives the sophisticated and modern literary point of view with regard to Negro novelists, received the book favorably. His article reads:

> The South is also the locale in *Seraph on the Suwanee,* Zora Neale Hurston's novel of the poor white and her marriage to a man whose ancestors once owned huge plantations before the Civil War. It gives a few glimpses of the Negro worker's relationships to the white boss. It has the other incidental interest of being a literary dissection of Southern white culture by an anthropologist, an authority on folk culture, who happens to be a Negro.[95]

---

[94] Frank G. Slaughter, *New York Times Book Review,* Oct. 31, 1948, p. 24.

[95] Eddie Shimano, *Common Ground,* Spring, 1948, p. 107.

Worth Tuttle Hedden, critic, New York *Herald Tribune Book Review,* writing about the latest novel by Zora Neale Hurston expresses astonishment at the literary achievement of a neighbor rather than a member of the ethnic group. The reviewer gives her critical evaluations this way:

> . . . an astonishing novel. It seems incredible that one not born to the breed, even . . . neighbor and an anthropologist could be its biographer. . . . *Seraph on the Suwanee* is the love story of a daughter of Florida crackers and of a scion of plantation owners, it is no peasant-marries-the-prince tale. . . . Beginning conventionally enough with a seduction . . . it ends twenty-odd years later when the protagonists are about to be grandparents. In this denouement the divergent lines of (Zora) Hurston's astonishing, bewildering talent meet to give us a reconciliation scene between a middle-aged man and a middle-aged woman that is erotically exciting and a description of the technique of shrimping that is meticulously exact.[96]

Edward W. Hamilton, critic in the periodical, *America,* gives this novel a favorable review. Indeed, he hailed *Seraph on the Suwanee* with a flavor of excitement as he says:

> The first two-thirds of this novel is an incredibly good job. The author has caught the idiom of backwoods-Florida whites beautifully, and she presents the relationship between an insecure woman and her adequate and resourceful husband with a fidelity and delicacy that I think excels anything that other writers have achieved.[97]

One feature about reviewers of Negro works is evident (if this is typical); they do not read pertinent biographical information about the Negro author. For instance, this favor-

---

[96] Worth Hedden, New York *Herald Tribune Book Review,* Oct. 10, 1948, p. 2.
[97] Edward W. Hamilton, *America,* Jan. 1, 1949, p. 354.

able review of the novel contains an error. Zora Hurston has
written several novels and anthropological studies also.

> *Seraph on the Suwanee,* (Zora) Hurston's first novel,
> shows promise if ever a book did. The author deserves
> credit for portraying a man's man successfully—something
> that I don't recall a woman's having done before. She
> shows great sensitivity in tracing emotional sequences and
> reasoning processes, and high skill in setting scenes,
> utilizing regional phraseology, phrasing sprightly con-
> versation.[98]

Ann Petry's *Country Place* is one of the major contributions of the Negro to American literature in 1947. This is her
second novel and was warmly received by the leading periodicals. Bradford Smith in the *Saturday Review of Literature*
gives a point of view which the novel for him evinces:

> . . . *Country Place* is an interesting book because it re-
> veals, as better books might have concealed, a fault not
> . . . Petry's but of our time. It is the fallacy that literature
> must reduce itself to the common denominator of glands
> and hormones at a time when the reverse effect of mind
> upon body has become pretty clear. It is, in larger terms,
> the lack of faith in a moral universe. Once you accept
> an automatic theory of conduct, men's actions become
> more violent as they lose purpose. Hence the violence in
> . . . Petry's story. It is the lack of moral logic that turns
> drama into melodrama. Not that violence has no place
> in literature. But in Greek drama, in Shakespeare, the
> characters are responsible for their actions; they gen-
> erate events and events have their consequences upon
> them. Then, out of materials very like those of *Country
> Place,* you get a *Madame Bovary.*[99]

Along with this rather remarkable précis Bradford Smith
explains the artistic flaws in the novel in this passage:

---

[98] *Ibid.*

[99] Bradford Smith, *Saturday Review of Literature,* Oct. 18, 1947,
pp. 17, 21.

A design somewhat too apparent, a rather too skillful contriving, adds to the quality of artificiality . . . her bad people lack motivation . . . the reader is made to understand the social forces which produced Studs Lonigan, [but] there is no comparable explanation for . . . Petry's characters.[100]

The *New Yorker* in its section "Books Briefly Noted" had this to say:

. . . on the whole the author has kept up to the form she displayed in *The Street*. . . . [Ann] Petry has joined the company of the novelists who have described the American small town as a center of bigotry, marital infidelity, and astounding malice.[101]

John Caswell Smith, Jr., *Atlantic Monthly* reviewer, thought most of the characters were well done and he goes on to say:

Ann Petry's writing in this second novel shows much of the improvement one was led to anticipate on reading her first, [*The Street*]. *Country Place* is a fast-moving, somewhat melodramatic tale of a small New England town as seen through the eyes of its druggist, Mr. Fraser. . . . Taken as a whole, though, *Country Place* is a good story, worthy of the telling. It preaches no sermons, waves no flags. It tells a plausible narrative of, for the most part, some very human people in an earthy situation.[102]

Richard Sullivan, critic, *New York Times Book Review*, continues the favorable acceptance with a different slant as he writes:

Yet this is despite the violence of its events a rather quiet book, carefully and economically phrased, and a good

[100] *Ibid.*
[101] *New Yorker*, Oct. 11, 1947, p. 122.
[102] John Caswell Smith, Jr., *Atlantic Monthly*, Nov., 1947, pp. 178-182.

deal different from the author's best selling *The Street*. The novel deals . . . justice and injustice clashing in a New England town. *Country Place* is a novel which on the whole is decidedly better than average. Its style is bright and vigorous. Its feeling for place, for the small telling background detail, seems consistently right. Its characterizations are forceful. Its events, though weighted down with melodrama, come together into a satisfying whole design. There are . . . open and obvious touches of management at the end so that right seems to triumph almost at the author's direction and perhaps a few too many side issues are forced into a final situation that doesn't quite seem to justify them at all. But a passionate seriousness of intention, a good feeling of honesty and a general competence of execution make up adequately.[103]

Writing in the New York *Herald Tribune Book Review*, Rose Feld discusses favorably *Country Place*. Her first concern is for the tragedy of the returning soldier who finds that his wife has been unfaithful. An extract from her detailed account appears below:

Mainly, it is the Weasel who gives substance and shape to the events of the story. He is a Dickensian creature, compounded of slyness, cruelty and viciousness. It is he who throws the first suspicion of Glory into Johnny's mind; . . . .The story, with the Weasel acting as self-appointed spy and informer, is told on two levels, that of Johnny's tragedy and its resolution and that of Mrs. Gramby's conflict with her daughter-in-law, Lil, who is also Glory's mother. A storm of hurricane proportions, excellently described, serves as a backdrop for the intensity of the human drama that is enacted under two roofs. There is much that is exceedingly good in (Ann) Petry's book, the feel of a small town, the integrity of dialogue, the portrayal of Johnnie, of Glory, of Mrs. Gramby.[104]

───────────

[103] Richard Sullivan, *New York Times Book Review*, Sept. 28, 1947, p. 8.

[104] Rose Feld, New York *Herald Tribune Book Review*, Oct. 5, 1947, p. 6.

William Gardner Smith in his second novel, *Anger at Innocence,* attracted attention and received critical reception which added to his reputation. Nonetheless, the leading critics in periodicals were not as enthusiastic as they were over his controversial work *Last of the Conquerors.* Lloyd Morris, critic, in the New York *Herald Tribune Book Review,* wrote favorably of the book as this passage illustrates:

> Essentially melodramatic in its plot, frequently rising to scenes of painful violence, *Anger at Innocence* is nevertheless mainly pitched in a low key. Its muted tone is intentional. By consistent understatement Smith makes credible a peculiarly baleful environment, and persuades us to contemplate experience in which it would be intolerable fully to participate.[105]

Robert Kingery, author, writing in the *Library Journal,* appraised the book in this way:

> Violent, brutal in incident and language, this book seems to be (in spite of much bitterness), a serious attempt to examine the nature of good and evil through a number of characters clearly and realistically drawn. As such it is recommended for collections aiming to include contemporary fiction of literary merit.[106]

One of the major figures in developing the thesis of this book, that Negro novelists became inclusive in the selection of characters from all humanity, is Willard Motley. His reputation on the strength of his first novel, *Knock on Any Door,* was firmly established by critics. The reception of this work was especially favorable in the *Saturday Review of Literature* where Margaret B. Hexter, critic, wrote this favorable impression:

> Discerning readers were much intrigued a couple of years ago by an unusual book, *Rebel without a Cause,* by

---

[105] Lloyd Morris, New York *Herald Tribune Book Review,* Nov. 5, 1950, p. 18.
[106] Robert Kingery, *Library Journal,* Oct. 1, 1950, p. 1662.

a psychiatrist, Robert L. Lindner, the transcript of an actual hyno-analysis of a criminal psychopath. A far larger body of readers will doubtless be attracted to *Knock on Any Door,* a novel which is, to all intents and purposes, the biography of an imaginary criminal psychopath. If . . . Linder's work had much of the readibility of fiction, . . . Motley's has much of the veracity of science. . . . It is difficult to believe that there will be any to question his mastery of the novelist's art. *Knock on any Door* is a triumph of naturalistic fiction. The only question is whether in this phenomenal first novel . . . Motley has given us his all, or whether a major luminary has just arisen in the literary firmament.[107]

Margaret Hexter further compares the novel to the work of Richard Wright. But she remarks that Nick is a hero more engaging than Richard Wright's Bigger Thomas. Willard Motley is even more successful in persuading his readers that the criminal was a victim of society.

In a very complimentary manner Arna Bontemps, author of *Black Thunder* and *God Sends Sunday,* reviewing in the New York *Herald Tribune Book Review* establishes his favorable case by writing:

What James T. Farrell exposed of the South Side Irish of that city, and Meyer Levin of the West Side Jews, what Nelson Algren's *Never Come Morning* did for the Polish neighborhood and Richard Wright's *Native Son* for the Black Belt, Willard Motley now accomplishes for a community around Maxwell and Halsted (for the Italians). The novel is a substantial achievement by a new writer whose work is sure to be noticed and carefully evaluated.[108]

For Bontemps the author is painstaking, attentive to the

---

[107] Margaret B. Hexter, *Saturday Review of Literature,* May 24, 1947, p. 13.

[108] Arna Bontemps, New York *Herald Tribune Weekly Book Review,* May 18, 1947, p. 8.

small details of his projected work; his observation is photographic; his ear musical and retentive. Motley has the ability to realize and project multiplicity of characters, all vivid and recognizable, all clearly differentiated. The book as a whole despite its length is remarkable for its economy. It is a controversial book dealing with graphic material, and Motley handles his material with considerable restraint. There is certain relentlessness and insistence that can not be brushed aside. Nick Romano, named after St. Nicholas of Talentino and dedicated to the church from infancy, emerges finally with this motto, "live fast, die young, and have a good looking corpse!" and the saga yielded in his career is as sordid and moving, as sharply etched and disturbing as anything yet written in the great Chicago tradition of naturalistic fiction.

Charles Enoch Wheeler, critic in the *Crisis,* greeted the publication of Willard Motley's *Knock on Any Door* with a warm reception, and he lauds it as having been written with the power of "a Dreiser and the passion of a Dostoyevsky."

Phoebe Adams, *Atlantic Monthly,* mentions the fact that the work relates the damaging influence of environment upon a child. Society converts a nice little boy named Nick into a killer, Pretty Boy, as revealed in the first two-thirds of the novel. The last third shows this same society gathering its weapons in pious rage to take a highly personal revenge on Nick. Even though Motley does no preaching, the unmistakable indictment of society is crystal clear. The book compels attention by its honesty, thoroughness, and its deep concern for the people who appear on its pages. The trial scene gives a description of a legal and intellectual battle waged in the courtroom that is as exciting and as full of suspense as the best cloak and sword melodrama ever written. Motley has written a social novel, but he has created a complete and self-contained, absolutely convincing world.

Horace R. Cayton of the *New Republic* adds this favorable critical appraisal:

> Motley, in creating this monumental work, employs a technique not unlike that of Theodore Dreiser. . . . Motley has, indeed, stated the psychological problem arising out of the economic and social conflicts which face America and the world.[109]

Henry Rago of *Commonweal* agrees with Arna Bontemps and Phoebe Adams since he finds that *Knock on Any Door* has a Polish protagonist of Algren's work, the Bigger Thomas of *Native Son* and the Studs Lonigan of the Farrell trilogy.

> (*Knock on Any Door*) is a dramatization of the fate of a boy who lives and dies in the Chicago slums. (His) documentation is impressive, and (Willard) Motley has prodigality, . . . stamina, and that is as compelling as any evidence can be when we talk of writers of the future. . . . His description of the wretched neighborhoods of Chicago are as fine as anything on the subject.[110]

On the negative side where Motley violates the artistic properties of his medium, Henry Rago insists that Nick of *Knock on Any Door* is a somnambulist and the whole is melodramatic sometimes. The structure of the plot is rushed. It becomes apparent that Motley is forcing the novel to fit into the society nemisis pattern, and as such this approach is nothing new.

Another critic, Charles Lee, *New York Times Book Review*, writing under the heading "Disciple of Dreiser" has this account to give of his impressions:

> Let it be stated at once: an extraordinary and powerful new naturalistic talent herewith makes its debut in American letters. But let it be added immediately: Chicago's Motley has a deal of graduate work to do in litera-

---

[109] Horace Cayton, *New Republic,* May 12, 1947, pp. 30, 31.
[110] Henry Rago, *Commonweal,* July 25, 1947, p. 358.

ture's school of realism before attaining all the honors of his craft.

His resemblance to Farrell, and especially to Dreiser, is striking. Indeed, he has played clearly the sedulous ape to the latter; not a few readers will catch echoes in his book of *An American Tragedy*. And, though he lacks that master's qualities of cosmic brooding and massive eloquence, he has something of his rugged narrative drive, his cumulative emotional power and his kindling sense of compassion. Dreiser would have been proud of his disciple.[111]

Charles Lee, who strongly supported Motley with honest appreciation of the novel, nonetheless, takes him to task for his shortcomings and flagrant defects of narrative technique. These are the faulty qualities which may very well be corrected. Motley, according to Lee, is not a subtle writer. Indeed, he writes like a whole glee club of sob sisters and in the continuous wailings and shreiking his book is a sordid sequence of heartbreak in Chicago slums, suicides, desertions, lost loves, and a multitude of others until the still small voice of critical reason may be overwhelmed. Furthermore, there is room to disagree with his concept of naturalism. The theory upon which Motley works is not necessarily valid. Actually, people with a very undesirable environment overcome the depressing effects and attain stature of importance in particular communities as responsible citizens. *Knock on Any Door* is in this case a dramatized slice of sociology. The crux of the matter rests in the enigma man himself, for men from the best regulated homes in the world become criminals. Therefore Motley's novel is distorted to fit the rule. Nick belongs to Freud as well as to sociology, a fact which Motley fails to take into account. "What remains . . ." Phoebe Adams remarks, "is a truly remarkable first novel."[113]

---

[111] Charles Lee, *New York Times Book Review*, May 4, 1947, p. 3.
[113] Phoebe Adams, *Atlantic Monthly*, July, 1947, pp. 126-127.

CONCLUSIONS

My mother bore me in the southern wild,
And I am black, but O! my soul is white;
White as an angel is the English child,
But I am black, as if bereav'd of light.

. . . .

For when our souls have learn'd that heat to bear,
The cloud will vanish; we shall hear His voice,
Saying: come out from the grave, my love and care,
And round my golden tent like lambs rejoice.

Thus did my mother say, and kissed me;
And thus I say to little English boy:
When I from black and he from white cloud free,
And round the tent of God like lambs we joy.
    Little Black Boy   William Blake

In the introduction, critical method, definitions, and thesis
were given. The following chapters dealt with discussions of
two prevailing tendencies among Negro novelists of the decade
1940-1950. On the one hand, they described the specialized
condition of the Negro in American society. The Negro world

in isolation, where the protest theme does not give a sharp edge to the novel, was discussed. The problem of miscegenation was treated as a group of novels belonging to the category of novels of purpose. On the other hand, novelist's delineations of characters from all ethnic groups in American society displayed a second tendency with its correspondingly broadened view and understanding of life. Periodicals with favorable criticism of Negro productions established the reputations of some Negro novelists as serious writers.

This chapter gives an estimate of the writers and the novels of the forties. It views the whole as a body of literature which indubitably belongs to the American scene. As such it has the faults and the virtues of American society reflected in its content.

American literature in the hands of Negro practitioners is impressive indeed during the forties. It reflects aspects of American society. American literature was enriched with the publication of Wright's *Native Son*. This "masterly novel"[1] by the "apostle of race"[2] was the culmination of the novel of protest along with Petry's *The Street,* Himes' *Lonely Crusade,* Offord's *The White Face,* Lucas' *Third Ward Newark,* Attaway's *Blood on the Forge,* and Smith's *Last of the Conquerors.*

Impressive as it is, like American literature in general during the forties, the Negro's output has numerous defects. One is struck immediately with the limitations imposed by a narrow range of subject matter. Varied as it is and inclusive of American interests, Negro writing concentrates on one weakness of American society rather than its virtues. Admittedly, all of America is not good; conversely, all is not bad for the Negro. An unhappy fact of American life is inequality of races. Especially marked conflicts exist between whites and

---

[1] Van Wyck Brooks, *The Confident Years: 1885-1915,* p. 550.

[2] Alfred Kazin, *On Native Grounds,* p. 372.

blacks. This theme attracts novelists because of its dramatic potentiality. The Negro novelist's failure to disassociate himself from this peculiarity of American life, significant as it is, impoverishes the thematic content of his body of literature. Variations on the same theme are hardly conducive to producing a great literature.

Protest literature by category deals with sociology since it propagates the idea of change in American social conditions. Fictionalized accounts of observable life omit other important disciplines such as philosophy, economic theory, experience in other lands, and ordinary American successes.

These, in accordance with American ideals, are valid materials too. Negroes have attained success in some exceptional cases, far too few granted, despite insurmountable barriers. These chosen few enjoy a reasonable share of the good things of American life and spiritual tranquility. Instead of the self-consciously accusing complex of race, the triumph of these few may very well make exciting drama. Such a novel would reveal human beings with lofty aspirations led to logical conclusions. To date no Negro has written a political novel which grapples with the colorful drama of national interests. Motley's *We Fished All Night* deals with political life in Chicago.[3] No novel gives the story of religion in rationalistic terms which show spiritual developments as products of a philosophical system. The war novel of strategy and tactics applied to battles in which Negroes fought and died has failed to appear. The philosophical novel in which some system of thought as it affects the life of the Negro has yet to appear. The novel of international intrigue has been neglected. No artist has given a fictionalized version of his life. Obviously, Negroes indicate limitation of activities which make up the full life in their novels. Few, if any, Negroes occupy positions either politically or economically in higher

[3] Willard Motley, *We Fished All Night*, p. 6.

administrative echelons where policy making is involved. The Negro in America, for the most part, remains an unassimilated mass of humanity, echoing but not shaping the culture.

Organized society has defects always; conversely, it has instruments by which these faults may be corrected. Human nature which is unpredictable does not permit social perfection. So, there will invariably be some deviation from the ideal. Man will not be satisfied with a Utopian existence, for his flexible character will not permit him to achieve such a state. Organization of human beings into society presupposes imperfections and flexibility, and the articulate minority is expected to voice dissent. Negro novelists have not failed to take advantage of this. They have written continuously novels which attack some inherent weakness in the social order. Their works protest against social conditions which are unfavorable to them. To register their protest they document carefully an issue, thereby propagating the idea of change. What these books really demand is not fundamental change in the social structure; rather they insist on making the letter and spirit of our Constitution and the Declaration of Independence,[4] indispensable to American social structure a reality. Experiences in American society demonstrate quite clearly that equality does not mean literally "all" people. Negro novelists interpret this double meaning as being incompatible with the ethos of the society. So, in the forties, less exclusively than in other decades of the century, the novels by Negroes concentrate on this weakness. Their contention centers about two basic demands, namely, job security and security of personality. On the surface this would appear to be needless ranting and pamphleteering because in theory this condition exists. As the novels of protest indicate, surface features are misleading, for these two very desirable, indeed, indispensable attributes of American democracy are denied Negroes. These

---

[4] Howard Mumford Jones, *Ideas in America*, p. 186.

novels list systematically those areas in society and those social institutions wherein this occurs.

Native Son clarifies the issue by giving the two essentials for integration and self-realization of the Negro race in American society. Attaway's *Blood on the Forge* extends the protest to labor where the Negro's job security is threatened. Labor so utilizes Big Matt, Chinatown, and Melody that job security and personality security are taken away. Himes in *Lonely Crusade* and *If He Hollers Let Him Go* varies the setting, but the crux of the matter is the same. His protagonists in the two novels, Bob and Lee, find both attributes impossible to achieve. Petry's *The Street,* which depicts life in an unwholesome environment, gives us Lutie Johnson who contends for personality and job security by making these two mean a home for her son and a job in keeping with her ability and training. Circumstances, however, destroy her values of respectability and independence in Negro womanhood. She takes into account the segregation from local environment to national policy by citing the army. Curtis Lucas in *Third Ward Newark* presents an extreme case of a woman who develops a psychotic personality[5] because of a sexual crime perpetrated by a white man. More disgusting and destructive is the low repute in which a Negro woman's life is held. Negro womanhood is not respected in Wonnie's case. In *Flour Is Dusty* social features in public places of amusement merely point up organized personality insecurity because of the policy of discrimination.

The Negro novelist's protest has an ironical bent because the specialized conditions and concepts of race become more complicated, for a white face does not necessarily mean a white man or woman. Conflicts between individuals are inevitable, but this situation presents conflicts between races where American minorities are overwhelmed by sheer num-

---

[5] Abram Kardiner, *Psychological Frontiers of Society,* p. 8.

bers, and more important, wealth, and power. Social definition
and not biological fact of man operates in the case of Kern
in *Alien Land*. Here is a white man of Negro ancestry, and
he is, therefore, defined Negro. Liom in *Counter Clockwise* is
a white woman, but she is socially defined Negro. Insecurity
of personality is the main complication in this dilemma.
Naturally, these characters seek the advantages which they
feel their color should give them in America. Confronted with
the knowledge that these whites are Negroes by definition,
their white suitors reject them promptly. *God Is for White
Folks* poses the same widening condition in the character,
Beau. Taken as a group, these novels suggest that society
should make an attempt at reorientation in thought and action
on this social condition.[6] This type of Negro, who is a periphery case, seeks personality security through identification
with the majority group in American society. Each of these
characters manages to secure job security.

The *Last of the Conquerors* poses significantly the differences between the European continent and North America,
the United States in particular, in the concept of race. In
Europe, regardless of skin coloring, man belongs to the human
race, and color does not cause immediate rejection as in most
cases in America. Personality and the ability to assimilate
European culture seem to be the prerequisites of life. This is
quite a picture in contrast to the American way where the
white majority refuses to accept the Negro as another man,
thereby depriving him of personality security. In fact, a Negro
has no identity, individuality, nor image of himself if he is a
Bob Jones of *If He Hollers Let'm Go* type. On the other
hand, in Smith's experiences in Germany there was no display
of anti-Negro feelings on social levels by the Germans. Personality security a fact of life, love affairs, amalgamation, and
cultural development resulted. This personality security was

---

[6] C. V. Terry, *New York Times Book Review*, April 3, 1949, p. 20.

counterbalanced by complete personality destruction in the army, especially in housing, discipline, work, and transfer of men. White men lived peacefully with black men in Germany, an astonishingly democratic condition in a dictatorship, enemy of democracy.

Negro novelists through their characters make a trenchant exposé of conditions in life and anticipate a time when insecurity of a black man in a majority white world may be eliminated with job security and personality inviolate. Meanwhile social commentary indicates that some Negroes view other continents with admiration or a means of possible escape. Indeed, the novels imply that exodus from American injustices and discriminatory practices may be the Negro's means of "self-realization."[7] Perhaps the process of assimilation may be facilitated or human dignity of individuality maintained. In any case Smith in *Last of the Conquerors* permits his characters to say that they prefer life with the Germans to life in America. By such a statement this character does not mean an admission of racial inferiority, but he does disclose a preference for a life devoid of racial pressures. More disastrous and demoralizing to the American point of view, one Negro soldier escapes to the Russian border. For him this unknown life, whatever it is, offers an escape from American dominance which starts with an emasculation of Negro personality.

Even though Europe may very well be *No Green Pastures*,[8] Smith's *Last of the Conquerors* shows that acceptance of Negroes is a part of the German Weltanschauung. In no cases do racial pressures or social pressures assume American proportions in Europe. But the *Last of the Conquerors* indicates a paradox too. For the forties was a period in which American dollars proved to be a means of sustaining Europe which means, perhaps, an Americanization of Europe in

---

[7] Erich Fromm, *Escape from Freedom*, p. 267.
[8] Roi Ottley, *No Green Pastures*, pp. 60-68.

matters of race. Furthermore, life of Negroes in European dominated colonies[9] is another matter and does not rightly belong to the present study. One is aware of a difference between life in the European controlled colonies in Africa and life for the black man transplanted to Europe.

South America and Australia appear to be places of escape, especially Brazil. But the minor difficulty of language would have to be surmounted first. Negroes, it appears from the novels of protest, do not yearn for mere assimilation. They want security and the ability to maintain their individuality as well. The escape of the American Negro is not a geographical one. But it is integration into the American dream of self-realization of all men.

The Negro authors in the forties sensibly point out, for they know, that the world of western civilization offers no Utopia. But they insist that social pressure on account of different skin coloring is an illogical and untenable position. Life for the Negro does not proceed on a logical basis and, therefore, in no instance in America is the life of the Negro as even and as free from pressures as that of the majority group. Controls, it would seem, will not permit it. The moral rightness or wrongness of the situation the novelist leaves to the American white conscience to decide. The novelist merely points up the fallacies and changes, both implicit and explicit, in his characterizations and problems which his material poses.

The protest novels by Negro authors, such as *Lonely Crusade* by Himes, say that the Negro is proud of his American heritage for the most part. He continues to point out in effect that by choice and birth he will remain a part of the American scene. He seeks an improvement of his condition nonetheless. Rejection of a contrary system and faith in the efficacy of the American experiment form the basis of his

---

[9] Harold Laski, *The American Democracy*, p. 454.

protest. The characters in no sense of the word fear the vicissitudes of life. On the contrary, they embrace life cheerfully, but they do express disillusionment over persecution because they are Negroes. The authors have their characters envision and, rightly so, a world where this insidious and pernicious practice, if not eliminated, will be reduced to a minimum.[10] Richard Wright with all of his vehemence and intensity asks for only two fundamental human qualities; namely, personality and security. Petry raises the same question from a feminine point of view, and she protests against the low esteem in which Negro women are held, Lutie Johnson insists that Negro women may be physically beautiful and morally good. For Lutie a fair amount of happiness consists of a home for her son, Bub, and a job. In fact Lutie prefers a Negro world with economic security. Attaway and Himes give the same point of view and make the same demands. For them economic security, while working with all races, should be accorded the Negro. Qualified people of all skin coloring should do jobs in common, exacting the same respect for technical knowledge rather than open resentment of the type Bob Jones gets as foreman of a mixed crew in *If He Hollers Let Him Go*. The novels advance the idea consistently that job security is the most important matter of life for some Negroes. They realize, as do assimilated Negroes in ultra modern, American circles, that social acceptance is a matter of individual choice. American leadership in selling the world on its system has to face the charge always of nonassimilation of Negroes.[11]

Now because life in the situations in which the Negro novelists' characters find themselves is just the reverse of the stated principles of democracy, accompanying frustrations

---

[10] Jones, *op. cit.*, p. 186.
[11] *Ibid.*, p. 188.

and psychological states of anxiety bedevil the Negro's existence. These characters insist that a land of plenitude which
makes Negroes live in poverty because of job opportunity
difficulties[12] is intolerable. Since the two fundamental demands of economic security and personality security have
never been met, there is justification for demanding change
by Negro novelists. In the few instances where Negroes have
attained job security and personality security, the results have
not been disastrous nor inimical to the interests of the country.
Observable reactions of these few are lives pursued and lived
in conventionally accepted taste as useful American citizens.

Historically speaking, great novelists are remarkably productive in a decade. Sir Walter Scott is the prime example.
With the majority group, American authors such as William
Faulkner, John Steinbeck, Sinclair Lewis, Ernest Hemingway,
and Edna Ferber fertile productivity is in evidence. Com-
paratively apparent at once is the lack of sustained talent
among Negro novelists. With the notable exception of Frank
Yerby, there is no Negro novelist of the forties with more
than two novels to his credit. Richard Wright's important
novel, *Native Son* was not followed in the forties by another.[13]

---

[12] *Ibid.*, p. 202.
[13] Richard Wright, *The Outsider*. *The Outsider*, by Richard Wright,
appearing thirteen years after his initially successful novel discussed in
this period shows the maturity which the intervening years of silence has
given him. Evidence of the intellectual stimulation which Paris, France,
gives the hypersensitive artist is best seen in Wright's growth. Especially
true of Wright, he has mellowed his bitterness and frustration which
marked his earlier *Native Son,* and placed both in a frame far more
universal in scope. *The Outsider* is of remarkable literary stature. The
newly created character, Cross Houston, is a Negro with intellectual
acumen which can hardly be ascribed to Bigger Thomas of *Native Son.*
The Outsider may be discussed on three levels. First, it is a story of a
man, very human, beset with the twin polarities: fear and desire. Secondly, Negro man is elevated to the universal man category. Thirdly,
conflicting ideologies may be viewed to advantage.
Caught in a difficult marital situation, Cross Houston, a frustrated
intellectual and school teacher, works in the Post Office. This is the first

It is true that he has written an autobiography and articles, but no solid piece in his initially successful medium. Zora Neale Hurston, on the other hand, has sustained talent, but her work belongs to another decade for the most part. She has written works in other fields and improved in her technique as a novelist. Since Ann Petry made her debut with *The Street,* she has followed this performance with another novel, *Country Place,* which is a solid piece. One expects from her competently executed works, *The Narrows* (1953). George Henderson's first novel was successful, but his second work, *Jule,* which belongs to the period under discussion, proved disappointing. Himes' *Lonely Crusade* is better than his first work, *If He Hollers Let Him Go,* and the same may be said of William Attaway's *Blood on the Forge* in comparison with his first successful novel *Let Me Breathe Thunder.* One deplores the fact that no new novel has appeared since the early forties. Oscar Mischeaux has determined effort, but he lacks the true narrative gift. All of his works bear the stamp of the theatrical scenario writer, and his two books appearing during the forties have shown little, if any, improvement in artistic execution. Willard Savoy's *Alien Land,* Carl Offord's *The White Face,* John Lee's *Counter Clockwise,* and Lewis Caldwell's *The Policy King* are just authors of the one first

---

of the three sets of difficulties in which Cross Houston is involved. Secondly, he escapes and enters into another world of conflicting ideologies. Thirdly, Houston murders out of fear. Cross, an alcoholic, is estranged from his predatory wife, Gladys. Sexually vigorous, he indulges indiscriminately and impregnates Dot, his latest conquest, who is a minor. His mother intervenes with religion which has no appeal to Cross. Saved from legal action by a train accident in which he is reported killed, Cross flees to New York. When he encounters one of his old, fellow workers in a house of prostitution, he murders out of fear. He then joins a group of subversives, the Communist party, causes Eva Blount to commit suicide, and actually murders Herndon and Hilton. Instead of death in the electric chair when he is apprehended, he is set free, free to have his old fears and desires as the ambivalence of man gains control. The conclusion is a tour de force in surprise endings in literature.

novel of promise. In the case of Adam C. Powell Sr., one admires his skillful performance but hardly expected him at his age to enter upon a literary career. Indeed, he had given before his death most of his duties as minister to his capable and dynamic son, Adam Clayton Powell, Jr.

Even though these books propagate the idea of change within the American frame of reference, they do not adhere to any conflicting political ideology. *Lonely Crusade* is a novel in which Himes paints a distasteful picture of the Communist party activities in America according to Lee Gordon's experiences. His book is tantamount to a Negro writer's complete estrangement from such a conflicting ideology. So far as the Negro novelist is concerned, the possibility for realizing his persistent demands is in the American scene. One insight impresses itself upon the reader of this fiction, namely, that political fervor among the Negro characters is generally lacking. This is one of the faults of the articulate Negro character because he makes his demands through protest rather than the more practical channels of party politics. Lee Gordon knows that the Communist Party is not the right choice, but he is wary of the other parties if the intellectual Jew's description is correct with whom he talks. Most political parties, according to the expressed view, are designed for selfish purposes—the usurpation of power. The underprivileged are exploited merely for political gain.

In particular, melodrama is an overworked device in the novel of protest by Negro authors. Very often this fails to achieve or present the tragic view of the common man which should be the intent of the author who essays a protraction of persecution. In far too many cases, an unhealthy bitterness comes from the character, rather than a three-dimensional figure serving as an explanation of the principles of modern tragedy. Very often this defect causes a dismissal of the work by some readers because the book gives the impression of distortion. The line of fact to truth becomes improbable. Melodrama as a literary device and technique should be employed less frequently for the sake of proportion in the novel.

Many exciting events mark the forties, and the American Negroes have participated in them. One looks to serious writers for fictionalized versions of this Atomic Age.[14] The dawn of a new age alone, with all of the prospects of an unknown future, should be stimulating. Motley, one of the successful Negro novelists of the forties, in his second work, *We Fished All Night,* gives a mirror of Chicago life. In this protracted work he catches the turbulence of the forties. If anything, he attempted too much. In the work appear unionism, politics, psychiatry, vacillation of Jewish characters in the war and in the creative arts.

White patronage of professional "race" workers crowds his thickly populated world. We follow his hero from the ghetto of youth and an amateurish acting career through the war and ultimate success as the political "boss" of Chicago. Don Lockwood, Polish hero, feels that the life he has led is not satisfying. He uses a technique of reporting events in flashbacks and in the musings of his characters. As to the mechanics of the novel he manages to tie up all of the threads by interweaving the lives and fortunes of four families so that an effective conclusion is reached. Certainly, one expects from this powerful writer a more finished product subsequently.

Willard Motley is significant for his conception of the world which is a broad view filled with compassion and concern for man in society. In his novels he has shown how forces are at work in society which operate against all groups of people in the American scene. His artistry is not a mere light stroke of the paint brush; he paints on a broad canvas with

---

[14] René Wellek and Warren, *Theory of Literature,* p. 89.

thick oils so that the colors and conflicting forces stand out in bold forms and shapes which strike the reader with the essence of truth.

His drawn characters from other minority groups in America is not a mere transference of the race problem from one group to another. On the contrary, he digs at the roots of American society and unearths the basic negative forces which pertain to all people.[15] He is concerned with universal man, for fundamentally man in America, as everywhere, has a common origin and will suffer the same common end. The period between these absolutes should not be marked with separateness on the basis of kind but should be resolved in a mutual understanding of life with its problems common to all men. His psychological insights into character are realistic interpretations[16] so that flesh and blood figures move in his drama. His broad understanding of the complications life holds for most people makes him a writer of stature. Among other things Motley demonstrates that man in a social mileu has far more similarities than dissimilarities. The interpretation of society rests, as all sociologists inform us, upon our derived norms and sense of morality which is a socially evolved set of values common to all in a free country.

In the literature of protest by the more serious Negro authors, violence occurs frequently. This indicates another parallel between writers of the main stream and the Negro authors. Steinbeck in his *Grapes of Wrath* has violent scenes. Farrell in his Studs Lonigan has his share, while Faulkner seems obsessed with it in his novels, *Intruder in the Dust, As I Lay Dying,* and *Absalom-Absalom*. Richard Wright in his *Native Son* has two crimes, while Attaway's *Blood on the Forge* has an overwhelming scene of violence in the labor

---

[15] Horace R. Cayton, *New Republic,* May 12, 1947, pp. 30-31.

[16] Robert Spiller, Thorp, Johnson and Canby, *Literary History of the United States,* vol. 2, p. 879.

battle where Big Matt kills several men before he is killed. Chinatown and Melody present a horrible picture after their eyes have been gouged out during the labor battle. Big Matt's brutal flogging of his little Mexican mistress is another example of violence in the same novel. Lewis Caldwell in his *The Policy King* presents a racket warfare, and a time bomb planted in the church kills thirty people. Himes in *Lonely Crusade* permits Luther to commit a heartless murder without compunction. In fact, Luther delights in killing Paul because he breaks the code of honor among criminals. Curtis Lucas' *Third Ward Newark* contains rape, murder, and a race riot for the elements of violence. The rape scene of the fifteen-year-old girl by a white man and this Negro's brutal murder is very unpalatable indeed. Lutie Johnson murders in a highly dramatic scene which closes Ann Petry's *The Street*. Even though it is accidental, *Country Place* has a violent ending, a work by the same author. Motley's *Knock on Any Door* has sadistic scenes, murders, and fights. The needless murder of the inmate, Tony, at the reform school by overexposure to water is repugnant. The episode serves as a striking commentary upon the strong-arm methods of the officers in institutions of correction. Nick's wanton murder of Riley and then kicking the dead man's face show extreme violence.

Violence for the sake of violence as a structural part of literature has a long history in the art of the novel.[17] In the forties this device is used to secure certain effects. Often in the Negro's world hostility is directed toward them, and in many cases conflict results in violence. In order to reach a majority white audience, violence is directed toward them, which is the process operating in reverse in order to evoke a reaction. In *Native Son* by Wright, this process of reversing violence occurs. Curtis Lucas gives the rape theme in reverse in *Third*

---

[17] Percy Lubbock, *The Craft of Fiction*, pp. 9-11.

Ward Newark, and he is in keeping with the commentary which Wright makes in *Native Son* in the case of Bessie's murder. Negro womanhood commands very little, if any, respect is what he is saying. Wonnie becomes a psychopath as a consequence of this knowledge. Ernie's rape of her colors her whole existence, and when she is contemptuously dismissed by the authorities, her mental condition becomes that of anxiety.[18] This is another situation in reverse, for a Negro man would be lynched for the same offense.

So much violence in Negro novels may very well be interpreted by some majority group readers as proof of a common generalization about Negroes. That is to say, if not all, most Negroes are violent and brutal anyway, killing each other with knives and razors as *Nigger Heaven* by Carl Van Vechten in the twenties and Maxwell Anderson in *Dark Laughter* in the thirties *show.* To attack this existing fallacy Negro novelists in the forties direct the violence toward whites. It does become a different matter when the generalization is exploded into an attack upon white complacency. Naturally, thinking Negroes nor whites appreciate such an anticipation of Negro violence.

Although Frank Yerby is the popular author of the decade, his novels contain a great deal of violence. In *The Foxes of Harrow,* a period piece, there is violence because war itself by definition is violent. Laird's slaying of Hugh has more than a melodramatic flavor in *The Vixen.*

The novels which were examined show a wide selection of materials and varied fables. These incidents and situations arise from the American scene. They, therefore, have as many manifestations of problems as the vast country affords. Depending upon geographical locations, the authors have consistently rendered pictures with fidelity of particular regions.

---

[18] Rollo May, *The Meaning of Anxiety,* p. 220.

For instance, Chicago is the scene of *Native Son*, but Mississippi is part of the whole story. Georgia and New York provide the setting for *The White Face*, while *Jule* paints pictures of Alabama and New York. *It Was Not My World* concentrates on Mississippi with unhappy results. Florida is the scene of *Seraph on the Suwanee* which is authoritatively presented. *Lonely Crusade* makes sections of California real, and *The Wind from Nowhere* takes excursions into South Dakota. *The Foxes of Harrow* describes New Orleans of another era. *Country Place* gives a panoramic description of Connecticut and its countryside. So, the Atlantic seaboard, North, and South, along with the Middle West, practically the whole American topography appear.

The literature, although nationalistic viewed as a whole, has a regionalistic, tonal quality. The authors know that certain factors operate more pronouncedly against the Negroes in some sections than others. It is quite clear that there is hardly any section where Negroes are free from racial pressures. The degree to which these pressures affect the Negro, however, is decidedly different as, for instance, in the Deep South as opposed to the more enlightened North.

Two prevailing tendencies have been characteristic of novels by Negro authors of the forties. On the one hand, they have been preoccupied with racial themes which by implication means a critical comment upon American society. On the other hand, there emerges an unmistakable departure from this practice. The parallel tendency to portray life and delineate character of humanity wherever sufficient dramatic conflict is found is in evidence. That is to say, the Negro authors become writers about life and problems of any race in the American scene. With such an advantageous move, the Negro writer gains in maturity and stature. For such a broadened perspective provides an opportunity to display under-

standing about the human race. Thinking men have known
for centuries that the doctrine of race is far less significant
than the universal fact of man. Humanity is inclusive while
race is obviously exclusive.

This wider perspective eliminates the Negro novelist from
literary specialization with its corresponding emphasis upon
injustices and discrimination against a single minority in a
polyglot population. At the same time this trend of Negro
novelists indicates a favorable literary horizon. It is only in a
positive affirmation of American democratic heritage that any
American author can point the way of truth. The flexibility
of the novel as a medium makes it ideally suited to transmit
the best thinking on social problems. Among Negro authors
the question of assimilation in the written word is a fait
accompli.

During the forties there is with the Negro author far less
sentimentality than is generally ascribed to him. There
abounds in his novels a strong sense of feeling, a brooding, a
sense of frustration and inadequacy. In fact, there is a continuous purging of the reader with this feeling and sense of
inevitable frustration on account of his race. This is not a
universal condition. The American Negro is in a specialized
condition in terms of universal man. Furthermore, this is not
the general case with dark people throughout the world. In
other societies in the world, black or dark skin coloring is not
held in low esteem. So, since the Negro is in a specialized
condition on account of his color, he is eliminated initially
from heroic tragedy in the classical sense. There are dark
kings and black princes in the world, but they do not rule in
America. In this sense the Negro misses the rule of a stratified
order where nobility gives stature to personality.

But in the everyday world where the common man can
not find the simple happiness which a job affords, he can

qualify. For the sense of the inevitable in terms of the industrialized, modern world is inability to achieve success.[19] To be forever facing frustration, poverty, and a feeling of isolation, estrangement, as it were, from the source of things in society is tragic indeed.

Even though Negro novels are defective, they are not without positive virtues. The most striking quality about them is their authentic interpretation of Negro life and the Negro world from experiences inside the restricted and isolated Negro world. Another significant aspect of the novels is their characterization of Negroes. Finally, the Negro novelist of the forties has given the aspirations and hopes of the American Negro in the novel. Realistically drawn pictures of the Negro life in American society are actually shocking because of the deviation from publicized and ordinary patterns of American life in the sense of standardized living. Sections of novels dealing with pertinent issues and positing demands of the Negro for a larger life become brochures of Negro life in the American cultural pattern. All of them have parallel cases among the majority group writers of American literature. What is life like in the Negro world? The competent Negro novelist answers this question by beginning with race. Racial ancestry in America and the concomitant conflicts which accrue from the American concept of race are tremendously important to thousands of people in America. Even though scientific advances will not validate the white's contention of superiority and the Negro's inherent inferiority, actual life continues on this premise no matter how fallacious it is. Prejudices of whites against Negroes accompany this position of whites and since they control affairs, the Negro novelist describes existing attitudes which are negative toward Negroes.

Native Son begins with a list of such attitudes. The lawyer

---

[19] Annis Sandvos, "Flight from Aristotle," p. 328.

for the State of Illinois calls Bigger "a lizard, a snake" and
insists that all whites should be happy to prevent this black
monstrosity from continuing to crawl on his belly. Some whites
feel that Negroes will rape white girls and Bigger is charged
with rape at once. Of course, Bigger did not rape Mary
Dalton.

Beneath the Sky by Jarrette continues this theme and
shows an extreme case of this negative white attitude. Jake
Logan without any reason at all insists that Willie, a Negro
youth, will rape his daughter, Margaret. Obsessed with this
notion, he succeeds in lynching Willie although Jane tells him
that she has not been raped at all. Isolated, the Negro world
has all of the external features of the white world. The most
objectionable side of this life is the poverty and lack of opportunity to share in the good things of American life.

The characters live in homes ranging from shanties in
Blood on the Forge, Jule, The White Face, and *High Ground,*
to rather stately and comfortable homes in *Living Is Easy,*
Taffy, and *The Policy King.* Politically, the novels give evidence of a growing militancy among Negroes who attempt to
fight for the ideals of American democracy. From such a novel
as *Jule* one finds absolutely no interest in politics. But with the
transition made from Georgia to New York in the case of
Taffy, Mrs. Johnson, his mother, is a political leader who runs
for an important office in Brooklyn city government. Religion,
it seems, is always with the Negro, for no matter how ineffectual it may be, it still inspires and appeals to most Negroes.
From the unique Father Divine cult and store-front churches
to the dignified rector in *Living Is Easy,* describes best the
range and variety of ministers treated. Rev. Snow in *The Policy
King* is an ideal portrait of a modern Negro minister while
Rev. Marshall is the hypocritical type. Mischeaux in his *Wind
from Nowhere* draws a very despicable and low character in

the minister. On the other hand, Dr. Tern in *Picketting Hell* is touched with satiric flourishes in an admirable portrait with sustained emotionality and dignity of a Baptist minister. Most denominations are represented, and *The First Night* has a Catholic priest. The doctrine which instructs adherents to accept this life as only a transitional period of persecution and suffering which leads inevitably to an eternally blissful, heavenly home has psychological value. As to education, the Negro world presents the very inadequate school facilities from *Flour Is Dusty* to the very best school in Brooklyn for *Taffy*. Of course, Bub attends a New York school which has only one system, but *The Street* indicates that the white teacher finds him intolerable and intellectually not so bright as the white students in the class. On the college level, Jerry of *The Policy King* goes to Northwestern in Illinois, Howden in *Stranger and Alone* takes his advance degree from New York University while Kermit in *The Case of Mrs. Wingate* takes his advanced degree from Harvard in Massachusetts.

Sex is taken as a matter of course in the Negro novels. Conventional sex expression appears in the novels, for Bigger has his lover, Bessie. Bob in *If He Hollers Let Him Go* has Alice and indulges in an affair with his landlady. Lee Gordon in *Lonely Crusade* has his wife, Ruth, and his affair with Jackie. Luther is the stock notion of whites about Negroes in matters of sex, for he is ignorant, big like a giant, and has a nymphomanic white woman for a sex partner. Lutie Johnson is the type for Negro women. Her existence is a commentary upon prevalent notions of whites about the sex life of Negro women. She is beautiful and appealing. "Any man with a spark of life in him would want Lutie."[20] Yet she finds white men repugnant to her. The current notion is that Negro women are not respectable if judged by the puritanical cri-

---

[20] Ann Petry, *The Street*, p. 87.

terion of repression, but they all subscribe to the Freudian idea of uninhibited sex life or the free love cultist. Likewise, that Negro men crave white women is another stock idea which the novel refutes. Lutie, of *The Street,* enumerates the features about white men which are repellant to her. She dislikes their white skin, hairy body, and the ashen dead look on Junto's face disgusts and horrifies her. *Third Ward Newark* by Lucas has its Wonnie who goes insane because she is raped by a white man. She leaves her husband because they live in a hotel where a white man desires to sleep with her. Cissie in *High Ground* has the same idea about matters of sex. Cleo in *Living Is Easy* is a mulatto who prefers a Negro man. All of these say that they prefer sleeping with Negro men rather than to become a tool or instrument for white men's lust and nothing more.

Economics with the American Negro can not be stressed too much for it is here that few, if any, cases amount to a one-to-one correspondence in America. Job distribution, wealth, and the control of wealth, general turnover in supply and demand make of the Negro worker a clean cut case of exploitation. The Negro in the South in such a work as *The White Face* or *Blood on the Forge,* or *Jule* is primarily an agricultural laborer. These novels show destitute and impoverished farmers. In the East menial and domestic jobs supply the largest markets for Negroes. Jule does any available job. Lutie Johnson in *The Street,* Cleo in *Living Is Easy* are domestic workers. Bob Jones advances to the position of supervisor in *If He Hollers Let Him Go,* along with his fianceé, Alice. They experience frustrations because they are not permitted to supervise. Whites refuse to take orders from Negro supervisors. In the union relationships Negroes are destroyed by certain union policy in *Blood on the Forge* and *Lonely Crusade.* The Negro businessman is a failure if *Living Is Easy* is an example. *The Policy King* urges patronage of Negro business.

One particularly noteworthy aspect of the Negro novel of the forties is the creation of literary types. Two distinct types emerge who are contrary to the general stock Negro characterization. Bigger Thomas of *Native Son* is the prototype. He is a truculent and calloused Negro who is a psychopath because he has been punished because he is a Negro. Dominating the type created in the novel of the forties, Bigger anticipates Bob Jones of *If He Hollers Let Him Go*. Bob, more or less, is an educated Bigger who takes arrogance with him when he enters the hostile white world which makes it quite clear that they do not want Negroes about, particularly educated ones who dare to say that they are equal to whites. Bob Jones does not succeed, but he makes a courageous effort. Ed Tyler in *Behold a Cry* is a study in reverse; he accepts the Negro world for what it is worth and confines his activities to sexual pleasures, ignoring his responsibility to his wife and family. Jule is another impervious type. Of the women, Lutie Johnson in *The Street* is the prototype, for she is intelligent, beautiful, respectable, and insists upon living a life oriented in a Negro world. She is much more vividly drawn than Nella of *The White Face* or Marianne of *High Ground*. She anticipates Cleo of *Living Is Easy* and Helen of *The Policy King*. Along with these prototypes go the familiar, even conventional, Negro type who is intelligent, aggressive, and conscientious. These are qualities which are not only acceptable in terms of basic American personality traits but also essential for the functioning individual in a society. Another contribution to the type of character is the collaborator, Shelton Howden, of *Stranger and Alone*. Here, a Negro, possessing a share of security, maintains his position by accommodating white leaders who insist that the Negro must be kept in a subservient

position. Wimbush in the same work is a master in this art
of collaboration which is contrary to the principles of democratic living in America.

Ralph Ellison's *Invisible Man*, outside the chronological
limits of this study, is inclusive of racial themes discussed in the
period. Stress upon dispossession, underprivileged Negroes,
and insecurity of black men in white America continues the
protest motif. Leadership among Negroes in *Invisible Man* is
unlike that of Shelton Howden in *Stranger and Alone*. But
militant leadership of the Brotherhood crushes invisible man.
Indeed, the forces from without and internal dissension from
within reduce invisible man to the state of flight.

In recounting the experiences of a college trained, black
man, Ellison has his hero mount similar hurdles as Howden
in *Stranger and Alone*. Beginning in Greenwood in the deep
South, invisible man migrates to Harlem and remains. Here,
he has better opportunities for full participation in American
life. A different set of complexes greet him, for competition
in vicious dress at Liberty Paints on Long Island temporarily
defeats his "blackness of blackness." Life in Harlem offers
diversion for him with Emma. Significant momentum to life
begins for invisible man when he becomes a part of the
Brotherhood. This organization seeks to end oppression of
Negroes by challenging illegal evictions, police brutality and
other wrongs in Harlem. Through this group invisible man
meets Sybil, a white girl. His sexual escapade with her merely
points up a mistaken notion commonly held by the whites, of
the preference of white women by American, invisible black
men. The Brotherhood disintegrates in a crisis, and invisible
black man retires to his hibernation in a cellar. Monopolated
light and power has been and continues to be his theme for
reflection. Indeed, he needs must ponder the American scene.

The prelude in the admittedly James Joycean technique

anticipates the epilogue written in the same style.[21] The cultural correspondence between the two American groups is a part of the artistic design of the novel. The racial conflicts center about skin coloring and sectionalism in America. From the "Cast down your buckets where you are" philosophy, with separateness of ethnic groups an accompanying feature, to the all-Americans, remain the problem of those who are black and discover that they are invisible men. Far more rationality comes from this work than its surface bitterness indicates, for there is an optimistic message underlying the whole: Hope! Think! Endurance! Artistically designed and skillfully executed, *Invisible Man* richly deserved the National Book Award.

With the air cleared of racial tensions the Negro author gives his work a different tone. Even though Frederick Hoffman in *The Modern Novel in America* could find nothing in Motley's *Knock on Any Door* of "intellectual or moral purpose" only "muddled affair of confused emotion and sentiment,"[22] critical opinions differ with him. At the time of publication, the novel was favorably received by Charles Lee of *New York Times Book Review* who felt that it was the work of an "extraordinary and powerful naturalistic talent."[23] Later Paul Bixler in *Antioch Review* gave the same type of appraisal. A far more acceptable evaluation of the novel was given by E. M. Forster, British novelist and man of letters, who is the author of *Passage to India, Howard's End, A Room with a View,* and more recently, *Two Cheers for Democracy.* To him *Knock on Any Door* is a promising novel, and the very aspect which Hoffman finds objectionable struck Forster as significant. He said of the work: "In the middle of all that

---

[21] Alain Locke, *Phylon*, Spring, 1953, p. 34.

[22] Frederick Hoffman, *The Modern Novel in America, 1900-1950,* pp. 187-190.

[23] Charles Lee, *New York Times Book Review,* May 24, 1947, p. 3.

drunkenness and violence which I don't take to—I saw human values and human warmth."[24]

Certainly, the development of upright American citizens is of paramount importance. If juvenile delinquency is not to be handled properly, surely America has become insensitive to basic growth. The existence of institutions for delinquents is known to everyone. To show the underlying reasons for this problem is a noble cause. Most thinking Americans desire a means of prevention of crime. One suspects that such an observation has an unmistakable tinge of bias and belabors the point to maintain the idea that only the majority group writers have anything significant to say to all Americans.

Most critics were unaware of the existence of Chesnutt's works or considered them of insufficient literary quality to mention in connection with the works of Attaway, Hurston or Motley. Neglect of the earlier Negro authors may be an indication of the low esteem in which these works are held by critics and publishers. The notion that Negroes write only about Negroes and Negro life has been shown to be invalid in the productions of Negro novelists of the forties. Reception of works by Negro novelists makes it reasonable to assume that there will be continued widespread acceptance of novels by talented Negroes. Willard Motley's *Knock on Any Door* represents one of the most notable contributions to the trend under discussion, it does not stand alone and has parallel cases. Although other Negro writers made their debut in works which describe Negro life, such as Zora Neale Hurston in *Jonah's Gourd Vine*, written in 1934, over a decade later she wrote her most finished novel dealing with whites in her Native Florida. The same trend may be noted in the work of Ann Petry who published her first successful novel, *The Street*, an indictment of American society on account of inadequate

---

[24] Harvey Breit, *New York Times Book Review*, June 19, 1949, p. 35.

housing conditions and lack of a wholesome environment in certain sections of Harlem for a growing child. Her second work, *Country Place,* tells the story of whites in her native Connecticut.

Frank Yerby, in direct contrast, made his initial appearance as a popular novelist delineating white characters. In the works to his credit, however, there emerges slowly his development from a merely competent writer of historical narrative to a serious student of labor issues involved during the nineties as appears in his treatment of strikes in *Pride's Castle.* His lectures on slavery and his Negro characterizations in *Floodtide* show an acute interest in presenting a favorable attitude toward Negroes. Alain Locke, critic, observes: "Yerby has the talent to write of serious matters if and when he chooses."[25]

The fact that Negroes interpret life of other ethnic groups in their novels aids in resolving some of the difficulty posed by racial barriers in America. For when a reader has to be told that the author belongs to the Negro group, it is surely impossible to insist that his racial characteristics are so dominant that he does not belong to the white cultural world. Society in general is responsible for literature. Any one of several groups living in the same society may describe and interpret aspects of it with fidelity. Literary people are among the first to recognize this, as evidenced by Diana Trilling's remark: "Surely if literary people had their way there would be no Anti-Negroism or Anti-Semitism in this country."[26]

Fortunately or unfortunately, depending upon one's point of view, the Negro lost all traces of his African cultural heritage hundreds of years ago. He substituted therefor the American cultural pattern, and he is truly an American cultural product. He subscribes to, fosters, and writes in the American

---

[25] Alain Locke, *Phylon,* Jan., 1948, p. 202.
[26] Diana Trilling, *Nation,* March 9, 1946, pp. 290-291.

tradition. Malcolm Cowley, critic, remarks of this fact: "The Negroes act, speak, and think exactly like the whites . . . and even writes like them."[27]

In depicting the characters of other ethnic groups, Negro novelists confirm Cowley's observation of the cultural correspondence in America among literary people. Ann Petry in creating The Weasel in *Country Place* develops a character around the eccentric motif. This type is not unfamiliar to American literature, but he is not conventional. He has a passionate obsession for knowing the details about his neighbor's affairs. This type is realistic enough when one considers those unfortunate people who have prying neighbors. Petry succeeds with Mrs. Gramby as a woman of means who insists upon the manner of society. This approach to manners is in accord with the prevalent notion among some critics that America should admit that it has defined classes on the basis of wealth. Mrs. Gramby with her fleeting memories and delicate tea cups gives much of the flavor of this life of leisure where sensibilities and genealogy become important considerations.

Zora Hurston in *Seraph on the Suwanee* similarly achieves success with characterization. But hers is at the opposite extreme of the social ladder, for she portrays a group of people who are Florida crackers, that is to say, they are far removed from the gentility and manners of Gramby house. Nonetheless, Hurston triumphs in a way that few women novelists are able to do. She portrays a man's man. Jim Meserve answers the requirements of personality criterion for the aggressive, bold, and earthy he-man type. He makes it known at once that he is a man who knows what he wants and gets it. It is this aggressively confident manner which subdues Arvay cutting through her subterfuge immediately. As a consequence, she is

---

[27] Malcolm Cowley, *New Republic*, Sept. 27, 1948, p. 467.

never quite adjusted to him, but she finds him irresistible. The two complement each other for fictional purposes.

Motley gets inside Nick in *Knock on Any Door;* he moves in front of us as a full-blown, three-dimensional character. He is a type that is conventional and familiar to American literature. In naturalistic tradition Nick has many counterparts, but Motley gives to Nick and this type a new interpretation. Nick has a headiness about him, a headiness without the reality of exhiliration. It is a rather foreboding cockiness of despair which presages his disintegration and tragedy. Emma's poetic rendition denotes Motley's creative ability with another type, for she impresses her tragic role of the tender and truly sensitive literary figures. She has delicacy and character, but this same forceful character unfortunately must suffer anxieties and untimely death. Motley has several other characters. Deservedly, he receives from E. M. Forster such questions: "Is it true that he is a Negro? How incredible, how very nice, for there is no inkling of it in his writing."[28]

If the Negro novelist has not produced a classic during the forties, such productions as Richard Wright's *Native Son,* Ann Petry's *The Street,* William Attaway's *Blood on the Forge,* William Smith's *Last of the Conquerors,* J. Saunders Redding's *Stranger and Alone,* Zora Neale Hurston's *Seraph on the Suwanee,* and Willard Motley's *Knock on Any Door* make a bid for permanency in American literature. The forties sparked the Negro producing novels of high levels of competence and literary merit. Laski confirms such a critique when he observes that the Negro's "work in literature and music is second to none."[29] Paul Bixler of the *Antioch Review* agrees. Indeed, Mumford Jones, like Bertrand Russell, emi-

---

[28] E. M. Forster, *New York Times Book Review,* June 19, 1949, p. 35.

[29] Harold Laski, *The American Democracy,* p. 466.

nent British sage, in his brighter moments of contemplation, forsees the acquiescence of whites in favor of black men. That is to say, full and unquestioned equality in the conduct of affairs in western civilization will be accorded black men. May the powers and forces that be combine to facilitate the process in the American here and now.

In the case of the Negro novelist, his prime need, a creative imagination, has no limitation. Disassociation from racism may be, and indeed is difficult, but some gifted Negro writer in the transcendent process of literally entering another world will write his classic. In the throes of surging creativity, race, as Negroes know it in America, has no place. Vital humanity involved in dramatic situations in the national scene provide limitless supply of material for continued interpretation, illustration, and comprehension of life.

BIBLIOGRAPHY

FICTION

Attaway, William, *Blood on the Forge*, New York, Doubleday Doran, 1941.

Bland, Alden, *Behold a Cry*, New York, Charles Scribner's Sons, 1947.

Caldwell, Lewis A., *The Policy King*, Chicago, New Vistas Pub. Co., 1945.

Deaderick, Jenkins, *It Was Not My World*, Los Angeles, Author, 1942.

Henderson, George, *Jule*, New York, Creative Age Press, 1946.

Himes, Chester, *If He Hollers Let Him Go*, New York, Doubleday Doran, 1945. *Lonely Crusade*, New York, 1948.

Hurston, Zora Neale, *Seraph on the Suwanee*, New York, Charles Scribner's Sons, 1948.

Jarrette, A. Q., *Beneath the Sky*, New York, Weinberg Co., 1949.

Kaye, Philip B., *Taffy*, New York, Crown Publishers, 1950.

Lee, John, *Counter Clockwise*, New York, Wendell Malliet Co., 1940.

Lucas, Curtis, *Flour Is Dusty*, New York, Dorrance Co., 1943. *Third Ward Newark*, New York, Ziff Davis Co., 1946.

Mischeaux, Oscar, *The Case of Mrs. Wingate*, New York, Book Supply Co., 1948. *Masquerade*, New York, Book Supply Co., 1947. *The Story of Dorothy Starfield*, New York, Book Supply Co., 1946. *The Wind from Nowhere*, New York, Book Supply Co., 1946.

Motley, Willard, *Knock on Any Door*, New York, Appleton-Century-Crofts, 1947. *We Fished All Night*, New York, Appleton-Century-Crofts, 1952.

Offord, Carl, *The White Face*, New York, Robert McBride Co., 1943.

Petry, Ann, *The Street*, Boston, Houghton Mifflin, 1946. *Country Place*, Boston, Houghton Mifflin, 1947.

Powell, Adam, Clayton, Sr., *Picketting Hell,* New York, Wendell Malliet Co., 1942.

Rasmussen, E. M., *The First Night,* New York, Wendell Malliet Co., 1947.

Redding, J. Saunders, *Stranger and Alone,* New York, Harcourt Brace, 1950.

Savoy, Willard, *Alien Land,* New York, Dutton, 1948.

Smith, William Gardner, *The Last of the Conquerors,* New York, Farrar, Straus & Young, 1948. *Anger at Innocence,* New York, Farrar, Straus & Young, 1950.

Swados, Felice, *House of Fury,* New York, Doubleday, 1946.

Thomas, Will, *God Is for White Folks,* New York, Creative Age, 1947.

West, Dorothy, *Living Is Easy,* Boston, Houghton Mifflin, 1948.

Wood, Odella, *High Ground,* New York, Exposition Press, 1945.

Wright, Richard, *Native Son,* New York, Harper, 1940.

Yerby, Frank, *The Foxes of Harrow,* New York, Dial Press, 1946. *The Golden Hawk,* New York, Dial Press, 1947. *Floodtide,* New York, Dial Press, 1950. *Pride's Castle,* New York, Dial Press, 1949. *The Vixens,* New York, Dial Press, 1948.

NON-FICTION

Ahnebrink, Lars, *The Beginnings of Naturalism in American Fiction,* Cambridge, Harvard University Press, 1950.

Aldridge, John, *After the Lost Generation,* New York, McGraw-Hill, 1951.

Barton, Rebecca, *Race Consciousness and American Negro Literature,* Dallmeyer, Greifswald, 1934.

Barzun, Jacques, *Race: A study in Modern Superstition,* New York, Harcourt Brace, 1934.

Beach, Joseph, *American Fiction 1920-1940,* New York, Macmillan, 1941. *The Twentieth Century Novel,* New York, Appleton-Century-Crofts, 1932. *Forms of Modern Fiction,* Minneapolis, University of Minnesota Press, 1948.

Beard, Charles A. and Mary, *Rise of American Civilization,* New York, Macmillan, 1944. *America in Mid-Passage,* New York, Macmillan, 1939.

Beardsley, Grace, *The Negro in Greek and Roman Civilization,* London, H. Milfors, 1929.

Benedict, Ruth, *Patterns of Culture,* Boston, Houghton Mifflin, 1934. *Race: Science and Politics,* New York, Viking Press, 1945.

Brawley, Benjamin, *The Negro in Literature and Art,* New York, Duffield Co., 1918.

Boyton, Percy, *American Contemporary Fiction,* New York, Macmillan, 1941.

Brooks, Van Wyck, *The Confident Years: 1885-1915,* New York, Dutton, 1951.

Brown, Sterling, *The Negro in American Fiction,* New York, J. B. Lyon Press, 1937.

Burgum, E., *The Novel and the World's Dilemma*, New York, Oxford Press, 1947.

Calverton, V. F., *The Liberation of American Literature*, New York, Charles Scribner's Sons, 1932. *The Newer Spirit*, New York, Boni & Liveright, 1925. *Anthology of American Negro Literature*, New York, Modern Library, 1929.

Campbell, O. J., *Living Shakespeare*, New York, Macmillan, 1949.

Carlyle, Thomas, *Sartor Resartus*, London, J. Dent's & Sons Ltd., 1948.

Cash, W. F., *The Mind of the South*, New York, A. Knopf, 1941.

Cassirer, Ernest, *Essay on Man*, New Haven, Yale University Press, 1944.

Chesnutt, Helen M., *Charles W. Chesnutt*, Chapel Hill, University of North Carolina Press, 1952.

Coleridge, Samuel Taylor, *Biographia Literrati*, London, Blackwell, 1940.

Commager, H. Steele, *The American Mind*, New Haven, Yale University Press, 1950.

Conrad, Earl, *Jim Crow America*, New York, Duell, Sloane & Pearce, 1947.

Cowie, Alexander, *Rise of the American Novel*, New York, American Book Co., 1948.

Cowley, Malcolm, *Exile's Return*, New York, Viking Press, 1934.

Crossman, Richard, *The God that Failed*, New York, Harper, 1949.

Curti, Merle, *Growth of American Thought*, New York, Harper, 1942.

Daiches, David, *Literature and Society*, New Haven, Yale University Press, 1940. *The Novel and the Modern World*, Chicago, University of Chicago Press, 1939. *A Study of Literature*, Ithaca, Cornell University Press, 1948.

De Voto, Bernard, *Modern Fiction*, Boston, Houghton Mifflin, 1951.

Du Bois, W. E. B., *Black Folk, Then and Now*, New York, Henry Holt, 1931. *The Souls of Black Folk*, Chicago, A. McClurg, 1924.

Eliot, T. S., *Criticism in America*, New York, Harcourt Brace, 1924.

Embree, Edwin, *Brown America*, New York, Viking Press, 1945. *American Negroes*, New York, Day, 1942.

Emerson, Ralph Waldo, *Complete Works*, vol. 12, ed. by Edward Emerson, Boston, Houghton Mifflin, 1906.

Ford, Nick, *Contemporary Negro Novelists*, Boston, Meador Co., 1936.

Forster, E. M., *Aspects of the Novel*, New York, Harcourt Brace, 1927.

Freud, Sigmund, *Civilization and Its Discontents*, London, Hogarth Press, 1949. *Basic Writings of Freud*, ed. by A. A. Brill, New York, Modern Library, 1938. *Civilization: War and Death*, ed. by John Rickman, London, Hogarth Press, 1939. *A General Introduction to Psychoanalysis*, New York, Norton, 1949.

Fridell, Egon, *Cultural History of Modern Age*, New York, Knopf, 1932.

Frohock, Wilbur, *Novel of Violence in America*, Dallas, Southern Methodist University Press, 1950.

Fromm, Erich, *Escape from Freedom*, New York, Rinehart, 1941. *Psychoanalysis and Religion*, New Haven, Yale University Press, 1950.

Gholson, Edward, *The Negro Looks into the South*, Boston, Chapman & Grines, 1947.

Glicksburg, Charles, *American Literary Criticism*, New York, Hendricks House, 1950.

Gloster, Hugh, *Negro Voices in American Fiction*, Chapel Hill, Univ. of North Carolina Press, 1948.

Haines, Helen, *What's in a Novel*, New York, Columbia University Press, 1942.

Hall, Thomas, *Religious Background of American Culture*, Boston, Little, Brown, 1930.

Hart, James, *The Popular Book*, New York, Oxford University Press, 1950.

Hatcher, Harlan, *Creating the Modern American Novel*, New York, Farrar, Rinehart, 1935.

Henderson, Philip, *The Novel Today*, London, Boriswood, 1940.

Hicks, Granville, *The Great Tradition*, New York, Macmillan Co., 1935.

Hoffman, Frederick, *The Modern Novel in America, 1900-1950*, Chicago, Regenery Co., 1951. *Freudianism in Literary Mind*, Baton Rouge, Louisiana State University Press, 1945.

Horney, Karen, *Neurosis and Human Growth*, New York, Norton, 1950. *The Neurotic Personality of Our Times*, New York, Norton, 1937.

Hyman, Stanley E., *The Armed Vision*, New York, Knopf, 1948.

James, Henry, *The Art of the Novel*, ed. by R. P. Blackmur, New York, Charles Scribner's Sons, 1950.

Johnson, Charles, *Into the Main Stream*, Chapel Hill, University of North Carolina Press, 1947. *Patterns of Negro Segregation*, New York, Harper, 1943.

Jones, Howard Mumford, *Ideas in America*, Cambridge, Harvard University Press, 1944. *Major American Writers*, New York, Harcourt Brace & Co., 1935. *The Theory of American Literature*, Ithaca, Cornell University Press, 1948.

Kazin, Alfred, *On Native Grounds*, New York, Reynal, 1942.

Kardiner, Abram, *Psychological Frontiers of Society*, New York, Columbia University Press, 1948. *The Mark of Oppression*, New York, Norton, 1951.

Klineberg, Otto, *Characteristics of the American Negro*, New York, Harper, 1944. *Race Differences*, New York, Harper, 1935. *Social Psychology*, New York, Holt, 1940.

Kroeber, A. L., *Anthropology*, New York, Harcourt, 1948.

Laski, Harold, *The American Democracy*, New York, Viking, 1948.

Leavis, Frank, *Culture and Environment*, London, Chatto, 1933.

Leavis, Q. O., *Fiction and the Reading Public*, London, Chatto, 1932.

Leisy, Ernest, *The American Historical Novel*, Norman, University of Oklahoma Press, 1950.

Levin, Harry, *Perspectives of Criticism*, Cambridge, Harvard University Press, 1950. *Towards Standards of Criticism*, London, Hogarth, 1947.

Lewisohn, Ludwig, *Expression in America*, New York, Harper, 1932.

Locke, Alain, *The New Negro*, New York, Boni & Co., 1928.

Loggins, Vernon, *The Negro Author*, New York, Columbia University Press, 1931.

Lubbock, Percy, *The Craft of Fiction*, New York, P. Smith, 1945.

May, Bernard, *Negro's God as Reflected in His Literature*, Boston, Chapman Grines Inc., 1946.

May, Rollo, *The Meaning of Anxiety*, New York, Ronald Press, 1950.

Matthiessen, F. O., *American Renaissance*, New York, Oxford University Press, 1941. *Theodore Dreiser*, New York, William Sloane Associates, 1950.

Millet, Fred, *Contemporary American Literature*, New York, Harcourt Brace, 1929.

Morten, M. Dauwen, Zabel, *Literary Opinion in America*, New York, Harper, 1942.

Muir, Edwin, *The Structure of the Novel*, London, Land. U. Woolf, 1928.

Myrdal, Gunnar, *An American Dilemma*, New York, Harper, 1944.

McIver, R., *Civilization and Group Relationships*, New York, Holt, 1948.

McDowell, Tremaine, *America in Literature*, New York, Macmillan, 1940.

Nelson, Eldred, *Our Atomic World*, Albuquerque, New Mexico University Press, 1948.

Nelson, John Herbert, *The Negro Character in American Literature*, Lawrence, University of Kansas Press, 1926.

Odum, H., *The Way of the South*, New York, Macmillan, 1947.

Ottley, Roi, *The Black Odyssey*, New York, Charles Scribner's Sons, 1947. *No Green Pastures*, New York, Charles Scribner's Sons, 1951.

Parrington, Vernon, *Main Currents in American Thought*, New York, Harcourt Brace, 1930.

Pelham, Edgar, *The Art of the Novel*, New York, Macmillan, 1934.

Pritchett, V. S., *The Living Novel*, New York, Reynal & Hitchcock, 1947.

Redding, J. Saunders, *On Being a Negro in America*, New York, Harcourt Brace, 1951.

Reisman, David, *The Lonely Crowd*, New Haven, Yale University Press, 1950.

Riley, Isaac Woodbridge, *American Thought*, New York, Holt, 1923.

Sandvos, Annis, "Flight from Aristotle," unpublished Columbia University Ph.D. Thesis, 1950.

Scally, Mary, *Negro Catholic Writers, 1900-1945*, Detroit, W. Roeing, 1945.

Schnieder, David, *Psychoanalyst and Artist*, New York, Viking, 1950.

Schlesinger, A. Fox, *History of American Life*, New York, Macmillan, 1944.

Smith, Bernard, *Forces in American Criticism*, New York, Harcourt Brace, 1939.

Smith, J. H., *The Great Critics*, New York, Harper, 1948.

Spiller, Robert, Thorp, Johnson and Canby, *Literary History of the United States*, New York, Macmillan, 1948.

Stauffer, D., *The Intent of Critic,* Princeton, Princeton University Press, 1941.

Taylor, F. Walter, *A History of American Letters,* New York, American Book Co., 1936.

Trilling, Lionel, *The Liberal Imagination,* New York, Viking, 1950.

Van Doren, Carl, *The American Novel,* New York, Macmillan, 1940.

Van Doren, Mark, *The Private Reader,* New York, Holt, 1934.

Warren, Robert, and Brooks, Cleanth, *Understanding Fiction,* New York, F. S. Crofts, 1943.

Wells, Henry, *The Realm of Literature,* New York, Columbia University Press, 1927.

Wellek, René and Warren, *Theory of Literature,* New York, Harcourt Brace, 1948.

Worfel, Harry, *Modern Novelists,* New York, American Book Co., 1951.

Whitman, Walt, *Complete Works,* ed. by Louis Untermeyer, Simon Schuster, 1949.

Wilson, Edmund, *Classics and Commercials,* New York, Farrar Straus, 1950. *Axel's Castle,* New York, Charles Scribner's Sons, 1950.

Wright, Richard, *Black Boy,* New York, Harper, 1946.

PERIODICALS

The following articles are representative but not inclusive:

Bascoe, B., "Negro Novel and White Reviewers: Richard Wright's Native Son," *American Mercury,* May 1940, pp. 113-17.

Bell, Lisle, "Novels of Cities in War Times," New York *Herald Tribune Book Review,* May 16, 1943, p. 12.

Bontemps, Arna, "Chicago in a Naturalistic Novel," New York *Herald Tribune Book Review,* May 18, 1947, pp. 8.

Brown, Sterling, "Insight, Courage, and Craftsmanship," *Opportunity,* June 1940, p. 185.

Butterfield, Alfred, "Dark Heartbeat of Harlem," *New York Times Book Review,* February 10, 1946, p. 6.

Cohn, David, "The Negro Novel," *Atlantic Monthly,* June 1940, pp. 826-828.

Cook, Fannie, "Somebody," New York *Herald Tribune Book Review,* October 20, 1946, p. 10.

Cowley, Malcolm, "The Case of Bigger Thomas," *The New Republic,* March 1940, pp. 382-383.

Daiches, David, "The American Scene," *Partisan Review,* May-June 1940, pp. 244-245.

Daniels, Jonathan, "Man Against the World," *The Saturday Review of Literature,* March 2, 1940, p. 5.

Dempsey, David, "Uncle Tom's Ghost and the Literary Abolitionists," *Antioch Review,* September 1946, pp. 442-447.

Ellison, Ralph, "Richard Wright Blues," *Antioch Review,* Summer 1946, p. 652.

Fadiman, Clifton, "Native Son," *The New Yorker,* March 2, 1940, pp. 60-61.

Hexter, Margaret B., "From Altar Boy to Killer," *The Saturday Review of Literature,* May 24, 1947, p. 13.

Ivy, J. W., "Mrs. Petry's Harlem," *Crisis,* May 1946, p. 436.

Jack, Peter Monro, "A Tragic Novel of Negro Life in America," *New York Times Book Review,* March 1940, p. 20.

Lee, Charles, "Disciple of Dreiser," *New York Times Book Review,* May 24, 1947, p. 13.

Lewis, T., "Saga of Bigger Thomas," *Catholic World,* May 1941, pp. 201-206.

Locke, Alain, "Negro Fiction," *Phylon,* March-June 1947, p. 18.

—— "Reason and Race," *Phylon,* May 1946, p. 21.

Marshall, Margaret, "Black Native Son," *The Nation,* March 16, 1940, p. 367.

McBride, James, "Homme Fatale," *New York Times Book Review,* May 4, 1947, p. 22.

Pickrel, Paul, "Outstanding Novels," *Yale Review,* March 1950, p. 576.

Rago, Henry, "Knock On Any Door," *Commonweal,* July 25, 1947, p. 358.

Rice, Jennings, "Noble, Rash and Rakish," *New York Times Book Review,* February 4, 1946, p. 4.

Rugoff, Milton, "A Feverish Dramatic Intensity," New York *Herald Tribune Book Review,* March 1940, p. 5.

Smith, Bradford, "Glandular Balance," *The Saturday Review of Literature,* October 18, 1947, pp. 17, 21.

Stanford, Don, "The Beloved Returns and Other Recent Fiction," *The Southern Review,* Winter 1940, pp. 618-619.

Tracy, Henry, "Answered in Fiction," *Common Ground,* Summer 1946, pp. 109-110.

Trilling, Diana, "Fiction in Review," *The Nation,* June 5, 1943, p. 815.

Van Doren, Mark, "Literature and Propaganda," *Virginia Quarterly Review,* April 1938, pp. 203-208.

Wright, Richard, "How Bigger Was Born," *The Saturday Review of Literature,* June 1940, pp. 1-3.

—— "I Bite the Hand that Feeds Me," *Atlantic Monthly,* June 1940, p. 826.

Wyke, Marguerite, "South Side Negro," *Canadian Forum,* May 1940, p. 60.

INDEX OF AUTHORS

INDEX OF NOVELS